Wild Things

Nature, Culture, and Tourism in Ontario, 1790-1914

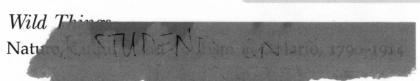

Europeans in the nineteenth century were fascinated with the wild and the primitive. So compelling was the craving for a first-hand experience of wilderness that it provided a lasting foundation for tourism as a consumer industry. In this book, Patricia Jasen shows how the region now known as Ontario held special appeal for tourists seeking to indulge a passion for wild country or act out their fantasies of primitive life. Niagara Falls, the Thousand Islands, Muskoka, and the far reaches of Lake Superior all offered the experiences tourists valued most: the tranquil pleasures of the picturesque, the excitement of the sublime, and the sensations of nostalgia associated with Canada's disappearing wilderness.

Jasen situates her work within the context of recent writings about tourism history and the semiotics of tourism, about landscape perception and images of 'wildness' and 'wilderness,' and about the travel narrative as a literary genre. She explores a number of major themes, including the imperialistic appropriation and commercialization of landscape into tourist images, services, and souvenirs. In a study of class, gender, and race, Jasen finds that by the end of the century most workers still had little opportunity for travel, while the middle classes had come to regard holidays as a right and a duty in the light of Social Darwinist concerns about preserving the health of the 'race.' Women travellers have been disregarded or marginalized in many studies of the history of tourism, but this book makes their presence known and analyses their experience. It also examines, against the backdrop of nineteenth-century racism and expansionism, the major role played by Native people in the tourist industry.

The first book to explore the cultural foundations of tourism in Ontario, *Wild Things* also makes a major contribution to the literature on the wilderness ideal in North America.

PATRICIA JASEN is a professor in the Department of History, Lakehead University, Thunder Bay.

Wild Things

Nature, Culture, and Tourism in Ontario, 1790–1914

Patricia Jasen

University of Toronto Press
Toronto Buffalo London

© University of Toronto Press Incorporated 1995
Toronto Buffalo London
Printed in Canada

ISBN 0-8020-0684-1 (cloth)
ISBN 0-8020-7638-6 (paper)

Printed on acid-free paper

Canadian Cataloguing in Publication Data

Jasen, Patricia Jane, date

Wild things : nature, culture, and tourism in Ontario,
1790–1914

Includes index
ISBN 0-8020-0684-1 (bound) ISBN 0-8020-7638-6 (pbk.)

1. Tourist trade – Ontario – History.
2. Ecotourism – Ontario – History. I. Title.

G155.C3J37 1995   338.4'791713   C95-930450-9

University of Toronto Press acknowledges the financial assistance to its
publishing program of the Canada Council and the Ontario Arts Council.

This book has been published with the help of a grant from the Social
Science Federation of Canada, using funds provided by the Social Sciences
and Humanities Research Council of Canada.

For Angela

Contents

Illustrations following pages 54, 104, and 132.

Acknowledgments

The research for this book was made possible by the Social Sciences and Humanities Research Council of Canada through a Canada Research Fellowship, a Research Grant, and support from the General Research Grant Program. Lakehead University provided financial assistance for the purchase of photographs.

Portions of this book have been published elsewhere in somewhat different form. Material in Chapter 2 appeared in an article entitled 'Romanticism, Modernity, and the Evolution of Tourism in the Niagara Frontier,' *Canadian Historical Review* 23, no. 3 (September 1991) 283–318, and is reprinted with permission of University of Toronto Press Incorporated. Much of Chapter 3 was published in 'From Nature to Culture: The St Lawrence River Panorama in Nineteenth-Century Ontario,' *Ontario History* 85, no. 1 (March 1993), 43–63. Portions of other chapters appeared in 'Imagining Fort William: Romanticism, Tourism, and the Old Fort, 1821–1971,' Thunder Bay Historical Museum Society *Papers and Records* 28 (1990), 2–29; and in 'Native People and the Tourist Industry in Nineteenth-Century Ontario,' *Journal of Canadian Studies/Revue d'études canadiennes* 28, no. 4 (winter 1993–4), 5–27.

At the University of Toronto Press, I would like to thank Gerald Hallowell, Robert Ferguson, and Patricia Thorvaldson for their assistance and editorial advice. I am indebted to numerous archivists and librarians for their help, but special thanks go to the inter-library loan staff at the Chancellor Paterson Library and to photographer Peter Puna at Lakehead University.

The aid of friends and colleagues must also be acknowledged. Julie Byzewski, Margaret Frenette, Eileen Pope, and Gerald Ross acted as research assistants, and I am grateful for all their work. Peter Bailey,

Angela Davis, Paul Driben, Debra Lindsay, Dennis McPherson, Douglas Rabb, and Helen Smith read portions of the manuscript and helped me to improve them. Any errors in fact or judgment are, of course, my own. There are also many people who have passed on references and bits of information just in case they might prove useful; they usually were, and I thank you.

My greatest debt is to my family. My parents have always been generous with their love and support. My son, Paul Jasen, has cheered me on and shared ideas about this mysterious thing called culture. My husband, Rick Holmes, has lived intimately with this book for years, and I am grateful to him beyond words for his help, faith, and companionship.

Wild Things

1

Introduction:
Nature, Culture, and Tourism

Dreams of wild things brought hundreds of thousands of tourists to the region now known as Ontario during the nineteenth century. Tourists made pilgrimages to Niagara, so that they could experience the wonder and terror of its wild, foaming waters. They floated down rivers, crossed vast inland seas, glided through wild archipelagos, and crashed through tumbling rapids. They ventured into the depths of the primeval forest, thrilling to think what wild things lurked there, unseen and unheard. They sought out the Iroquois, the Ojibway, and other Native peoples to act as picturesque figures in the landscape, as wilderness guides, and as makers of keepsakes, imagining that these so-called wild men and women might unlock the secrets of the primitive past and reveal the true meaning of the wild and the civilized. And as the century wore on and fears about the effects of urban life mounted, they flocked from the enervating city to the exhilarating wilderness, hoping to cast themselves under the care of Mother Nature and to rediscover the power of the primitive within themselves.

This book is about that search for wilderness and wildness. It recognizes that the meanings conveyed by these words are human inventions which are rooted in a particular cultural context. In other words, there is no perception of wilderness that does not take its meaning from whatever we believe civilization to be, just as no meaning accrues to the word *wildness* unless we know its opposite, that is, the cultural norms which the 'wild' has violated.

Wild Things is set in the nineteenth century and the years before the First World War, an age of imperialist expansion and an overwhelming preoccupation – in 'Western' middle- and upper-class patterns of thought – with matters of racial health and the rise and fall of civilizations. This introductory chapter is devoted to thematic and theoretical issues. The remainder of the book is organized more or less chronologically, each chapter dealing with a particular kind of tourist experience. Chapter 2 analyses the early history and meaning of Niagara Falls and its transformation from a wild place into the prototypical tourist destination in North America in the nineteenth century. Chapter 3 looks at how the tourist industry's model of the 'panorama' was employed along the St Lawrence River, and at how landscape, historic sites, and Native communities were all used in marketing this popular excursion. Tourism in the upper Great Lakes is the subject of Chapter 4, which examines how European ideas about the forest and the wilderness were applied to this region. It also studies the involvement of Ojibway communities in the steamer excursion business, and considers the broader meaning of tourists' incursions into 'Native lands.' Chapter 5 focuses on the growth of the therapeutic back-to-nature holiday among Torontonians, and the development of Toronto's recreational hinterland, with particular attention to Muskoka and Toronto Island. Chapter 6 studies the complex relationship between wilderness tourists and their Native guides in northern Ontario, and confirms that tourism before the First World War in Canada was closely tied to the expansionist cause.

But the history of tourism in Canada and throughout the Western world encompasses a number of issues which transcend geography. Historians are concerned not only with where the tourists have gone and why, but also with the maze of cultural and economic relationships they entered into, and upon which they left their mark. For example, the question of what, exactly, a tourist is must be reconsidered in light of recent writings which constructed (and then demolished) the tourist-traveller dichotomy. This book argues that being a tourist means being in a state of mind in which the imagination plays a key role, and each variety of tourism it examines reveals the central and enduring importance of the 'romantic sensibility' to the culture, economics, and politics of the tourist industry. Another theme is the role tourism played in the colonization process in nineteenth-century Canada: tourism often preceded – or accompanied – immigration and resource exploitation, and the tourist industry made its own contribution to a distorted representation of Native cultures and the transformation of their economies. The following chapters also consider questions of class and gender: who was privileged to become a tourist, and what sorts of people left records of their experiences.

This chapter introduces these organizing themes and the theoretical considerations to which they give rise, and provides, where necessary, some historical context which predates the period covered here. I have attempted to do this with a minimum of theoretical name-dropping and a maximum of accessibility to the interested general reader, on the assumption that analytical precision need not be sacrificed along the way. This strategy is motivated in part by a suspicion that the process of containing cultural criticism within a tight web of theoretical discourse, especially where the power relations between Europeans and indigenous peoples are part of the subject being studied, itself involves a kind of intellectual imperialism too little understood at the present time.

TOURISTS, TRAVELLERS, AND THE SEMIOTICS OF TOURISM

Those working in the field of tourism history will be familiar with the debate over tourists versus travellers. James Buzard began his recent study of nineteenth-century British tourists and the Continental holiday, aptly titled *The Beaten Track* (1993), by quoting Evelyn Waugh's quip that 'The tourist is the other fellow.'[1] Waugh, of course, was referring to tourists' habit of seeing *themselves* as travellers and *others* as tourists – a defensive position also employed by some widely quoted scholars who have studied tourism themselves. Daniel Boorstin and Paul Fussell, in particular, denounce the tourist as an empty-minded consumer, a 'fantasist equipped temporarily with unaccustomed power,' who seeks the illusion of a higher social status, who vastly prefers pseudo-places to anything authentic, and whose ubiquity has made 'real travel' – the pursuit of genuine experience in truly strange places – a thing of the past.[2] In turn, Boorstin and Fussell, as cultural critics who should know better, are themselves maligned by other writers for missing the key point that the tourist-traveller dichotomy is in fact an invention, a rhetorical device we all employ to convince ourselves that *we* are not tourists. As Jonathan Culler says, 'the desire to distinguish between tourists and real travelers is a part of tourism – integral to it rather than outside it or beyond it.'[3]

Culler argues further that tourists do set out in search of authentic experience. What distinguishes them, in fact, is their perpetual quest for signs of authenticity, for essences of the cultures they examine. Tourists are interested, he says, 'in everything as a sign of itself, an instance of a typical cultural practice,' and therefore they read entire 'cities, landscapes, and cultures as sign systems.' Perhaps Culler underplays many tourists' easy satisfaction with the supposed 'realness' of things – the kind of reality they are encouraged to experience, for example, at living history museums where having fun is given greater priority than historical accuracy. But he also recognizes how slippery the whole concept of authenticity is, for the process of identifying anything as authentic involves turning it into a sign: the 'authentic is not something unmarked or undifferentiated; authenticity is a sign relation.' To dismiss the tourist as a unworthy subject of study, he reminds us, is to miss seeing this army of semioticians at work, entangling itself in the paradox of authenticity, engaging in the 'modern quest for experience as a quest for an experience of signs.'[4]

If such an uncertain relationship with reality is part of our modern predicament, how and when did this come about? The whole notion of tourism's modernity is more complex than some writers have recognized. The historian can easily dismiss Fussell's claim that *travel* was possible until the Second World War but since then has been totally displaced by *tourism*. However, Dean MacCannell's insistence that modern ('socially organized') tourism dates back no further than the beginning of this century, and that before then 'sightseeing ... was mainly speculative and individualistic,' does not stand up to scrutiny, either.[5] Studies such as S. Piers Brendon's *Thomas Cook: 150 Years of Popular Tourism* (1992) illustrate just how well organized the industry was by the midnineteenth century, and other works record the laments of early nineteenth century observers over the growing hordes of tourists swarming through Britain's countryside and to the great cities of Europe.[6] But tourists knew they were despised; hence their anxiety to identify themselves as travellers. As Chapter 2 of this book shows, the kind of tourist angst that MacCannell sees as a microcosm of the modern predicament was already in evidence by the early nineteenth century, if not earlier, as tourists became enmeshed in the conflict between image and reality, began to fear that they were not enjoying themselves as they should, and acquired the habit of condemning, sometimes with a sharp sense of irony, the industry that supposedly served their multifarious needs.

For any number of reasons the tourist-traveller dichotomy seems to miss the point, for the relationship between tourism and travel is more a matter of subjective experience than objective reality. This book includes the testimonies of many kinds of people on the move, and it does so on the assumption that anyone – including immigrants and those travelling on commercial, government, or military business – became a tourist whenever the pleasures of sightseeing, or the pursuit of new experiences and the sensation of physical or imaginative freedom, emerged as the main priority.

The study of tourism in the nineteenth century in fact reveals that the tourist sensibility was overwhelmingly a romantic one. Though it may be argued that so large and diverse a body of people as the pleasure-travelling public could hardly be characterized by a particular, identifiable ideology, this book seeks to show just how intimate and enduring the connection between romantic values and the workings of the tourist industry was. It remains so today: as tourists we like to have our feelings aroused and our imaginations stirred, and we look for images of 'otherness' that might evoke such responses. We are indeed engaged in a quest for signs, and it is the role of the tourist industry to point them out for us, however innocent or invidious that process turns out to be.

TOURISM AND ROMANTICISM

The story of Ontario tourism begins not in North America but in Britain (and elsewhere in Europe), with a cultural transformation that accompanied the beginnings of the romantic movement. Such so-called movements are notoriously difficult to define in any satisfactory manner, but here romanticism refers to the tendency, widespread among members of the middle and upper classes by the end of the eighteenth century, to value feeling and imagination, or sensibility, far more than before, to extend or transfer feelings formerly associated with religious experience to the secular realm, and to imbue 'wild nature' with new meaning and value.[7]

In the wake of this transformation, travellers' interest in the wild places of what they called the New World steadily grew. Clearly the gradual improvement in transportation facilities and the rising wealth of the middle classes provided the material basis for the growing habit of travel, but new cultural priorities spurred the demand for fresh sights and experiences essential to the creation of a tourist industry. Many factors were involved, including the emergence of the 'picturesque' and the 'sublime' as major aesthetic categories; the rising importance of landscape as an element of taste; growing links between concepts of landscape, nationalism, and history; and a deepening fascination with aboriginal peoples. To some degree each of these elements predated the romantic movement, and reflected changing ideas about good and evil in nature and the relations between human society and the natural world.

The importance of the 'sublime' as an element in both elite and popular culture was well established by the late eighteenth century, and represented one important aspect of this changing mentality. The craze for sublime experience entailed a new appreciation of natural phenomena, which in earlier times had been generally regarded as unpleasantly frightening, unattractive, or even demonic. Among these were 'scars' on the earth's surface such as mountains and ravines, and other gloomy or violent phenomena such as cascading waters, bleak moors, dark forests, and thunderstorms.[8]

This shift in taste was gradual, and began sooner than is sometimes assumed. In 1709 the Earl of Shaftsbury declared in *The Moralist* that 'I shall no longer resist the passion growing in me for things of a natural kind ... Even the rude rocks, the mossy caverns, the irregular unwrought grottos and broken falls of waters, with all the horrid graces of the wilderness itself, as representing Nature more, will be the more engaging.'[9] But as Malcolm Andrews points out, in the early eighteenth century 'wilderness and mountain scenery were a minority taste,' and the passion for them had yet to be named.[10] The word *sublime* was of course very old, but its earlier use in rhetorical theory had referred to the quality in literature or art (that is, in culture not nature) which induces awe or 'throws an audience into transport,' as Longinus explained.[11] In the eighteenth century the word was newly employed to describe a response to natural phenomena, and Edmund Burke's *Philosophical Enquiry into the Origin of Our Ideas of the Sublime and Beautiful* (1757) led the way. Kant and others would dispute the emphasis Burke placed on the importance of terror in the sublime experience, but his *Enquiry* was the single most important influence in establishing the link between landscape, emotion, and pleasure. As Andrews has argued, Burke's *Enquiry* gave a 'dignity to primary emotional drives' which was extremely influential, for it helped to discredit rationalism and prepare the way for the romantic movement.[12]

The idea of the sublime was not only debated by philosophers, but it also permeated many aspects of culture. In popular literature and art, the passion for terror and gloom was expressed through the Gothic movement. The art of landscape gardening was transformed as estate owners strove to create fantasy worlds of man-made hills, lakes, and waterfalls, and curious members of the middle class, who were allowed to tour these estates, passed judgment on the effectiveness of their efforts.[13] Tourists also rediscovered or reinterpreted the Alps, and flocked to Wales and the Highlands. The most ambitious journeyed to the place where the sublime was said to be incarnate: Niagara Falls, where this intensity of experience became firmly established as a measure of a holiday's success.

Another aspect of the growing preoccupation with nature and landscape was the idea of the picturesque, a particularly English aesthetic category which had equally important implications for the rise of a tourist industry in both Britain and North America. The picturesque referred to a distinctly different and less spectacular quality of landscape, one that was visually pleasing but lacked the emotional impact of the sublime.[14] This term would long outlive *sublimity* as a tourist industry catchword ('The picturesque is found any time the ground is uneven,' says Roland Barthes in his criticism of the Hachette guidebooks),[15] but in the late eighteenth century its specific qualities were variety, intricacy, roughness, and the quality of being paintable. Like the sublime, it had its predecessors, in this case the eighteenth century's mounting admiration for European landscape painters such as Rosa, Poussin, and Claude Lorraine, as well as the growing affection for representations of British pastoral scenes.[16]

The relationship between the picturesque on the one hand and notions of civilization and wildness on the other was rather complex. Of vital importance to the picturesque tradition was the belief that nature, at its best, seemed to imitate art; that is, it conformed to the aesthetic principles of European artistic traditions. As Joseph Addison remarked in 1712, 'we find the Works of Nature still more pleasant, the more they resemble those of Art.'[17] Eighteenth-century landscape gardening embraced this idea most vigorously, and, as Denis Cosgrove and Stephen Daniels point out, 'a landscape park is more palpable but no more real, nor less imaginary, than a landscape painting or poem.'[18] The great gardeners strove to arrange nature into a series of artfully composed views, educating the visiting public on matters of taste and setting new standards in landscape perfection that would be emulated in painting (and later in photography), thus more or less completing the circle. Similarly, in tourism the commonplace goal of sightseers by the late eighteenth century was to find nature's most artfully composed views, and this preoccupation, combined with their use of such paraphernalia as the camera obscura and the Claude glass, was all part of the new enthusiasm for turning nature into art.[19]

Not many years would pass before the service industries learned to cater to this new obsession. But one element of the tourist industry, the production of guidebooks, had a particularly early start. Among the first guidebook writers, the Reverend William Gilpin was likely the most influential in moulding tourist taste. During the 1770s and 1780s, he wrote a series of travel guides (*Picturesque Observations*) that not only gave detailed advice on how to reach places of beauty in Britain, but also instructed tourists where to pause in their ramblings to get the best view, how to react to what they saw, and how to reproduce it in paintings so that they could 'take it home.' The Wye Valley tour, with Tintern Abbey as its highlight, was extremely popular by the 1770s and was soon thoroughly commercialized, with covered boats providing regular passenger service and Gilpin's guidebook offering careful analysis of each passing view. Elizabeth McKinsey credits Gilpin with proselytizing the charms of travel 'in search of the picturesque,' with 'democratizing' tourism by creating itineraries that all could follow, and with putting, figuratively speaking, a camera in the hands of every sightseer.[20] By 1790 this way of seeing landscape had become established as an integral part of the tourist experience. It encouraged the growth of hotels and other trappings in areas deemed picturesque, with Keswick on Lake Windermere becoming one of the first vulgarized tourist towns.[21]

Nature, culture, and tourism were brought together in another manifestation of these new aesthetic principles. The romantic sensibility, especially when infused with nationalism, encouraged an appreciation of those scenes in which landscape and history, especially in the form of ruins and graveyards, were blended together. The fascination with nature's ruins, such as mountains and ravines, was thus extended to the ruins of civilization and the emotions they evoked, such as nostalgia and melancholy. Advocates of the picturesque, notably Gilpin and Uvedale Price, took a gloomy yet delicious pleasure in scenes of age, decay, and desolation, and Gilpin's travel guides disclosed his fondness for 'old, unhappy, far-off things / And battles long ago.' They agreed that these qualities could be found in the 'elegant relics of ancient architecture; the ruined tower, the Gothic arch, the remains of castles, and abbeys,' and Price expanded his definition of the picturesque to include rough vernacular architecture such as cottages and mills, preferably in a state of dilapidation.[22] Such scenes had even more appeal if they were inhabited by quaintly clothed, preindustrial people apparently doomed to extinction, such as Highland crofters or the aboriginal peoples of distant continents. Thus the evocative power of 'oldness,' so thoroughly exploited in present-day Britain but much used in Canada as well, became part of the tourist industry's arsenal at least two hundred years ago.[23]

While it is easy to see the sublime and the picturesque as part of the reaction against rationalism which culminated in romanticism, such set aesthetic conventions were, at least in theory, anathema to the romantic movement's revolutionary agenda. Wordsworth, in his *Prelude*, specifically denounced the picturesque habit of viewing nature as a series of approved scenes that were supposed to elicit a set of predictable responses. The picturesque was not only formulaic, it objectified nature; what did it matter, it seemed to say, if the Scottish crofters were starving as long as they played out their lives as part of a well-composed Highland landscape?[24] The romantics, on the other hand, promoted *feeling* and the sanctity of the deeply personal response to nature. They sought to regain the initiative from the arbiters of so-called civilized taste and introduce a higher morality to their relationship with nature, whose existence was not, they insisted, dictated by the needs of human beings; 'everything has a Life of its own,' as Coleridge said.[25] And yet, as is often pointed out, the romantics' belief that nature mirrored their own moods and emotions was subjective enough that it denied, as often as not, that separate reality which they had claimed to restore, and in their hands both animate and inanimate nature were mined for their associative uses and symbolic import.

In turn, the works of the famous romantic writers provided fodder for the tourist industry. James Buzard shows how Byron's ways of seeing places were recycled over and over in travel writings and in guidebooks: he also shows how Byron provided imitators with 'accredited anti-touristic gestures that were performable *within* tourism.' Romanticism not only clothed places and cultural objects with thick layers of meaning, it offered an ideology which enabled travellers to these places to see themselves as more sensitive and original than other tourists, as members of 'an aristocracy of inner feeling.'[26]

Despite the contradictions inherent in romanticism, the movement elevated the pleasures of the imagination to a higher moral plane than they had enjoyed for a very long time, and endowed the idea of the individual with greater value than had perhaps ever been possible within traditional Christian culture. The implications of this process were extensive, and it is not far-fetched to suggest that romanticism's association between images, commodities, feelings, and personal fulfilment was a vital contributing factor in the development of consumer capitalism, including the growth of the tourist industry.

The uses of romanticism have so thoroughly suffused modern consumerism that their importance may go unnoticed, but by examining the interplay of culture and economy in an earlier era the historian finds that, as Cosgrove puts it, 'the dialectic of material conditions and human consciousness, of material production and symbolic production' becomes remarkably clear.[27] One recent work which considers this relationship is Colin Campbell's *The Romantic Ethic and the Spirit of Modern Consumerism* (1987). Campbell argues that the Industrial Revolution cannot be fully explained by concentrating on such factors as changes in production, population growth, or the demands of foreign markets. According to Campbell's account, the romantic movement ushered in a new hedonism in which the stimulation of the emotions or feelings became one of the most valued pleasures. Inspired by the association of objects and images with feelings, an inexhaustible lust for consumer goods and services fuelled the ever-expanding production and perpetual innovation that is characteristic of capitalist society. Campbell's analysis often fails to make the connection between demand and supply, and he has nothing to say about the tourist industry himself, yet the applicability of his ideas is clear enough. Romantic values endowed a host of places with evocative meaning, luring ever-growing numbers of people to travel, to use trains and boats, carriages and hotels, guidebooks and other paraphernalia in their quest for pleasurable sensation, and to be ready purchasers of any goods that might serve as souvenirs through which the essence of these precious experiences could be captured.

Campbell relates this process to the secularization of European culture, which had accelerated since the eighteenth century. The romantic imagination served the growth of capitalism by assuming some of the power that religion had once possessed. In a related fashion the practice of tourism, particularly at special places such as Niagara Falls, has been aptly compared to a secular pilgrimage; tourists went there to worship Nature and to feel its power, in the hope that the awe it inspired would bring about a brief or lasting transformation in themselves.[28] John Sears sees this as especially significant in the case of tourism in the United States, for strong religious traditions combined with postrevolutionary nationalism predisposed Americans to look in their landscapes for what they called 'sacred places.' Sears says little about the romantic movement, but his studies of attractions such as Niagara, Yosemite, and Yellowstone show the key role played by romantic nationalism in giving these places meaning for Americans.

Ian McKay's recent studies of twentieth-century tourism in Nova Scotia demonstrate the enduring commercial value of romantic imagery, and they show, in a Canadian context, that such images can be translated into both economic and political capital. Although he suggests that the passion for wild nature developed far later than was actually the case, he shows how the state in the inter-war years was motivated to enter the tourist business, and how bureaucrats quickly learned to exploit images of rugged scenery (and an equally rugged but idyllic rural past) in order to sell such places as Peggy's Cove and its fisherfolk to tourists.[29] Throughout the country as a whole – in fact, before the First World War – federal and provincial government involvement in tourism was minimal, but as the following chapters show, romantic nationalism was exploited shamelessly by tourism promoters as diverse as the Canadian Pacific Railway and the Toronto *Globe*, to serve the expansionist goals of Ontario's elite.

What is being argued here is that tourism as a consumer industry was built upon selling images and arousing romantic fantasies, and that romanticism in fact established the cultural foundations of the tourist industry and supplied its strategies for success. When historians of tourism write about places becoming 'commodified,' they are referring to the process by which meaning was encoded, saleable imagery was identified, and tourist sights were made to speak to consumers on an imaginative level, through the language of signs. But this process is not unique to capitalist cultures. There is little insight to be gained, as Culler points out, in looking nostalgically to a time when 'use-value' still mattered more than 'exchange-value,' even if our modern condition (as tourists or historians) compels us to believe in part that authenticity belongs to the past.[30] It is important, however, to try to understand the structures of meaning employed by tourism and the power relations embodied in them, particularly in those places where tourists were the agents of a larger colonization process.

TOURISM AND COLONIALISM

An element of romanticism which calls for closer examination because of its central role in wilderness tourism is the appeal of so-called primitive places and peoples. Of course this aspect of European culture predated the romantic movement, and merely entered a new phase with the writings of Rousseau and his followers. Europeans had scrutinized the Americas for centuries in their attempts to understand themselves, and later, as tourists and recently settled North Americans, they continued that search for meaning, reworking old images and ideas to serve new purposes. More than ever, as the nineteenth century progressed, notions of wilderness and 'wild men,' or the 'otherness' of non-European cultures, were used to confirm the values of their own civilization.

Images of wildness had served for millennia as the necessary counterpoint to notions of civilization, safety, and order in Western culture. In the Bible (and elsewhere) such imagery was largely negative: a Biblical wilderness was far more likely to be a barren land than a forest, and signified, as Roderick Nash says, 'any place in which a person feels stripped of guidance, lost and perplexed.'[31] Related words in the Teutonic and Norse languages were first used to describe human behaviour that was wilful or out of control; later they also came to mean places where a person might easily get into a confused or disordered state of mind. In Greek and Roman cultures, where nature was admired primarily in the pastoral sense, wilderness was associated with supernatural and frightening things. The word *panic*, for example, derives from the Greek god Pan, lord of the forest, whom one hoped to avoid meeting when alone in the woods. Thus classical, biblical, and European tribal beliefs all contributed to the vast body of medieval mythology where wild places and strange creatures abounded.[32]

The predominance of fearful and threatening wilderness imagery, however, did not mean that wild places and peoples were without value. Keith Thomas explains how both Christian and folk traditions held that everything in nature, whether good or bad, had some direct use or meaning for the human species that was only waiting to be discovered.[33] The wilderness, therefore, was full of symbolic meaning for humans to decipher, full of clues by which the progress of civilization – a European obsession – could be measured.

There is no single model for describing early Europeans' understanding of the relationship between themselves, as humans, and the rest of the natural world. Christian attitudes towards wilderness, for example, were neither consistent nor necessarily in agreement with popular beliefs. In support of its claims for humanity's singular place in God's scheme, church doctrine argued that there was a total separation between the human and animal worlds (or between spirit and nature). Humans had souls, other creatures did not, and the gulf between them was complete. Popular wisdom, on the other hand, clung to the much more ominous understanding that the boundary was not so distinct or secure. Thus medieval mythology was full of ambiguous and fantastic entities, and these tales maintained their literal credence and their symbolic import well into the early modern period. The church had its own doubts about the integrity of the human species, and was in practice an institution dedicated to the task of curbing the animal within. The notion of the subhuman has in fact been pervasive throughout European history, for there have been countless instances in which subordinate groups (women, the Irish, the poor, the insane, children, and non-white races) have been defined by church or state as being closer to animal nature than members of the dominant group.

It is hardly surprising, therefore, to find that the literal existence of the mythological wild man, who was half-man, half-beast, was taken for granted for hundreds of years and was still very influential at the dawn of European imperialism. Such images guided explorers in their interpretation of the aboriginal peoples they encountered, while the tangible reality of beings quite different from themselves reinforced the wild man myth. Europeans flocked to see the unfortunate individuals whom explorers and traders brought back from the New World for display, and the so-called wild boys purportedly found now and again in the woods were exploited as popular curiosities well into the eighteenth century. Part of this fascination derived from the Europeans' haunting fear that their superiority and dominance were not assured, and that civilized humanity could slip back into more savage ways. A growing belief in polygenism (the idea, condemned by the church, that God created more than one species of humans) helped to explain why some races could be closer to animal nature than themselves, but no one theory, however flattering to the European, was enough to lay this fear of the savage to rest.[34]

If the wild man stood for savagery, however, he also stood for freedom. As urban life became steadily more complicated, people naturally wondered what might have been lost through the processes of civilization. Even as early as the fifteenth century in Germany, for example, there were those who suggested that city dwellers might be able to learn something from the wild man.[35] Rousseau's tribute to primitivism in *Emile* (1762) and in his other works reinforced a steadily mounting fascination in western Europe with both the wild man and the noble savage, and by the late eighteenth century this preoccupation had become a significant element in the passion for travel to wild places.[36] It was about this time, as well, argues Hayden White, that the wild man image was transformed from the mythical to the fictional – a 'fiction' being an image not *literally* believed in, but useful on a symbolic level.[37] Thus the image of the wild man became infinitely malleable, to be emulated, pitied, or despised as the needs of the moment dictated.

In no aspect of the process of contact was this more true than in the practice of tourism, as this book will show. Not only places but people became objects of the commodification process when they fell under the tourists' gaze, and the act of defining them, of endowing them with meaning, itself involved a kind of appropriation or assertion of control. As Edward Said observes, in nineteenth-century travel narratives European 'consciousness was represented as the principal authority, an active point of energy that made sense not just of colonizing activities but of exotic geographies and peoples.'[38] The effects and implications of this process were highly varied, but in British North America the growing tourist industry was one aspect of the association between imperialism and culture which historians have largely overlooked.

The subject of Mary Louise Pratt's *Imperial Eyes* (1992) is neither tourism nor North America, but her study of travel and exploration narratives illuminates the extent to which such writings functioned to produce 'the rest of the world.'[39] That world was produced by and for the European imagination, but the impact of such cultural constructions was far from imaginary. Pratt and other cultural historians show how, as Marianna Torgovnick says, 'ideas about primitive societies ... have made things happen in the political world,'[40] and they have made things happen in the economic world as well. Ideas and images produced by the European imagination were given both political and economic reality because of the power exercised by the colonizing nations, and their meaning must be understood in that context. In W.J.T. Mitchell's words, such images ought not to be regarded as 'providing a transparent window on the world' but 'as a sort of sign that presents a deceptive appearance of naturalness and transparence, concealing an opaque, distorting, arbitrary mechanism of representation.'[41]

Wilderness tourism in nineteenth-century Ontario took place in, or infringed upon, regions occupied mainly by Native people, particularly the Ojibway. It occurred in what Pratt calls 'contact zones,' a term she uses to mean 'the space of colonial encounters, the space in which peoples geographically and historically separated come into contact with each other and establish ongoing relations, usually involving conditions of coercion, radical inequality, and intractable conflict.'[42] The effects of wilderness tourism on Native peoples were profound and remain largely undocumented, but some discussion of those interactions will be found in later chapters. Here the focus is confined to the role imagery played in predetermining how tourists saw, defined, and made use of Native peoples in their travels.

Behind these images, whether their users knew it or not, lay a particular ideological agenda – the imagery constituted a kind of language for signifying the meaning and fate of the Native population of North America. Virtually all tourists visiting the Canadian wilderness, whether European, American, or urban Canadian, saw themselves as agents of, or temporary refugees from, the civilized world. The relentless march of progress, they believed, would inevitably triumph in all parts of North America, but in the meantime they looked to the Native inhabitants to satisfy their curiosity about humanity in its wild state and to confirm their confidence in their own civilization. Regardless of whether Native people were seen as good or bad, noble or ignoble, innocent or demonic, they were cast in the role of a race in decline. Tourists might idealize or condemn them, but the belief that Native people belonged to the past and were without a future supplied a powerful, unifying theme. Confining 'Indians' to the past had a particular advantage for tourists, for it allowed them to see Native people as 'authentic' and yet ineffectual and unthreatening at the same time.

The range of varied and contradictory images employed by Europeans, Americans, and Euro-Canadians in order to 'understand' the Native population have already been the subject of many studies.[43] The images which affected tourists most, however, judging from references made in their travel narratives, were those which pervaded popular culture, especially novels and other literature. Especially influential were the works of certain American writers widely known throughout North America and Europe, most notably James Fenimore Cooper's *Leatherstocking Tales* of the 1820s, Washington Irving's *Astoria* (1836), and Henry Wadsworth Longfellow's *The Song of Hiawatha* (1855).

The priorities of tourism favoured the romantic version of the wilderness and its peoples, and Cooper's Indians, not surprisingly, were particular favourites. He did not portray them as perfect, for their heroic qualities were undermined by their violence in hunting and in war, but still they possessed what he called the red gifts: a marvellous physique, a keen eye and quick reflexes, amazing stamina, a natural wisdom, a simplicity of manners, a poetic way of speech, and all the other attributes of a people totally in tune with nature.[44] More often than not these attributes, real or imagined, were what the tourists looked for in an Indian, and their absence, even the absence of the chilling ferocity which these people were supposed to exhibit, was sometimes a source of disappointment and wry comment.

Just as nineteenth-century tourism cannot be divorced from the larger context of colonialism, such literature cannot be separated from the much broader effort to define the character of North American civilization and to limit Native people to certain prescribed roles. Cooper, for example, knew the wilderness was bound to disappear, but he took part in a movement of writers and artists which was very much in tune with one stream of middle-class thinking. This movement was aimed at creating an American past as romantic and exciting as that of Europe – an invented past for which urbanized Americans could feel a pleasurable nostalgia and pride but no guilt for their role in displacing Native people from their lands, for that was part of the inevitable march of civilization. Art rather than history and feeling rather than fact were what mattered most in this endeavour. Washington Irving was part of that school of thought, though he sometimes questioned the idealized portrayal of the noble Indian. 'As far as I can judge,' wrote Irving, 'the Indian of poetical fiction is like the shepherd of pastoral romance, a mere personification of imaginary attributes.'[45] Cooper defended the process of image-making as precisely the writer's prerogative. That is what poetry is, he pointed out, and 'to suppose that the redman is to be represented only in the squalid misery or in the degraded morals that certainly more or less belong to his condition, is, we apprehend, taking a very narrow view of an author's privileges. Such criticism would have deprived the world of even Homer.'[46] But if the novelist could use primitive imagery to create a mood or draw a moral lesson in which the Indian's role was mainly metaphorical, the sightseer could assume the same prerogative, and throughout the nineteenth century we find tourists constantly reconstructing the image of the Indian to serve as some sort of symbol in a larger world view.

Not surprisingly, the habit of idealizing the Indian had some bitter detractors. Overall, during the nineteenth century the status of Native people in Western culture was in decline, and as Hayden White says, they came to be regarded by a majority of non-Natives 'less as an ideal than as an example of *arrested* humanity, as that part of the species which had failed to raise itself above dependency on nature.'[47] Negative images of wilderness man had always existed, but Native people, like European women, suffered during the nineteenth century from a proliferation of pseudoscientific theories aimed at proving their inferiority. Some influential American ethnologists, by the 1840s, had reacted against the sentimentalism of writers such as Cooper and had come out in support of polygenism; that is, they persuaded themselves that the Indians had been created as a separate race. By examining the skulls of Native North Americans they sought to prove that the race had never progressed, and this view was used to justify conquest and extermination.[48] In popular literature, romanticism was countered in so-called Indian-hater fiction which appealed particularly to settlers in the western United States, who, as Helen Harris says, had been incensed by Cooper's 'elevation of the Indian to the level of an articulate human.' Mark Twain deliberately set out to show easterners that Cooper's Indian had never existed, and some of his lesser known works portray Native people as utterly debased and mock them and their defenders viciously.[49]

The hostility towards Native people displayed by some American tourists on their 'Northern Tours' is best understood in the context of a culture bent on justifying the expansionism of the United States. But such views were prevalent enough in Canada, and there was a growing tendency during the latter half of the nineteenth century to apply theories of racial degeneracy in this country as well. Darwin's *Origin of Species* weakened the influence of polygenism, but it could be used to support the idea that some races were below others on the evolutionary scale. This belief was not incompatible with a romantic admiration for the traditional qualities of the wild man, but people could easily decide that such attributes were only suited to life on a lower evolutionary plane. Historian Francis Parkman's popularity in Ontario was certainly not marred by his portrayal of Native people and the Métis as backward races bound to succumb to Anglo-Saxon superiority, and much of the literature of English Canada, by the closing decades of the century, was in tune with the need of Ontario expansionists to justify their own conquest of the West.

But the image of the Indian still had a part to play in Canadian and American culture, one as divorced from reality as earlier imagery had been. As Native people were pushed from the everyday lives and consciousness of urban Canadians, and as the latter became more and more preoccupied with the debilitating effects of city life, the wild man image was, as White says, despatialized, or internalized.[50] This simply meant that the Indian no longer needed to exist 'out there' to provide imaginative satisfaction; it could be enough just to 'play Indian' on one's own – when on holiday, for example.[51] Wilderness was a product of perception more than an objective reality, and an individual's ability to rediscover 'the wild man within' was a very personal affair. White sees this use of the wild man image as both new and old, as a remythification, in fact, in that it works in the 'same way that the myth of the Wild Man did in ancient cultures, that is, as a projection of repressed desires and anxieties.'[52]

WHO'S SPEAKING? CLASS, GENDER, AND THE NATURE OF TRAVEL NARRATIVE

All of this sounds very bourgeois, and so it was. The tourist industry mainly served the propertied classes in the nineteenth century, and it is members of the middle and upper classes whose experiences – whose ways of seeing – are documented in the vast majority of sources. The final section of this chapter will consider some questions of historical evidence and 'voice,' which affect our understanding of nineteenth-century tourism. Were working-class people participating in tourism? Why is the historical record so heavily weighted in favour of men's experience as travellers? If the genre of the travel narrative is our richest source of information about the experiences of tourists, how are we to read and interpret these works?

The history of tourism is imbued with the language of class. Historians have recognized that the dominant ways of interpreting landscape, for example, were rooted in the cultural values of people with leisure, literacy, and freedom of movement, people who found it natural to take a proprietorial view of the land, whether in relation to distant regions of empire or the shores of a nearby lake. Moreover, because the language of romanticism was so widely employed to inspire consumption and describe its delights, a link between a rising middle class which enjoyed growing powers of consumption and the enduring influence of the romantic aesthetic upon tourism can certainly be suggested, though hardly proven.[53] One observation that can be made with confidence is that middle-class people, by the latter decades of the nineteenth century, were increasingly anxious to identify themselves as the class most needful and deserving of holidays and best able to make good use of them. A yearly holiday was part of the pattern of consumption to which they laid claim. It was their reward for coping with the stressful world of business and social obligation, the one sure cure for 'brain fag' to which they were all entitled.

The extent of working-class participation in tourism is difficult to determine, not least because the boundaries of class in nineteenth-century rural Ontario are rather vague. Contemporary observers sometimes spoke of the holiday habits of 'the masses,' but in most instances we must assume that they were referring to activities enjoyed by a lot of people at once, rather than the full participation of all classes in the tourist industry. Many newly settled farmers were hardly people of means, but no doubt some travelled for pleasure when they could – to see Niagara, for example, if they lived close by. Urban workers, however, were more constrained in their use of leisure, as most did not have paid holidays even by the beginning of the First World War. Canadian labour historians are virtually silent on the question of the working-class holiday, perhaps mirroring the silence of workers for whom hours, wages, and security of employment were still the vital issues.

This neglect parallels the slight attention paid to general questions of working-class leisure in late Victorian Canada, compared, for example, with Great Britain in the same period. This may be partly because Britain had begun to industrialize a century earlier and there was time for a new recreational culture to develop among urban workers by the end of the nineteenth century, a culture which has now come to be seen as traditional. Economic supremacy also encouraged Britain's growing middle class to accept recreation as part of their own lives earlier than their Canadian counterparts, and some saw that workers, too, needed the occasional holiday, such as a day's rail excursion to the sea, if efficiency was to be maintained. In addition, with the rising respectability and strength of labour unions in Britain, paid annual leave began to be granted in a few industries as early as the 1870s, although most unions saw shorter hours and better wages, not holidays, as the important issues. But by 1900 many white-collar workers, including shop assistants, were getting paid holidays, perhaps as belated compensation for their seldom having been granted the Saturday half-holiday most skilled workers received. The advent of the bicycle gave many clerks a new mobility, while the friendly society or 'going-off clubs' helped families save for an annual trip to the sea.[54]

We know less about Victorian Canadian working-class leisure, but many workers immigrating to Canada from Britain probably encountered an even bleaker picture than the one they had left behind. Labour unions generally ignored the issue of holidays in favour of improved hours and wages, and according to Michael Piva, the sixty-hour week was still common among blue-collar workers in turn-of-the-century Toronto, though construction workers had won the eight-hour day and the Saturday half-holiday by 1903. Most workers, however, were not granted the half-holiday until well into the First World War.[55] What is striking about the Canadian situation is how little progress seems to have been made over time, and how precarious even the observance of statutory holidays seems to have been. In the late 1880s the Royal Commission on the Relations of Labor and Capital found many instances of workers losing wages where such holidays were observed, or being forced to work them to avoid dismissal. In some cases these were new rules, justified by rising competition, and the *Labour Gazette* in 1908 recorded that a law subjecting employers to a thirty-dollar fine for not shutting down on holidays had been rescinded.[56] Many Toronto factories closed down for some weeks each year for repairs, but this can only be understood as an imposed economic hardship for most, rather than a chance for holidays.[57] In such a climate it is no wonder that, for the majority of the urban working class in central Canada, the question of paid annual holidays was barely an issue, even in the early twentieth century.

If the holidaying public remained predominantly middle class throughout the period before the First World War, was it also dominated by male travellers as many historians have assumed? Travel has a good deal to do with physical and imaginative freedom, and therefore the question of women's experience as tourists is bound to be contested ground. Did Victorian society allow women to be at large to the same extent as men? When the author of a travel narrative is male, do we assume, if no female companion is mentioned, that she was not there? How exceptional were the women who not only travelled but published their experiences as tourists? Did travel mean different things to men and women?

The woman traveller has been rather neglected in recent works on the history of tourism, especially those that deal with the relationship between travel and the romantic ideal of personal freedom. Dennis Porter, for example, includes no women travellers in his *Haunted Journeys: Desire and Transgression in European Travel Writing* (1991), while Eric Leed's *The Mind of the Traveller: From Gilgamesh to Global Tourism* (1991) sees women only as objects of the male traveller's imagination. Leed defines travel as a masculine activity given *meaning* by the existence of the non-travelling woman; there is, Leed imagines, 'no free and mobile male without the unfree and sessile female.' As an historian Leed confidently maintains that 'historically men have travelled and women have not, or only under the aegis of men,' and by way of negative evidence he excludes women's voices and experiences from his study. He concentrates instead on such matters as 'sexual hospitality' and its role in the 'erotics of arrival' which brings 'the spermatic journey' to its climax.[58]

James Buzard's study of British tourists in Europe recognizes that women did travel, and it pays much more attention to the question of gender than most other works. He examines how the Byronic model – the romantic image of 'the lone male wanderer' freed from the constraints of home, and tasting life at its most intense – served men much better than women throughout the Victorian age. The dominant culture, he maintains, construed northern Europe (including Britain) as masculine and southern Europe (especially Italy) as feminine, though this gendered geography, as he calls it, was clearly the product of male perceptions and fantasies. He also observes, as part of his study of the tourist-traveller dichotomy, that many literary works employed the 'family abroad' plot to expose women as tourists by nature, condemning them on the grounds of their superficiality, their need to travel in the constant protection of others, and their habit of recreating the domestic atmosphere wherever they travelled abroad. Because Buzard relies heavily upon fictional works written by men for his evidence, the reader learns little about the true influence of women's dissenting views, or for that matter, about what they really did when they went abroad.[59]

There are studies, of course, which focus exclusively on the travelling woman, although these tend to be about highly exceptional individuals – intrepid world travellers who gained some fame or notoriety in their own time. Nonetheless, these works show that women travelled for many of the same reasons as men, including the search for adventure, freedom, and mystery, but that it was frequently much harder for them to escape home, family, and social conventions. Sometimes younger women managed a journey before family duties conspired to tie them down; others took to travel to avoid marriage, having witnessed the physical or mental illness brought upon their mothers or other women by domestic boredom and too many pregnancies. Those who spent their later years travelling were often making a break from a stifling, housebound existence, suddenly freed, in some cases, by the death of aged parents or a spouse whom they had nursed through long illness, or by the collapse of a marriage.[60]

The kind of prolonged 'adventure tourism' in which these women engaged was an exceptional practice for either men or women. To the original question of whether women were well represented within the ordinary travelling public, however, the answer must surely be yes, for the casual observations of nineteenth-century tourists everywhere confirms the presence and participation of women, young and old, married and single, as this book will show. John Sears goes so far as to say that nineteenth-century tourism was not 'gender-identified' because 'both men and women participated in it, often together, sometimes with children, and in so doing shared the same space.'[61] But the possibility that men's and women's experiences of travel may have been different should not be dismissed; instead, historians need to consider how sharp contrasts in the ways in which men and women travellers were received and perceived by the world may have worked to create these differences. For example, Sara Mills's *Discourses of Difference* (1991) points out that differences in men's and women's writings, which may seem to be due to gender, are more likely the result of external pressures which women writers had to 'negotiate.'[62]

It cannot be denied that the genre of the travel narrative was dominated by the works of men. Did women feel free to write publicly of their adventures? Many did not. Even Anna Jameson, an established author determined to write 'for women,' initially shrank from the personal, daily journal style of commentary common to the travel narrative because she dreaded being accused of the vanity of placing herself and her emotions at the centre of the story.[63] A chilling bit of advice embedded in a *Quarterly Review* article on women's travel writings some decades later showed how biological determinism might be directed at stifling the voice of the Victorian woman traveller. Go ahead and write like a man, with wit and evocative detail – the reviewer warned – but you will be defying your nature and society will despise you for it:

Modern philosophers may think and write what they please about the mental equality of the sexes, but ladies may depend upon this, that some of the most vigorous and forcible writing in the English language would lose all of its charm with a woman's name prefixed to it. Women may become orators and heroes in sudden emergencies – they may do feats of mental or physical manliness to defend a parent, a husband, or a child, which command our most enthusiastic admiration; but take away the sacred object – remove the high occasion which nerved her nature, or suspended it – and however wonderful or beautiful in itself the power exhibited, she may be sure that the feeling she wounds is far closer to our heart than the feeling she gratifies.[64]

Even though women's experience of travel was very likely not the same as men's, this had less to do with different values and desires than with the different social roles they were expected to play. The evidence we have shows that nineteenth-century middle-class men and women were both infatuated with the romance of travel, and that many of them dreamed of 'savage lands' where they could escape the constraints of civilization as defined and enforced by their own social class.[65]

Some writers have accentuated the difference between men's and women's travel by confusing the immigrant's experience with that of the tourist, suggesting, for example, that women saw 'the unexplored less as virgin paradise needing to be possessed and more as an extension of the home needing cultivation.'[66] It is true that female immigrants' experience was likely quite different from that of the men, as it was women's duty to domesticate the landscape and create islands of European civilization amidst an ocean of supposed savagery. But the contrast between the tourist and settler experience should not be underestimated, for our understanding of Euro-Canadian attitudes to the wilderness, particularly in Ontario, has been dominated and distorted in recent decades by the useful but too pervasive notion of the garrison mentality.

Others have pointed out already that this idea represents only one aspect of the Canadian psyche, and indeed just one side of Susanna Moodie, that archetypal malcontent who has been commonly represented as a 'one-woman garrison,' totally at war with nature.[67] Even a quick browse through Moodie's *Roughing It in the Bush* reveals that while the mentality of the settler – the woman facing the terror of loneliness and cultural isolation – dominates the work, the mentality of the tourist, free to possess the landscape imaginatively, is present at intervals as well. The gulf between fearing and romanticizing the wilderness is not necessarily one of personality but of circumstance. During Moodie's first Canadian spring, for example, when there was little work to do, she wandered in the woods and paddled on the lake in their canoe, giving 'names to fantastic rocks and fairy isles.' Later she describes a trip to Stony Lake with her husband with all the romantic effusions of the tourist, full of praise for the wilderness, 'savage and grand in its primeval beauty.'[68]

It is worth emphasizing that tourists, unlike most settlers, gloried in the sense of something alien, such as a wilderness that could be enjoyed physically and imaginatively and then left behind. It is the possibility or experience of entrapment – of *losing* one's freedom – that terrified, and that is what prompted Moodie to warn other women by revealing 'the secrets of the prison-house.' Ordinary life, real life, cannot be lived inside the values of romantic tourism; there is not much room for reality in the two-dimensional world of the picturesque, the sublime is by nature inhospitable, and the very elements of separation and control that are implied by the word *landscape* soon diminish if one is forced to stay. As another potential settler put it, 'I could afford to admire the noble forest at a distance, but when the possibility of my being imprisoned within its depths for the remainder of my life was mooted, I shrank from such an ordeal.'[69]

The relationship between the tourist's and the settler's ways of seeing the wilderness is tied to the relationship between landscape and living space, which has recently drawn attention from cultural geographers. They have helped us to understand that landscape, as Cosgrove says, 'is an ideological concept. It represents a way in which certain classes of people have signified themselves and their world through their imagined relationship with nature.'[70] The settler, explains Paul Carter, engages in 'establishing symbolic enclosures' which depend upon creating 'a point of view with a back and a front, a place with human symmetry,' and Cosgrove points out that 'for the insider, there is no clear separation of self from scene, subject from object.'[71] Tourists, on the other hand, moved through the landscape and carried their centre of gravity with them, secure in the distinction between self and other, consuming images of landscape and people, moving on when the romance began to fade.

All this is much in evidence in the most abundant and problematic set of source materials available to the historian of tourism: the genre of travel narrative. How are these collections of letters, diaries, journals, and stories to be read? It would be naive to mistake such sources for objective fact, and yet it would also be misguided to read them as mere reflections of travellers' already fixed views. Even though tourists, unlike established settlers, retained their sense of autonomy or separation from each new environment, most did not remain untouched by what they saw or return home unchanged. In other words, while realizing that the amount of cultural baggage that tourists brought with them was formidable, we need not take too deterministic a view of their experiences. On the contrary, as Joan Corwin points out, travel is 'so conspicuously a trial of identity' that travel narratives almost inevitably recount a journey within as well as a journey abroad, and Carter rightly insists that to become too formulaic about the study of travel narratives 'is to exclude precisely what distinguishes them: their active engagement with the road and the horizon.'[72] Even published narratives, usually derived from journals and letters, seldom present a story that is tidy and complete, and Carter reflects that it is the very quality of 'open-endedness, their lack of finish, even their search for words,' which may give us the clues we need.[73]

This lack of finish has not contributed to the travel narrative's reputation as a literary genre or even as a source of historical knowledge. During the nineteenth century, however, the market for such works was enormous, resulting in the publication of hundreds of accounts following virtually the same itineraries. Their popularity was probably enhanced by their ability to satisfy many needs at once, combining romantic adventure and practical information within one volume, even though the result was often a seemingly formless mass. In a saturated market, writers became more and more concerned with conveying the singularity of their own impressions, often showing little regard for accuracy of observation, but at the same time remaining happily unaware of the triteness of much of their own experience. At intervals didactic, fatuous, derivative, self-conscious, and prone to coyness, exaggeration, and overblown rhetoric, this vast genre constitutes a gold-mine of information about the mental world of tourists.

The problem of form, as Robert Fothergill says, is at the same time a problem of consciousness,[74] and it is partly through the awkward ways in which travellers managed to structure their accounts that we learn more about the nature of travel, what happens when two cultures meet, and how difficult it may be to order that experience. Despite its typically unwieldy construction, the travel narrative has some features in common with the novel, a genre with which it shared some of the same didactic purpose and market appeal during the nineteenth century. In the travel narrative the traveller casts himself or herself in the role of the protagonist, the itinerary itself provides the plot, and the setting out and the going home provide a beginning and an end. The journey often takes the form, overtly or otherwise, of a quest, a search for knowledge or experience that propels both traveller and reader, and the journey through space is frequently paralleled, as already suggested, by some form of inward journey as well. The familiar components of the novel – the setting of scenes and the introduction of characters, themes of conflict, danger, and suspense, and lessons about good and evil – are almost uniformly present in the travel narrative, and through each of these, writers have revealed their allegiance to or defiance of conventional cultural norms. The same was true even in writings not intended for publication, for in letters home or in private diaries, the need to structure new knowledge in light of past experience remained paramount. All writing is intended for an audience, even if it is only oneself, and no form of discourse is more self-conscious in its search for meaning than the private world of the diary.[75]

But unlike many works concerned with nineteenth-century travel, this book is not primarily an exercise in literary criticism but a critical study of the cultural foundations of an industry. It assumes, to use Simon Pugh's words, that 'texts are inseparable from the conditions of their production and reception in history,'[76] and travel narratives, as well as many other kinds of documents, are used as sources of information at the same time as they are implicitly or explicitly examined to see what they say about the cultural biases of their authors. The difficulty of language is acknowledged (but not solved) through placing some problematic words (such as primitive) in quotation marks when it seems particularly important that they not be taken at face value. But as Torgovnick and others have already argued, quotation marks solve nothing and absolve no one, and are best used as sparingly as possible.

The following chapters demonstrate that the most powerful unifying theme in Ontario tourism before the First World War was the tension and interplay between notions of civilization and wildness. If these ideas were the product of the European imagination, aided and abetted by the pervasive ideology of romanticism, they were nonetheless produced and perpetually recast for concrete social, political, and economic reasons. The nineteenth-century passion for wild things belongs to the history of ideas, but it belongs equally to the history of real people, real power, and real money.

2

Taming Niagara

Why must a book about Ontario tourism begin with Niagara? The reasons are several. Niagara Falls was the place where the tourist industry began, not only in Ontario but in North America. By the late eighteenth century the falls had become world famous as an icon of the sublime, to use Elizabeth McKinsey's phrase, and before many more decades had passed Niagara was attracting tens of thousands of visitors each year.[1] The result, of course, was that Niagara was transformed by such an insistent human presence, and its descent from the wild to the tame made it the prototype of natural places considered 'spoiled' by tourism. Niagara was prototypical in other ways as well, for the falls and their environs, at least for a time, embodied many of the elements of romantic tourism, including picturesque views, the melancholy remains of bloody battles and dead heroes, an association with supposedly primitive people, and of course wild nature at its most sublime. Moreover, tourism in nineteenth-century Ontario had overwhelmingly to do with water and its effect on human sensibilities; as the tourist itinerary steadily expanded, the impact of new watery sights and sensations, such as running the rapids on the St Lawrence in a Durham boat, or passing on board a steamer into Lake Superior's Thunder Cape during a lightning storm, would be compared to the sublimity of Niagara Falls. Niagara became the established standard against which other tourist 'thrills' were measured.

As already discussed, the idea of the sublime as it was understood by the late eighteenth century played an incalculable part in the rise of a tourist industry. One of the sensations tourists sought was an intensity of imaginative experience, and an encounter with the sublime meant being swept away by the beauty and terror of some natural phenomenon – being transported (however briefly) into another realm of being or level of consciousness. 'The essential claim of the sublime,' as Thomas Weiskel says, is that people can 'in feeling and in speech, transcend the human.'[2] This chapter looks at how tourists were drawn to the notion of transcendent experience at Niagara and what their expectations were. Was the experience a religious or secular one? How could it be expressed in words? How difficult was it to be swept away once multitudes of other people were attempting to do the same? How did a nascent tourist industry capitalize on the notion of the sublime?

Studies of Niagara have already given some attention to these questions, but Elizabeth McKinsey's has done so in depth.[3] She looks at how the falls were interpreted in literature and art, explores their importance as an 'icon of the American sublime,' and shows how Niagara was used to symbolize the ideals of the American nation. McKinsey is concerned with how and why this image changed over time, and finds that the growth of industry and commerce at the falls, combined with a shift towards utilitarianism and sentimentalism in Victorian America, undercut the sublime experience and the potency of Niagara as a cultural symbol. The perspective taken in this chapter is somewhat different, for it concentrates primarily on the experience of tourists, and particularly that of visitors to the Canadian side of the Niagara River. It reveals that, for most, the falls were a symbol of the New World sublime rather than an icon of American nationalism; that is, they symbolized the primitive danger and mystery long associated with the North American wilderness.

Unlike McKinsey, I do not see the romantic and the commercial as purely antithetical forces, but suggest that romantic values provided the basic structure of the tourist industry on the Niagara frontier. Here I follow the development of that industry through three stages: the growing interest in the sublime and the beginnings of tourism before 1812; the creation of an itinerary encompassing the falls, battlefields, the Tuscarora village and other views and sights by the 1820s; and the transformation of the falls by tourism, which accelerated after 1825. Throughout this period the plentiful testimonies of the tourists themselves tell of the mounting sense of irony and tourist angst that became part of the Niagara experience.

TERROR AND TRANSCENDENCE

'Our forefathers crossed themselves when they passed such scenes, and regarded them as the abode of the devil and his angels,' wrote Johann

Georg Kohl in 1861.[4] Europeans first learned of Niagara Falls from Samuel de Champlain in the early seventeenth century. Having not seen the falls himself, he based his account on frightening tales told to him by Native people, who may well have been obliging their listeners' taste for the fantastic. Their descriptions tended to confirm European perceptions of precipices, abysses, and waterfalls as symbols of the dangerous, the primitive, and the ungodly, and thereafter, in travel literature, such images of the falls became common currency.[5] François Gendron's idea of Niagara, for example, was that it was a horrible place where savages lived, who fed off 'wild cows' and other beasts hurled down on the rocks by the cataract.[6] Louis Hennepin, travelling with LaSalle, was the first European explorer actually to see Niagara, and his descriptions and engravings would, as McKinsey says, 'dominate the Western imagination' until half way through the eighteenth century. While Hennepin could see a wild beauty in the place, he also found it terrifying and demonic. 'When one stands near the Falls,' he wrote, 'and looks down into this most dreadful Gulph, one is seized with Horror, and the head turns round, so that one cannot look long or steadfastly upon it.'[7]

By the middle of the eighteenth century, two basic changes in Europeans' understanding of Niagara were taking place which were part of a much broader secularization process. First, in the spirit of the Enlightenment, explorers and scientists such as Peter Kalm were making their way to Niagara and producing topographical descriptions of the falls. These would lay to rest the more fantastic stories about their magical properties, and undercut Niagara's potency as a symbol of the demonic. People who visited Niagara were still overwhelmed by its power over them, however, and the second great change (made possible by the first) was that the idea of the sublime was reinterpreted and employed in new ways. The word came into use to describe feelings of wonder and terror, which were now considered more good than bad. Niagara thus became an *icon of the sublime* for the entire Western world. It was special not only because of its immensity but because, unlike European waterfalls such as Terni and Tivoli, Niagara thundered in magnificent solitude through the primeval forest of the New World, far from civilization, it seemed, in both space and time. As one early visitor put it, Niagara was 'the most romantic of awful Prospects Imaginable.'[8] The falls were valued most for their intensity of effect upon the mind and soul.

Niagara was not easy to get to, but by the 1790s the stream of sightseers was steadily growing. At that time, understandably, the journey was undertaken mainly by adventurers of some means. Among them were business and professional men, both American and British, either living in or visiting New York. They followed a route up the Hudson River and across to Fort Erie from Buffalo, travelling by boat and stagecoach. Also numerous were British and European adventurers, both male and female, some of whom were thwarted in their plans for a Grand Tour by the wars with France, and chose a North American tour instead. Depending on their itinerary they made their way to the falls through Buffalo or came up the St Lawrence River from Montreal. Well-connected visitors often stayed with the governor or with military officers and were taken to see the falls by private coach, while others were forced to put up at taverns in nearby Chippewa and to take advantage of a daily public coach service to the falls. No provisions for tourists' safety were made, and although guides could be found, such arrangements were ad hoc and not always satisfactory. In spite of such inconveniences, however, touring North America without seeing Niagara was then unthinkable.

An itinerary of sights as well as certain patterns of perception developed early on at Niagara. As has been pointed out elsewhere, the approach to the falls took on the characteristics of a pilgrimage, as many travellers were aware.[9] First they underwent the long anticipation of the falls, then the breathless final approach, and then the all-important first glimpse. After gazing at the falls from above, some then ventured below the falls by means of a perilous climb, and then went on to visit a series of supplementary sights such as Goat Island, at that time a verdant wilderness, the famous Whirlpool, the view from Queenston Heights, and Devil's Hole, best seen with its gory history fresh in the mind (the massacre of British soldiers in 1763 by Native allies of the French). The main attraction was always, of course, the falls themselves, the true object of their quest.

But was this a religious or a secular pilgrimage? Edmund Burke had said that the terror inspired by such sights could bring a new appreciation of God's omnipotence. The Methodist and evangelical revivals had brought spontaneous and public declarations of faith, including the sudden conversion experience, back into fashion. Niagara itself had been interpreted in biblical terms in recent American theological writings, and it was not unusual for tourists to describe their reaction to the falls as a profound religious awakening. 'My whole heart and soul ascended towards the Divinity in a swell of devout admiration, which I had never before experienced,' wrote poet Thomas Moore, and man of commerce James Melish boasted that when he first saw the cataract 'My eyes were rivetted to the spot, while I exclaimed, "These are thy glorious works, Parent of good!"' Edward Wakefield's religious response, on the other hand, seems to have come almost as a sober second thought. 'For some time,' he admitted, 'I was lost in wonder, but collecting my thoughts, the sublime images before me excited a sort of devotional awe, and raised emotions of adoration to that infinite Power by whom the mighty torrent was created.'[10]

There was a profound difference, however, between these homages to a benevolent God and the demonic images once associated with the falls. What nineteenth-century tourists were really worshipping at Niagara was Nature, whether the power of God was believed to be manifest in the scene or not. Once Europeans had lost their literal belief in its magical properties, Niagara had been effectively secularized. No longer seen as a place governed by the supernatural, Niagara could still *remind* visitors of God's omnipotence and make them newly aware of his presence, but if tourists sought access to another reality at Niagara, they sought it primarily within themselves. The sublime as newly understood was a romantic concept, and it promised to unleash for the individual a new capacity for intense experience. Niagara had become the ultimate test of the 'civilized' man or woman's ability to feel deeply, to transcend the world of the mundane, to hear Nature speak, and to live abundantly.

Early signs that the kind of romantic ecstasy which tourists longed for might prove elusive began to appear by the 1790s. The problem was partly one of words, for tourists found that their experiences of the falls, however wonderful, were not easily translated into sublimity of language. This was a complex problem with several consequences. For one thing, it was hard to prove to others that one's quest for transcendent experience had been successful, and in their repeated attempts to do so travel writers quickly fell into a set of hardening rhetorical conventions that undermined the very qualities of spontaneity and originality that they were trying to convey. They were self-consciously aware of this predicament, and the habit of alluding critically to the works of earlier travellers was already widespread by the 1790s and often focused on confirming or casting doubt on the veracity of other people's emotional responses to the falls. Self-consciousness also led them to feign reluctance over attempting yet another description of Niagara, protesting that language fell too far short of the actual experience. 'No words can convey an adequate idea of the awful grandeur of the scene,' wrote

Isaac Weld in his widely read *Travels*, and George Heriot found that the falls surpassed 'in sublimity every description which the powers of language can afford.'[11] To declare oneself speechless before the great cataract was offered as proof, however, of the intensity of one's experience, and the repeated use of the word sublime to encompass a combination of rapture, reverence, and fear might be taken to mean that the writer was struggling to describe the indescribable.

But travel accounts succeeded well enough in convincing others that Niagara was not to be missed, and also in setting certain standards in sublime experience. Even before the War of 1812 the romantic conventions surrounding tourism at Niagara had been established and their commercial usage begun. Travel narratives, when published, acted as advertisements for Niagara before a tourist industry came into existence, providing practical information for prospective travellers, enticing them through intimate revelations about the effects of Niagara, and arousing hopes and worries about whether their own feelings would be as authentic and profound. A sense of tourist angst was already becoming part of the experience of the falls, and would only increase as commercial tourism began to transform Niagara.

But these were early days. At the beginning of the nineteenth century Niagara was truly a wilderness, and tourists had, if they liked, the opportunity to experience real danger (and sublime terror) during their exploration of the falls. Male tourists probably felt a special obligation to prove their mettle by undertaking the most daring act of clambering down the steep bank to view the falls from below, though this demanding ritual soon became part of the regular itinerary for female sightseers as well. 'Mrs Simcoe's ladder,' built in 1795, remained in place for a number of years, though by all accounts it was a flimsy affair, insecurely attached to some small trees at the top. Things got no better once the descent was achieved. The path heading behind the column of water, wrote Timothy Bigelow in 1805, consisted of crumbling slate 'which was so mixed with the water that live eels were actually moving about between our feet, and a false step ... would have plunged us where nothing could have saved us from instant destruction.' Wakefield reported himself 'deprived of breath' by the whirling spray and 'stunned with the tremendous roar,' so that he was 'on the point of falling senseless in the awful chasm' when a friend came to the rescue. But some visitors, like Heriot, believed that danger was intrinsic to their quest, and that 'the train of sublime experience' was only intensified by 'the terror lest the treacherous rock crumble beneath the feet.' For a growing number, however, ease of access was important, and without it they were apt to feel that their enjoyment of the falls' sublimity had been circumscribed by a lack of local initiative.[12]

THE ROMANTIC ITINERARY

The War of 1812 kept tourists away from Niagara, but after peace returned, the Northern Tour – which took in 'the Springs, the Lakes, the Canadas, and the New England States' – grew more popular each year, and brought tourists by the hundreds to Niagara.[13] Travel for pleasure was sharply rising among Americans by the 1820s, and the northward flow would proceed unabated, curtailed only during years of epidemic disease. People who came long distances to see Niagara were almost universally members of the middle and upper classes, with leisure enough to put up with uncertain timetables and slow progress on bad roads, and money enough to pay the substantial costs of travel. By way of explaining his own motives for setting out, one anonymous traveller wrote that 'having a leisure month before me, and growing impatient of the confinement of a large and populous city, I thought I had a *moment to seize*; for the improvement of health; the enjoyment of a survey of the beauties and sublimities of nature, and the diversities of character which present themselves to a traveller.'[14]

The romantic foundations of tourism at Niagara were thoroughly developed by the early 1820s. While no one can speak for those whose impressions were not recorded, it appears that the majority of tourists, from far and near, were by this point well schooled in romantic rhetoric and used it readily at the falls. An expanded and established itinerary made the most of evocative natural and historic sights; in fact, this may have been Niagara tourism's Golden Age, when commercialization had not yet taken over, when things still seemed 'real,' and when some originality of response still seemed possible.

Tourist angst had become, nonetheless, a well-documented affliction, and disappointment in the falls was not an unusual confession. But its victims were far more likely to blame culture than nature; Niagara was not at fault, but rather their own over-exposure to descriptive accounts in which, as John Duncan wrote in 1823, 'all the parts of speech, and degrees of comparison, are fatigued by a seemingly fruitless effort to sketch the stupendous scene.'[15] But the great majority complained of no such troubling divergence of image and reality intruding upon their pleasure, and they were eager to confirm, as Richard Barrett told his diary, that 'although our expectation was wound up to the highest pitch by the numberless accounts we had heard of this great wonder, yet did the reality far exceed the description.' William Blane asserted that disappointment was unimaginable, and that for him the falls induced the most 'indescribable sensations,' falling back on stanzas from Byron's tribute to Terni as a means of expressing his ecstasy.[16] Even those whose principal purpose of travel was business, not pleasure, spoke the language of romanticism in attempting to describe the falls. Robert Gourlay, for example, whose *Statistical Account of Upper Canada* (1822) was intended as an immigrants' guide and an exposure of governmental abuses, found himself drawn into the rhetoric of the 'awful and sublime' while writing of Niagara (even while admitting that it was 'a beaten subject').[17] Written testimonies by Canadians are rare, but the number of colonists who ventured forth to see the falls probably increased steadily after the end of the war as transportation improved, and they, too, seem to have seen it through the same eyes. John Galt's *Bogle Corbet; or The Emigrants* (1831?) tells of settlers who in their second summer decide to visit the falls, and his characters display not only a basic knowledge of romantic values but an ironic understanding of their now hackneyed uses.[18]

Although a full-blown tourist industry at Niagara awaited the completion of the Erie Canal in the mid-1820s, it began to develop as soon as the war was over. In 1818 William Darby observed that 'in no other situation in the United States can buildings and other accommodations for the use of travellers be established with more certainty of remuneration' than at Niagara.[19] A Loyalist descendant named William Forsyth would be the first entrepreneur to exploit the tourists' demand for services on the Canadian side, and he helped to bring into existence a small but omnipresent 'service sector' whose intrusive and deceptive tactics soon became notorious.

A convicted criminal and former militia man who brought little credit upon himself during the war, William Forsyth was only the first of many unscrupulous tourism promoters at Niagara. His single-minded efforts to monopolize the tourist trade confirmed his reputation as a man bent primarily upon personal gain. But his rapaciousness was not unique, and his career would come to an abrupt end in the 1830s only because he was in continuous disfavour with the colonial authorities.[20]

Forsyth enjoyed the particular advantage of owning land inherited from his father, just downriver from the Horseshoe Falls. There he established Forsyth's Inn, which quickly became the favourite destination of visitors to the Canadian side, though their unpredictable host might prove obnoxious or obsequious depending upon his mood and the status of his guests.[21] From the beginning Forsyth had two priorities: to develop a range of services that would keep tourists within his grip, and to gain a monopoly of Niagara's most precious commodity, the view itself. His great opportunity came in 1820 when he bought the farm next to his own, thus achieving control over all the best frontage except for the sixty-six-foot-wide military or chain reserve that ran along the entire frontier. By 1822 he had erected the new, three-storey Pavilion Hotel, to be expanded in 1826. Visitors were soon being brought to the Pavilion in coaches operated by Forsyth's men, and would achieve their first glimpse of the falls by making their way from his hotel down a dense forest path which concealed the view 'till close at the place,' whereupon it burst upon them 'with astonishing grandeur!' As a less strenuous (and less sublime?) alternative they might gaze out of the hotel's upper storey windows or stand out on the balcony, from which an excellent view could be had. If they required a guide Forsyth could provide one, and if they wished to go into the gorge below the falls they could use the covered stairway he had erected in 1818, 'by which all who choose may go down on paying one York shilling.'[22] Forsyth had made a good beginning at turning tourists' desires into profit, and for the next decade he would try to tighten his control over their sightseeing itinerary.

These conveniences received much praise from tourists, even though they remained rudimentary. The trip below the falls, for example, usually involved a complete drenching, but Blane assured readers in the early 1820s that everything possible had been done 'to render access to different parts of the scene easy, even to the ladies.'[23] As yet, few predicted the ill effects of commercial tourism at the falls, and visitors generally lauded Forsyth's 'great desire to add to the unrivalled natural beauties of the wild and romantic scenery.'[24] But there were tourists who realized that the sublimity of the falls would not survive too great an ease of access. As one American put it in 1815, 'the enthusiastick traveller' should not arrive at the falls by some safe path; instead, 'His soul must be tuned by danger, obstruction, and novelty of situation, before it can be capable of the pitch to which it ought to be raised by this spectacle.' And Lieutenant Francis Hall warned that 'the effect produced upon us by any object of admiration is increased by the difficulties of approaching it: ... bring a Baptist's head, or even the wood of the true cross, to the believer's door, and they will soon lose all power over his fancy.' He based his fears on what he had seen of tourism in Britain, how 'the feelings excited by the Elgin marbles, for example, diminished when they were placed in a museum to be viewed by crowds of 'simpering fashionables' and 'gaping tradesmen.'[25]

Although the falls would always be the main attraction, the itinerary broadened after 1814 to include fields of battle where visitors could explore other kinds of intense experience equally in keeping with the romantic priorities of early nineteenth-century tourism. Traversing battlefields and imagining conflicts they had only read about was a popular pastime in postwar Europe and North America, for it afforded such romantic pleasures as the worship of the warrior-hero, the melancholy fantasy of violent death, the seeing and touching of the remains of battle (bones, 'blasted' trees, crumbling forts), and the association between history and landscape. In Upper Canada tourists' interest in such sites complemented the local residents' wish to keep memories of their ordeal alive and cherish the relics of war, and an itinerary quickly developed which commenced at the ruins of Fort Erie, took in the battlefields of Chippewa, Lundy's Lane, and Queenston Heights, and extended northward to include Fort George. For the average tourist the great appeal of this new history was the way it mingled with the landscape – the way, in imagination, they could hear the cries of the American soldiers being driven over the precipice at Queenston Heights, and hear the sound of guns mingling with the roar of the cataract at Lundy's Lane.

Despite their different nationalities, the adulation of General Brock was one emotion that a majority of the travellers could share with the local populace. The romantic cult of personality that instantly grew up around him exalted his devotion to his people, his statesmanship, his gallantry in war, his merciful treatment of American captives, and all those 'virtues which add lustre to bravery.'[26] Even though no memorial had yet been raised to his memory, local residents gladly escorted tourists to the spot where he had fallen, near the base of the escarpment, during the Battle of Queenston Heights.

As this piece of uncultivated ground became part of the tourist itinerary it took on a life of its own. John Howison called it sacred ground, for a view of it, he said, 'must awaken in the minds of all ... feelings as warm and enthusiastic as the contemplation of monuments consecrated by antiquity can ever do.'[27] The spot was distinguished, he said significantly, by 'an aged thorn bush,' and a natural, symbolically appropriate marker such as this had the additional appeal of being a living witness to the events of battle. To the romantic sensibility this means of connecting with the heroic past exerted a powerful attraction. Even though nothing could possibly be learned of Brock in his final moments by staring at a thorn bush, knowledge that this was the very thorn bush by which he had died satisfied a desire for intimate knowledge or contact through a train of association. In this sense the thorn bush was both marker and relic: it signified the place of Brock's death, and, as the only visible remains of his sacrifice, it became a treasured though perishable remnant of the past with its own aura of authenticity. But how real was it? Another tourist recorded seeing instead 'a number of thorn bushes which form a rude circle,' and slightly later accounts have Brock succumbing near some poplar trees or, alternatively, a cherry tree. As Donald Horne says, what matters to tourists 'is what they are told they are seeing.'[28]

The tourists' enjoyment of the battlefields circuit depended, in the absence of monuments, plaques, and guidebooks, on having some personal assistance in 'reading' the organic remains of war that might seem to the untutored to be quite unremarkable features of landscape. At Niagara all that was left at some sites were scars upon the ground and damaged trees, or at best the ruins of a stone fort or other military structure. In order for these to have meaning they had to be explained, and the tourists had to supply their own imaginative responses.

A journalist named Mrs Minot, who visited Niagara in the summer of 1815, provided one of the first detailed descriptions of these sites aimed at the potential tourist. No American could walk among the ruins of Fort Erie, she insisted, without intense emotion and an urgent curiosity. '[H]e will look round,' she wrote,

for some one who can describe to him, minutely, the unexpected explosion, and the brilliant sortie, who can point out the deep ravine and the difficult and till then impassable wood. He will examine the trees that are shattered, and the ground that has been torn up by the balls and rockets, on their passage from the British camp to the fort.

Her own description owed its imaginative force to sublime imagery: the deep woods, the shattered trees, the torn ground. Mrs Minot gave her readers a precise description of exactly what was left at Fort Erie: the structure itself was in ruins, with fragments of the east bastion at the water's edge; just to the north was a common grave containing the bodies of Colonel Drummond and 'a large number of the slain on both sides;' to the southwest lay the remains of Towson's battery; and behind the fort were the woods from which the British had laid seige. Dean McCannell points out that without permanent markers such sights are apt to 'wither away,' and that is exactly what Mrs Minot feared. She knew that the organic remains could not last, that grave sites would become indistinguishable, that foliage would grow back. She also (wrongly, as it turned out) believed that the ruined fort would shortly become 'indiscriminately mingled with the soil,' leaving 'the curious and feeling traveller' seeking in vain for any vestige of the war.[30]

The best guides that could be engaged along the battlefields circuit were the many veterans of the conflict who lived close by and made themselves readily available. With memories of the war still fresh, they could provide detailed and vivid accounts of each confrontation. Forsyth himself performed this service immediately after the war; Richard Barrett reported that at Lundy's Lane he showed them where American tourists had dug up the bones of the dead 'and carried them away as reliques.' William Dalton and his companions enjoyed guided tours of several battlefields, during which 'every attack and retreat was detailed to us, while standing on the very spot of action.' Another American visitor by the name of Stansbury was a guest of a 'staunch Loyalist' who had twice fought for the British, but these men shared a romantic fascination with the recent war and its visible remains. At the various battle sites Stansbury's host relived his memories, describing each battle while springing 'with the agility of a youth, over the ditches and upon the bulwarks of the fortifications.' Stansbury, meanwhile, gave free rein to his own melancholy yet intensely pleasurable reveries. At every step on Queenston Heights, he wrote, 'we hear in imagination, the shouts of the victorious, and the dying agonies of the conquered ... the thought intrudes itself, that on the very spot we are standing on, many have drank [sic] the crimson streams of some unfortunate husband or of some hapless son.'[31]

For many visitors such pleasant feelings of melancholy signalled the success of a battlefields tour. Both the dramatic topography and the events of war on Queenston Heights were conducive to unsettled thoughts, and tourists indulged unashamedly in fantasies of total human chaos. John Goldie, a Scottish botanist, described his haste to reach the field of battle as soon as he arrived at Queenston. After reaching the summit he 'sat down to enjoy the prospect before me, on the very spot where many a man had lost his life,' viewing 'with mingled sensations of pleasure and melancholy' the scene where 'many of my fellow creatures had been hurled into eternity.' Howison made sure that his first trip to Queenston Heights took place by moonlight. As he stood upon the precipice, he imagined 'the melancholy incident' in which American soldiers had 'wildly flung themselves over the steep,' whereby many were 'frightfully dashed to pieces by the rocks,' while others were 'transfixed and killed by falling on their own bayonets.'[32]

The contemplation of the gallant dead reached the level of sublimity where the wildness of the falls themselves was thought to have dominated the atmosphere of war. The battle of Lundy's Lane took place on an unremarkable piece of ground but 'almost within sight of the Grand Cataract,' and reached its horrific climax 'under a half-orbed moon ... which shed a pale and doubtful light upon the scene.' For Mrs Minot, proximity to the falls dominated the whole experience of this disastrous encounter, and even after the fighting stopped, 'the low moaning of the wounded and dying ... was confounded in the noise of the torrent.'[34] Many others would agree that the nearness of the falls inspired a higher bravery among those who fought and died at Lundy's Lane,[35] hundreds of whom lay heaped in a common grave – 'the most verdant spot on the whole plain,' according to Dalton, although legend would later have it that for years, on that spot, the grass refused to grow.[36]

The delight that tourists took in imagining such blood-letting combined strangely with their desire to see Native peoples as brutal and warlike, or at least as heirs to a savage past. Most tourists carried with them simple, romantic stereotypes and saw Native people mainly as part of the wilderness landscape. Images of exotically dressed or near-naked aboriginals were a conventional element of paintings and drawings of Niagara,[37] and therefore visitors were not surprised to see Native people fishing, portaging around the falls, or sometimes offering themselves as guides. They variously described them as noble and picturesque savages, a race sinking into decline, or as a combination of both, but they were preoccupied with assessing these people's chances of surviving the approach of civilization.

A few tourists had an opportunity for closer observation, which might confirm their preconceived ideas or lead to disappointment. A highlight of Edward Wakefield's extended visit was an invitation to take part in a bear hunt. He marvelled at his 'warrior' companion's innate abilities – to 'read' the forest, for example, detecting bear tracks in the fallen leaves – but he also saw the damage done by smallpox and drink, and predicted disaster for the race at large. John Duncan was exceptional in pointing out that the cruelty of Europeans towards the Native people made the former 'much better entitled to the appellation of *savages* than the poor despised Indians,' but he, like the rest, was preoccupied with the extent to which they could be civilized.[38]

By the 1820s a growing number of tourists at Niagara incorporated a visit to the village of the Tuscarora, near Lewiston, New York, into their itineraries. This was a practice which had parallels elsewhere; the Huron village of Lorette in Lower Canada fulfilled the same function as a tourist attraction – a place where visitors could assess the residents' capacity for civilization while picking up souvenirs at the same time. Some visitors admired the Tuscarora and other Iroquoians they met; some despised them. On the whole, the British visitors condemned them less totally than those from the United States, though virtually all assumed a patronizing tone. For example, one anonymous American traveller dismissed the Tuscarora as 'a falling race,' mere sorry remnants of those Indians who 'once reigned [as] lords of the forest.' In his eyes the Indian was not without virtues, but his fatal flaw lay 'principally in an unsubdued temperament of disposition, which disqualifies him for any change of primitive habit.' In this traveller's view it was simply impossible, despite the best efforts of government, to establish a 'connecting link between civilized and uncivilized society,' because when savage virtues are lost, nothing is gained. 'Scarcely an instance is known of an Indian emerging from an uncivilized state,' he maintained, 'without sinking in the scale of being.'[39]

William Dalton, on the other hand, was quite an admirer of the Tuscarora, and much more confident in their capacity for change. Like many tourists, he based his judgments on a rather detailed observation of the Native physique, as if he were assessing a breed of horse. Witnessing the men in ceremonial dress, he concluded that 'upon the whole, we admire their deportment. Their countenance is grave – their gait stately – and their behaviour respectful. They are, in general, tall, and remarkably well made ... But the scale of their strength is inferior to that of an Englishman.' Dalton concluded, however, that he had 'scarcely ever [seen] finer looking men,' and Elizabeth Harvey, holidaying at the falls in 1820, was of the same opinion. After an encounter with some men she understood to be Mohawk chiefs in the forest near Niagara, she pronounced them 'some of the handsomest young men I ever saw in my life – fine, tall and graceful figures and Spanish complexion ... one of them looked full of wit and fun.' In a letter home she describes herself as totally won over. 'People may talk of the high bred manners of fashionable circles. But I am sure they are surpassed by

these wild men of the woods – no awkward shyness – yet not forward.'
But what finally recommended them most in her eyes was that they
were *so civilized*, having their own 'pretty little church in which a
Mohawk clergyman does duty.' With no irony intended, she also observed that they were turning out to be 'pretty good farmers' on lands
'we have granted them.'[40] Comments such as these suggest the variety
of images which came into play. The noble savage image was appealing, but for the great majority who believed unquestioningly in
Europe's civilizing mission, such 'primitive' peoples had to be seen as
part of a disappearing wilderness.

DOING NIAGARA, OR NIAGARA UNDONE

The pace of change in all aspects of Niagara tourism would speed up
considerably after 1825, as Niagara's descent from the wild to the tame,
the sublime to the ridiculous, accelerated. The completion of the Erie
Canal and the steady improvement in transportation facilities hastened
the exploitation of Niagara's resources, both industrially and commer-
cially. Mills and other enterprises had been present on both sides of the
river since the turn of the century, but the new pace of development
soon transformed the landscape. Major industries were concentrated on
the American bank but were visible from the Canadian side, and as
McKinsey says, the fascination with nature's power over man was
giving way to satisfaction with man's power over nature.[41]

But changing feelings about Niagara owed even more to the growth
of a real tourist industry, fuelled by the northward flow of visitors each
year. Entrepreneurs scrambling for their share of the business became so
omnipresent that they virtually took control of the tourist itinerary, and
the neighbourhood of the falls was soon overrun, as Eliot Warburton
would complain, 'with every species of abominable fungus ... Chinese
pagoda, menagerie, camera obscura, museum, watch-tower, wooden
monument, sea gardens, [and] "old curiosity shops."'[42] Under constant
pressure to 'do' the falls as the locals would wish, tourists became even
more self-conscious about their responses and were often ambivalent
about the whole experience – dependent on the services provided, yet
often resentful that reality had diverged so far from the image of Niagara
they had carried in their minds. Their reactions, of course, varied enor-
mously, from sheer joy at all they beheld to genuine anger at the ravages
of commercialism, to bemused irony or perhaps a determination to find
some new delight not prescribed for them in the guidebooks.

Steamboat fares, hotel rates, and fees for coach travel confirm that the travelling public remained largely middle and upper class, and that many more now came with families. Americans from the southern states journeyed north *en masse* in the summer months to escape 'the sickly season' at home,[43] and Niagara remained the single most important destination in the fashionable Northern Tour. Novels and travel literature had popularized many romantic destinations; the Hudson River, for example, was a place of pilgrimage in its own right – especially after Washington Irving took up residence there – but the falls remained the ultimate tourist mecca, attracting, in Horatio Parsons estimation, some twelve to fifteen thousand people each year by the mid-1830s.[44] Some visitors stayed for several weeks while others just passed through, and tourism promoters now placed a new value on making it possible to complete the falls and battlefields circuit as quickly and effortlessly as possible.

Upper Canadians and New Yorkers also made quick jaunts to the falls, especially when something unusual was afoot. As if Niagara was not a wild enough spectacle in itself, a series of fantastic stunts began in the 1820s which would continue for decades, contributing much, by their very silliness, to the essentially ironic image of Niagara which gradually emerged. The most deplorable of these was staged by Forsyth in 1827, in cooperation with two other hotel-keepers. It involved sending a condemned Great Lakes schooner named the *Michigan* over the falls with a cargo of live animals aboard, originally advertised as a collection of the 'most ferocious animals' of the forest, but in reality consisting of raccoons, a goose, a dog, a buffalo, and two small bears.[45] Thousands of people travelled to Niagara by steamer, schooner, stagecoach, and wagon to witness this curious combination of mass tourist spectacle and pre-industrial fête. 'The roads to the Falls in every direction were like the approaches to a Yorkshire fair,' wrote William Lyon Mackenzie, and 'every place and every corner and nook was filled with human beings: bands of music enlivened the scene; and the roar of the African lion in the menagerie, and the din of the passing multitude, joined in the crashing of the cataract, was almost too much for human organs.' Mackenzie soon had the opportunity to report upon another romantic feat, as he himself called it, on the occasion of Sam Patch's jump from Goat Island into the gorge between the two cataracts.[46]

The use of animals at Niagara as tourist attractions, stuffed and alive, in museums, public thoroughfares, and in front of private homes, was increasingly commonplace and represented an effort to preserve the idea of wilderness where it was rapidly disappearing. At Mr Barrett's Museum, as *The Book of Niagara Falls* explained, the rooms were arranged 'very tastefully so as to represent a forest scene,' and contained 'upwards of eight hundred stuffed animals of various kinds and descriptions.' Johann Kohl found that he frequently met 'with wild animals where you do not expect them, according to a fashion prevailing in this country,' and among those he encountered was 'a very charming little bear playing every morning before one of the houses,' being fed biscuits by passersby. Another private yard contained 'half a dozen wolves of various colours and species, chained to blocks of wood,' while another displayed 'a few buffalo from the West, placed for a closer inspection than you could obtain on the prairies.'[47]

As traffic to the falls increased, travel narratives, guidebooks, and torrents of Niagara poetry – much of it dreadful – continued to pour from the presses. Both prose and poetry often attempted to capture the personal experience of the sublime, though with limited success, as this stanza amply demonstrates:

Niagara! to thee
    My spectacles I turn!
I see the waters boil,
    As if all ... did burn,
And Satan's imps, with ardour hot,
Were thrusting wood beneath the pot.[48]

Nonetheless, the number of tourists who arrived 'wound up' by what they had read and heard continued to grow. Descriptions of intense anxiety endured while approaching the falls, followed by affirmations of profound delight or confessions of heartfelt disappointment, were now commonplace.[49] Anna Jameson may have expressed the true dilemma of romantic tourism when she realized that the image may be more wonderful than the place itself, and that perpetual desire may be more exhilarating than fulfilment. She wished, at least at first, that she had never seen the falls, for 'the reality has displaced from my mind an illusion far more magnificent than itself ... yet I have not the presumption to suppose that all I have heard and read of Niagara is false or exaggerated – that every expression of astonishment, enthusiasm, rapture, is affectation or hyperbole. No! It must be my own fault.'[50] Jameson's own life was in disorder when she first visited the falls, which helps to account for her anxious response. But such excesses were common enough, though many other tourists were now inclined to blame the tourist industry rather than themselves if Niagara let them down.

Anxiety over the appropriate response to the falls had much to do with the fact that tourists had become the focus of intense entrepreneurial attention. The tourist industry was born in an age of uninhibited free enterprise, and stark competition governed the industry's development at Niagara despite Forsyth's efforts at monopoly. By the mid-twenties he already had a serious rival in John Brown, who ran a hotel upriver from the Pavilion and built a staircase down the wall of the gorge on property Forsyth considered his own: the portion of the chain reserve that ran between his land and the falls. In an attempt to get rid of Brown and prevent the reserve from being leased to others, Forsyth fenced in the land, only to have his fences twice torn down by agents of Sir Peregrine Maitland's colonial government. This so-called Niagara outrage became a symbol of the Family Compact's power and privilege in the colony (William Lyon Mackenzie, for example, sided with Forsyth during the years of litigation), and the men who bought him out in 1832 were both wealthy and well connected. They had secured the monopoly to ferry rights which Forsyth had sought in 1825 and now took over his hotel and staircase, but their larger plan was to subdivide the land and build a resort called the City of the Falls. That scheme failed, but they remained involved in many aspects of the tourist trade and transportation industry. Meanwhile countless other petty enterprises sprang up and new rivalries developed, sometimes leading to the intimidation of tourists and finally even to murder.[51] At Niagara, according to Charles Latrobe, the traveller had to contend with 'all the petty trickery of Matlock-Baths' (a notorious English resort), and Isabella Bishop complained that the entire strip fronting the falls on the Canadian side had become covered in 'a great fungus growth of museums, curiosity shops, taverns, and pagodas with shining tin cupolas.'[52] There was no relief from the chaos of *laissez-faire* until the government regained control of the chain reserve in the 1880s and created Queen Victoria Park.

It must be admitted that many tourists were frankly appreciative of the new conveniences, and made full use of them while touring Niagara Falls. Others were more selective, deploring only those contrivances which struck them as outrageous violations of taste while enjoying other provisions or taking them for granted. The most spectacular view at Niagara was to be had from a man-made construction called the Terrapin Tower, which perched precariously on the brink of the Horseshoe

Falls, and Bishop, who criticized much else, found it delightful – even the very flimsiness of the structure added to her exhilaration. But Edward Abdy had nothing but disdain for the 'barbarous and sacrilegious' individual who, for the sake of 'unfeeling trade and avaricious speculation,' had been 'permitted to outrage every feeling of taste, congruities, or common sense.'[53] Some visitors regretted any change; Latrobe, for example, was nostalgic for the old days when Niagara 'was still the cataract of the wilderness,' and the journey to it was full of adventure and peril. 'But how is it now?' he asked in 1835. 'The forest has everywhere yielded to the axe. Hotels with their snug shrubberies, out-houses, gardens, and paltry embellishment stare you in the face,' along with 'museums, mills, staircases, tolls, and grog-shops.'[54] The sublime experience, supposedly made more accessible, was for some more elusive than ever because of all the things they had to pretend *not* to see. Their writings contain many stories of irritations overcome (let not the reader think that 'we grew peevish and departed in wrath and disgust,' wrote Latrobe), but it required work. And part of the task was to escape, insofar as one could, the blandishments of an industry that professed to enhance, or make easier, the appreciation of Niagara's wonders while in fact undermining their evocative powers.

Many writers commented on the need for time at the falls, so that they might learn to concentrate on the sublimity of the scene and finally succumb to its power. Hotels obviously made this possible, for they enabled tourists to explore at leisure, rest when tired, and spend several days in the vicinity without inconvenience, while also accommodating the needs of children.[55] On the other hand, simply to enjoy the comforts of civilization at this place of wonder could undercut its primitive power, and Alfred Domett was surprised to find that a prolonged stay at the Pavilion allowed guests 'to look with listless eye even at this cataract of cataracts, to yawn [out the billiard room window] in the face of Niagara.' James Edward Alexander considered nothing 'so ill-suited to the scene as these abominations,' yet advised other tourists that, if one 'turns his back upon [the hotels], and looks towards the Falls and up the river, the scene is still ... wild.'[56] He himself took a room at Lundy's Lane, below the falls, and lay in bed and listened to the 'thunder of Niagara,' imagining the night battle that had occurred there years before.

Others, too, reported themselves affected in odd ways or at unexpected times by the proximity of the falls. Caroline Gilman remarked upon the wildness of her dreams, and Basil Hall found himself finally and poignantly aware of the 'true magnificence of the scene' when he happened by an open window in the dead of night, on his way to soothe a fretful daughter. Mary O'Brien spent her first night at Niagara listening to the noise of the falls, her mind swimming with 'the images excited by the sound and my preconceived notions of the scene,' which were dominated by feelings of passion, terror, and destruction. She was glad when morning came and she finally saw Niagara for herself, and felt 'none of the deep agony or the everlasting torment that Byron talks of,' but was filled with joy instead. Some tourists were able to convey the irony of the hotel experience. William H.G. Kingston and his bride joined the flow of newlyweds to Niagara in 1853, and he recorded their first glimpse of the falls from their balcony. 'As soon as our baggage was arranged,' he wrote, and 'the porters dismissed, our dresses dusted, and our hands washed, we opened the Venetian blinds with reverential awe, and stepped out together into the broad verandah, where a full and perfect view of the Falls appeared before our eyes.'[57]

When tourists emerged from their hotels they almost invariably went down to the river bank to gaze at the Horseshoe Falls, and then got on, as Warburton sighed, 'with the nuisance of sight-seeing.'[58] Any number of tourist handbooks were available to help them on their rounds, from the many editions of Davidson's *The Fashionable Tour*, first published in 1821, to the works devoted entirely to Niagara, which began to appear in the mid-1830s. The guidebooks' debt to the travel narratives was quite explicit, for they quoted (and plagiarized) voluminously from them, but the language of the sublime was now used in a prescriptive fashion: here is where you must go, and this is what you must feel. The guidebooks' function was to sell, and they not only reinforced the understanding that there was an itinerary of sights and experiences that must not be violated, they directed tourists to particular services, such as Mr Starkey's staircase and 'Fido's elegant and inviting confectionery establishment,' thus working in cooperation with other elements of the industry.[59] Determined for the most part to praise everything and say nothing that might deter, quidebooks took it for granted that the bene-fits civilization had brought to Niagara were unquestionable.

Tourists were also encouraged to believe that they could do no better than to turn themselves over to one of the guides, who beset them at every turn. Bishop complained that the visitor, 'yielding to the demands of a supposed necessity, is dragged a weary round,' and Francis Dun-can confirmed that at Niagara 'You can go nowhere without advice, and do nothing without suggestions. A large population have adopted the falls, as if they were some private dancing bear or talking fish; and you dare no more break through their dreary routine than you would venture to violate the etiquette of a court.'[60] Occasionally a tourist handbook took a different tack and offered itself as protection against a corrupt industry. *The Canadian Tourist*, for example, told the truth about Niagara's entrepreneurs, and warned that 'Tourists, to them, are but pigeons to be plucked.'[61] The notion that the guidebook's role was to protect tourists from other elements of the industry was implicit in another work entitled *Every Man his own Guide at Niagara Falls, without the necessity of inquiry or the possibility of mistake* (1853).

'One of the most disagreeable necessities of the tourist,' growled Warburton, remained the trip under the falls to Termination Rock.[62] This ritual still involved a good soaking; William Fleming found the spray so thick and violent that he gasped for breath and turned back, feeling as if he had been 'driven out for cowardice, lashed by a thousand hands, and hissed at by a thousand tongues.'[63] But it was a much more controlled and commercialized venture than it had been before the war, far less exciting and far less dangerous. As Thomas Fowler recorded in 1832, visitors descended the staircase from within 'a neat cottage' on Table Rock, where a register was kept and the keeper fitted out each paying customer in an aquatic costume consisting of pantaloons, 'a frock coat which buttoned close to the chin,' special shoes, and a waterproofed Dunstable hat. There were many variations on this garb; Alexander Dunlop complained to his journal that he was 'stript of my raiment - even to the last stitch' – clothed in a long red flannel shirt, white flannel culottes, wool socks, boots, and encased 'over all, [in] a sort of hooded surcoat of oilskin.' All felt ridiculously dressed and more than a little self-conscious, but women likely found the change of apparel liberating at the same time, better suiting them for climbing down the slope. As for the experience of 'going behind the sheet,' as it was now called, some dismissed it as 'nothing,' some found it unpleasant, while others were forcibly impressed. Dunlop called it 'sublime – and strange, *very strange*. The black man sat by me, grinning like a demon. I shall never forget the wonderful minutes spent there.'[64] Dunlop's so-called black man was his guide, and the blackness of the guides (or was there just the one black guide?) was a matter for occasional racist comment.

The village of the Tuscarora, some ten miles from the falls, continued as part of the tourist itinerary for several decades. 'I met a real Indian today,' crowed Isabella Trotter on her Niagara visit in 1858, and in order to see more Native people at close range she attended their village church service on Sunday to watch them at worship. She disapproved of the ceremony but found the people 'harmless,' though unremarkable except for their extraordinarily 'piercing and intelligent black eyes.' Horatio Parsons had warned some time ago that these Sunday visits were not encouraged by the Tuscarora, who – he claimed – easily tired of being made 'a gazing stock,' and regarded the tourists as notorious Sabbath-breakers who set a bad example for their children.[65]

Native people in the Niagara area produced (and made available through trade with regions to the south) a wide variety of souvenirs, which they marketed near the falls where the tourist traffic was the greatest. According to observers during the 1850s, these offerings included mohair items, 'selenite ornaments and bark trifles, curiously ornamented with colored grasses,' leather cigar cases embroidered with 'dyed elk's hair,' beaded moccasins, 'pin cushions, table-mats, baskets, and miniature canoes curiously dyed, and worked up with beads, porcupine's quills, &c, after their peculiar manner, with some taste, and by no means at low prices.'[66] Kohl was very taken with the quality of the work he found. 'They seem to have a very good eye for colour, and much richness of fancy; and they imitate strawberries, cherries, and other wild fruits of their woods ... in the most lively and natural colours and forms.'[67] Craft-making was primarily a women's industry, and while much Indian work was bought by dealers and ended up in curiosity shops (where its price was considerably inflated), it was offered for sale more directly by the women and children themselves, who sat near the falls 'with their wares spread out before them.'[68] In contrast with Niagara's other entrepreneurs, their style of marketing their goods tended to be unaggressive. Kohl described how he 'once met with a child of the wilderness who had undertaken to dispose of her own goods':

She was sitting wrapped in a black blanket, and as motionless as a statue, under a tree on Goat Island, with her little stock spread out very neatly on a cloth on the grass before her; she asked no one to buy, but waited in stillness and patience till a purchaser should present himself.[69]

Trinkets of non-Native manufacture, meant to remind one of the falls either through association or visual likeness, were also offered for sale at every turn. Among the souvenirs most commonly available were items cut from rock and wood, such as the walking sticks supposedly produced on Navy Island (a new sight in the itinerary after the Patriots' occupation in 1837–8), which one observer reported were 'as eagerly bought' as 'bullets and bits of iron are sought after by tourists on the plains of Waterloo.'[70] Also popular were the cheap prints of Niagara scenes sold at the curio stands. In these, typically, the employment of picturesque values domesticated Niagara and included the image of some tourists at play as part of the scene. With the invention of the daguerreotype, visitors were able to place *themselves* in the picture and take home material proof of their sublime experience. But the photograph can easily become more important than the experience, or, as Oliver Wendell Holmes predicted, the image may ultimately make the object itself disposable. Some tourists found it just as satisfying to have their picture taken in a studio, in front of a painted backdrop of the Horseshoe Falls.[71]

The unstable relationship between tourism and reality also affected the battlefields circuit, as did the broader process by which Niagara was tamed and demystified. Developments in transportation, such as the building of a railway from Chippewa to Queenston, helped to ensure that the battle sites remained part of the itinerary, and tourist promoters continued to run stagecoaches to and from the battlegrounds providing, in the words of one guidebook, 'an exhilarating and very pleasant excursion.'[72] But as Mrs Minot had predicted, after a generation or two the earth and grass and trees surrounding a crumbling fort had little to say to the curious traveller, though Fort Erie and Fort George retained a romantic charm and attraction as ruins 'deserted and desolate.'[73] The battleground at Chippewa, on the other hand, succumbed to advancing settlement; there, no vestiges of war were preserved, no monument was raised to the dead, and the battlefield gradually 'withered away' as a tourist sight.[74] Lundy's Lane became partially built over, but continued to be a popular place for an outing where tourists could visit 'the burying ground,' now contained within the yard of a newly built church. For a fee they could also gain a panoramic view of the battlefield from the top of one of the wooden towers which had been built by rival tourist promoters. In 1853 William Kingston found this whole excursion most unromantic, and for that matter, laughably unauthentic, for each of the towers was, he said, manned by 'an old soldier who was at the battle,' one of whom 'informs his visitors that the British won it,' while 'the other gives the palm of victory to the Americans.' The 'Irish cardrivers,' added Kingston, increased the levity of the experience by driving visitors 'about in all directions, [and] with naive discursiveness narrating events which never occurred.'[75]

The battle site which remained most stable in meaning was Queenston Heights, but it, too, lost much of its former mystery. The story of the battle and Brock's death as told in travel guides and narratives did not alter much, except for the elaboration of little myths such as those concerning Brock's last words, wherein 'Push on, Brave York Volunteers!' was by far the most favoured version. The site of his death remained in roughly the same place, though descriptions of it varied over time, with one guidebook advising in 1840 that it was to be found 'in a vacant lot in the village, since called Brock's lot.'[76]

For most visitors, however, interest in this spot gave way to the huge monument to Brock that rose upon the Heights in 1824, was later reduced to ruins, and was built again in the 1850s. On Queenston Heights the eye was naturally drawn to the column and away from the ground, and the way tourists now focused their attention on the Brock Monument instead of the whole field of battle constitutes a classic case of what MacCannell calls 'marker-site displacement.' In this process, what begins as a marker itself becomes the object of interest; it is built up 'to the status of a sight.'[77] Some visitors found it a highly evocative visual image (one fictional character even called it sublime),[78] but the fact that a single structure now seemed to embody all that was historically significant at this location made it possible to 'do' Queenston very speedily. Many tourists were simply driven by it and did not even alight from their carriages, for they could see the monument quite satisfactorily from where they sat. And many of those who did stop simply seemed to be performing a duty, and they subsequently recorded, in a rather flat or stilted manner, how they paid their respects to Brock by inspecting the column, reading the inscription, and relinquishing a York shilling for the privilege of ascending to the top. What most impressed them, ironically, was not the historical meaning of the monument but the view it afforded of the village below and the farms, orchards, forests, and distant lakes spread out beyond – a scene universally declared to be 'truly picturesque and pleasing.'[79]

With a tourist industry in full flower, Niagara was no longer a wild place. Its essential setting, the primeval forest, had disappeared from the rivers banks - 'of the ancient woods there is no trace, wrote Johann Kohl.'[80] But was Niagara still sublime? That was a matter of perception, for each visitor, as William Burr pointed out, 'is affected according to his own temperament,'[81] and each ultimately found in Niagara what he or she was able to create through the imagination. Tourists who found their desire for intense experience thwarted by an intrusive commercialism were forced to find ways of managing or retrieving those elusive feelings of romance; they might learn, for example, to subtract things from their field of vision so that they could *really* see the falls. If they were determined to become 'utterly Niagarized,'[82] then chances are they would succeed though it might require work, luck, planning, or the aid of additional sublime elements. A perfect day, the right view, and suddenly 'the thousand trumperies of the place' might be forgotten, but better still, as some visitors found, was the perfect night. 'We were so very fortunate,' crooned Emmaline Stuart Wortley, 'as to have a tremendous thunder-storm here on Tuesday night. The heavens seem literally opening just over the great cataracts ... It was a wild windy night, as if all the elements were revelling together in a stormy chaotic carnival of their own, till it really presented altogether a scene almost too awfully magnificent.'[83] Reading their accounts we can sense some tourists' joy and relief at having been able to recreate the experience that once came so easily, so irresistibly, at Niagara. Alexander Dunlop devoted himself to finding ways of avoiding guides and his fellow tourists, and spent many hours one night going over the same ground, his excitement slowly mounting into 'awe and *fear* – for they *are* fearful,' he insisted, 'when seen at midnight, and alone and close.'[84]

But despite such protestations Niagara had been tamed, and worse was yet to come. Contemporaries knew this, and a host of artists, writers, and other concerned individuals banded together in a campaign to save the falls which would go on for several decades. If people did not act, predicted Kohl at mid-century, they would soon find that they had 'crushed this prodigy of creation, like the ape-mother who kissed her darling to death.'[85] From having once symbolized some dark power that civilized humanity must protect itself from, Niagara had come to require human protection instead.

The interplay of romantic values and the growth of tourism as a consumer industry could not be better illustrated than it was at Niagara. Good timing was part of the process, for the growing fascination with the 'sublime,' which helped fuel the industry's growth in Britain and elsewhere, coincided with the wars with France which turned tourists' attention to North America. The northward flow of Loyalists produced settlements on the Canadian side which could take advantage of tourists' desire for better access to the falls and other picturesque views, and even the War of 1812, disastrous though it was at the time, created new tourist sights – battlefields, ruins, and graveyards – suited to the pleasures of romantic melancholy. Entrepreneurs such as Forsyth saw their chance, and the logic of a consumer industry in which images and feelings are offered for sale began to unfold at Niagara. Within a few short years the romantic itinerary had hardened into a commercial imperative, and the tourists' experience of Niagara had begun to accumulate the layers of ironic meaning which persist today.

W.T. Craig's *Falls of Niagara on the River St Lawrence* was published in England in 1801.

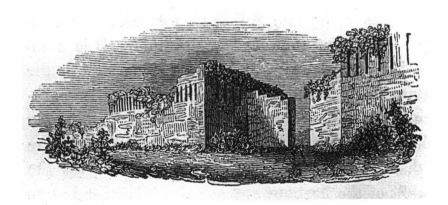

Guidebook view of the ruins of Fort Erie

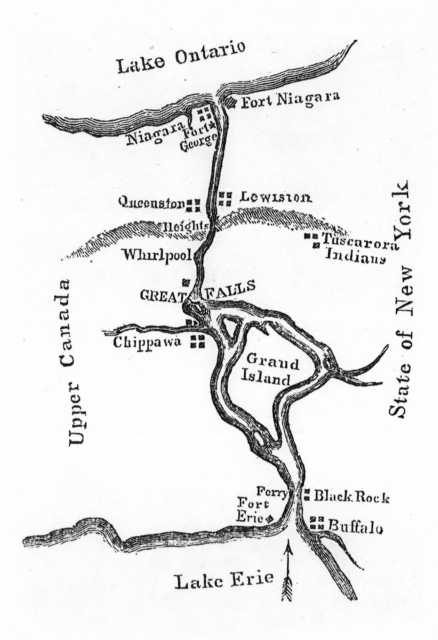

Tourist attractions along the Niagara frontier, 1823

The entrance to Horseshoe Falls cavern, c. 1830

English writer and feminist Anna Jameson on
her visit to North America in 1837

W.H. Bartlett's *General Brock's Monument, above Queenston*

Tourists posed in front of Horseshoe Falls, c. 1855

Scene among the Thousand Isles, engraving by W.H. Bartlett

Bartlett's picturesque view of Akwesasne, *St Regis Indian Village*

Timber Slide and Bridge on the Ottawa, engraving by W.H. Bartlett

A romantic portrait of an Indian pilot, steering a steamer down the St Lawrence rapids

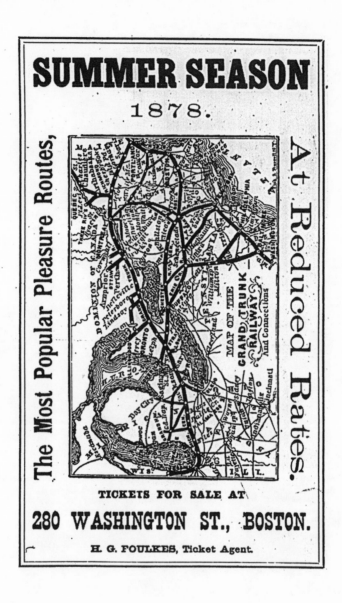

The Grand Trunk Railway and its connections linking the St Lawrence region
to the northeastern United States

The excitement of running the rapids in a steamer

The Duke and Duchess of York shooting the rapids and timber slide near
Ottawa, c. 1900

Lake of the Isles, Thousand Islands, by F.B. Schell

Schell's view of the Thousand Islands at dusk

A poster advertising an excursion
through the Thousand Islands,
c. 1899

3

Wilderness Panorama

Niagara Falls was a special place, unique in North America. The pattern of its development as a tourist attraction, however, would be more or less duplicated in countless other wilderness areas as the century progressed. As certain places of natural beauty were 'discovered' and found to conform to the values of romanticism, they were given new and seductive meanings. These were embodied in literary and visual imagery and then disseminated to a broader public. The transformation of such places into popular tourist sights thus depended, initially, on their ability to gratify the yearnings for beauty, romance, and adventure that drew travellers in the first place. Yet that phase was usually transitory. The process of mystification was followed by the demystifying effects of the human presence, and places once conceived by strangers as alien, evocative, and suffused with the unexpected fell victim to commercialization and domestication.

It would be simplistic, however, to see this latter change merely as a progression from the good to the bad, or the real to the artificial. The St Lawrence River and its islands, rapids, boatmen, and other sights all provided fodder for the tourist's imagination, but these romantic images were themselves constructions of the tourist mentality which performed their passing function and then faded away. The romantic iconography of rivers and their shorelines was in fact transferable from one place to another; images employed along the St Lawrence were also used to promote tourism on the Ottawa River and countless other waterways. What we learn from the story of the wilderness panorama, then, is how European notions of the wild, the picturesque, and the sublime could be used to package a touristic experience, and how the romantic imagination 'may recreate the world according to the mind's own desire.'[1]

By the 1820s the typical tourist's Canadian itinerary was bounded on the east by Montreal or the city of Quebec, and on the west by Niagara and the burgeoning towns on Lake Ontario. The St Lawrence River and its tributaries linked these places together, but during the first stages of tourism in the Canadas this river was little more than a waterway, the inconvenient and uncomfortable means by which most people travelled between the two provinces. Tourist traffic along this route grew quickly from the 1820s onwards, however, partly because both Niagara and the charms of old Quebec were drawing more and more visitors each year, and also because the fashion for the panoramic river cruise was turning the St Lawrence River into a major wilderness attraction in itself. This waterway not only transported tourists between their two principal destinations, but offered drama and variety, a kaleidoscope of landscapes, a visual banquet for the connoisseur of the picturesque. Moreover, it provided the setting for a very specific and fashionable European aesthetic to be acted out on a New World stage.

A growing tourist traffic both encouraged and benefited from improvements in transportation. Well into the 1830s, most visitors travelled by Durham boat or the smaller *batteau*, a flat-bottomed vessel with a lug-sail, 'a sort of mongrel between the canoe and the boat,' as Henry David Thoreau put it.[2] These were intended mainly for carrying freight, but passengers were commonly taken on as well. The journey upriver, the common fate of immigrants, could be extremely tedious, as the current was strong and the boats had to be poled up the rapids. Much faster and more popular with tourists was the descent to Montreal, a trip which might include a harrowing passage through the rapids, although a majority at this time still resorted to stage travel in order to avoid these wild waters. As the use of steamers developed in the 1830s, travellers could proceed in either direction in one day, getting off and on boats and coaches – still 'one of the most wearisome trips'[3] to be endured in Canada, in C.D. Arfwedson's opinion, but touted by others as one of the most picturesque and exciting on the continent. The Thousand Islands struck many travellers as most wonderfully 'wild and fanciful,'[4] and once steamers began to pass through the rapids in the 1840s, this new experience became a must for tourists. Growing importance accrued to other points along the route through association with history and legend. By mid-century the St Lawrence River had become thoroughly commodified and had taken its place among the world's great panoramas, while steadily losing any real association with the Canadian wilderness.

FAIRY ISLES AND VOYAGEURS

As had been true at Niagara, it was the travellers themselves who first initiated this transformation, for they endowed the St Lawrence River with new meaning and fame well before steamer companies became involved in its promotion. In doing so, however, they were following a familiar cultural pattern. Boat journeys were already common tourist fare in both Europe and North America by the early nineteenth century, and the experience was informed by the familiar values of middle-class tourism, much influenced by the romantic movement and its precursors. Again, the relationship between culture and tourism was a circular one in that the travel narratives of early tourists helped inspire the nature poets' interest in river imagery, while their poetry, in turn, encouraged others to set forth on their romantic journeys. Wordsworth especially was preoccupied with water's symbolic import; as one critic writes, 'Water in all its aspects – its sound and its quiet, its movement and its peace, its transparency and its power to reflect – is one of Wordsworth's most all-pervasive vehicles.'[5] His fascination with rivers sprang from his reading of North American explorers such as Samuel Hearne and Jonathan Carver; from his own European travels along the Loire and the Rhine; and from his appreciation of rivers close to home, already beloved by English tourists.[6]

Pleasure-boating on the Wye, for example, was a popular pastime by the 1770s, and the interpretation of its scenery was to be dominated by picturesque conventions. In 1782 the Reverend Gilpin published his first guidebook, *Observations on the River Wye*, and by the turn of the century a number of boats fitted out especially for the tourist trade (with tables for sketching and writing) were making their way up and down the river during the summer season.[7] The deck of a smoothly gliding vessel provided an ideal vantage-point for the appreciation of picturesque views. All tourists had to do was sit back and watch the show, and Gilpin encouraged them to feel as though a series of theatrical stage sets was being slid into place before them as they floated down the river. Each view, as Gilpin explained it, had 'four grand parts ... the *area*, which is the river itself; the *two side-screens*, which are the opposite banks, and mark the perspective; and the front-screen, which points out the winding of the river.'[8] This cinematic way of seeing landscape would persist throughout the nineteenth century, suited as it was to the pace and purpose of the river cruise.

On this continent the Connecticut and the Hudson Rivers both assumed a place in the American Grand Tour very early in the nineteenth century, to be followed soon after by the Mississippi. Americans hungered for scenery that could rival the European picturesque in its aesthetic value and in its wealth of romantic association, and the Hudson, in particular, met that need. Penetrating deep into the American continent, the Hudson was the principal route inland which had provided the setting for many a historic exploit. Along its banks unfolded the whole gamut of picturesque imagery: wild mountains and gentle valleys, quaint farms and tidy villages, nature mixed with culture in ever-changing configurations. As the century wore on, Washington Irving, Fenimore Cooper, and others unearthed and invented an array of heroic and patriotic meanings for the Hudson River and its valley, and the painters of the Hudson River School strove to create equally evocative effects through their art. A thickening aura of romance steadily reinforced the Hudson River's importance as a cultural symbol and a tourist attraction.[9]

The links between culture, tourism, and river scenery were drawn closer still by the popularity of a new art form, the panorama. Panoramas, cycloramas, and dioramas consisted of a succession of immense landscape paintings which vistors viewed as they walked along, usually in a circular gallery, or watched as the paintings passed before them on a giant roller. These panoramas were especially suited to the portrayal of New World scenery, for their size and scope could convey its vastness and the constantly changing landscapes one might experience when travelling by riverboat. In these huge topographical canvases, picturesque conventions still obtained to a degree, but the sense of perspective was reduced and the horizon placed at eye level so that the viewer would feel elevated – an experience similar to watching the scenery slip by from the deck of a steamer. In the 1790s a special building was opened in Leicester Square, London, for the viewing of circular panoramas, and similar facilities attracted mass audiences in both Europe and the United States during subsequent decades. As John Sears points out, this amusement was democratic in its appeal, for no special knowledge was needed for viewing panoramas, and they afforded the multitudes who could not afford to travel the chance to do so in imagination. Viewing a panorama, people could enjoy the sensation of moving through the scenery, dreamlike, enclosed within 'a magical circle,' as Alexander von Humboldt wrote, 'wholly removed from all the disturbing influences of reality,' pretending that they had suddenly become travellers in a foreign land.[10]

This, then, was the cultural context in which the aesthetics of the picturesque and the values of popular romanticism were brought to bear upon the St Lawrence River experience. Between the 1820s and the 1840s, as the tourist itinerary was formulated, travellers interpreted the journey according to their own priorities, teaching, in effect, the local populace and the nascent travel industry how to exploit the river's commercial tourist potential to best effect.

The Thousand Islands was the first feature of the journey to become a real tourist attraction. During the 1820s other stretches of the river still possessed little romance, but the passage through the Thousand Islands was recognized as Wordsworthian in the extreme. As when writing about Niagara, tourists vied with each other to produce the most lavishly romantic descriptions; but in contrast to Niagara, they seemed to value this archipelago less for its uniqueness than for the many aesthetic criteria that it managed to satisfy at once. As E.A. Talbot enthused in 1824, the 'Lake of the Thousand Islands' displayed 'all the features of the placid, the picturesque, and the sublime, with a striking intermixture of the savage and uncouth.'[11] The islands' endless variety and intricacy, their constant juxtaposition of rough and smooth enhanced by the delicate play of light upon water, foliage, and rock, satisfied the most demanding standards of picturesque taste. At the same time, literary allusions to labyrinthine rivers and fairy isles suffused travellers' descriptions, sometimes evoking memories of other romantic waterways such as Loch Lomond, the Straits of Malacca, an Italian lagoon, or 'all the enchanting visions of Arabian and Oriental description.'[12] Gliding unimpeded through this wonderland, tourists could dream what dreams they liked, drawing on a shared language of artistic and poetic imagery.

Movement was an essential element of panoramic tourism. Unlike the task of appreciating Niagara Falls, the Thousand Islands journey did not involve the contemplation of a fixed view but a series of perfectly composed scenes which dissolved each instant into something new, leaving viewers breathless, so they claimed, with admiration and anticipation. The most successful descriptions strove to create a sense of surfeit without admitting the possibility of boredom. 'The eye does not weary to see,' wrote Eliot Warburton in a much-quoted passage, 'but the hand aches, in ever writing the one word – beauty; wherever you steer over this great river – beauty, beauty still.'[13] And there were so *many* islands, 1692 of them, it was said, 'beyond each end of which,' explained Alfred Domett, trying his hand at a Gilpinesque metaphor, 'run out the green ends of other islands in regular gradations like the side scenes of a theatre.'[14] Some seemed to float on the surface of the river, calm and luxuriant, some were 'formed of fantastic rocks piled on each other,' creating 'endless varieties of shape, colour, height, size, and contour.'[15] Passing among them, sometimes so close that their verdure draped over the vessel, passengers could imagine themselves locked in a maze or labyrinth, now glimpsing a secret grove, a 'natural terrace, or a glade, peeping forth from its half-concealed position in a wood,' next seeming trapped among the islands – about to rush into a barrier of rock, 'a *cul-de-sac* from which no exit is visible.' But in the next second, 'a magnificent amphitheatre of lake' would open before them, until the islands enveloped them in mystery once again.[16] The term *fairy isles* or *fairy land*, was by far the most common romantic allusion to the Thousand Islands, suggesting not just their fleeting, ethereal quality, but the notion that in ancient times such 'woods and waves' were peopled 'in the imagination of the poets, with nymphs and goddesses.'[17]

The solitude and sense of timelessness that engulfed the Thousand Islands were gratifying to the romantic imagination, suffused as it was with European imagery of New World primitivism. While the Hudson River symbolized American progress, the St Lawrence transported many imaginative travellers into the primordial past, into a 'savage wildness,' an 'antediluvian scene' that had been there always, ever 'since God first spoke creation into existence.' Unlike a European river, its banks displayed no ruined castles, 'no rising turrets ... All was simple, primeval.'[18] Some preferred to imagine the shores devoid of human life, but of course this was not quite true. Native inhabitants of the region sometimes intruded upon the scene and imparted, Arfwedson allowed, 'a characteristic appearance to the landscape,' while Mrs Copleston achieved a state of 'perfect ecstasy' watching the Indians in their canoes, 'darting in and out from their numberless hiding places.'[19] By the 1840s the number of immigrant settlers along the St Lawrence was increasing as well, but among 'these fairy islands,' wrote Henry Tudor, one still saw only the odd 'speck of cultivation,' perhaps 'a cottage, or a log-house, of homeliness and silent beauty, ... affording a pleasing relief, in the symptom of human existence which it offers, to the otherwise unbroken solitude that reigns around.'[20] There was a sign of things to come, however, in the growing habit among settlers of offering occasional shelter and the rent of a canoe to tourists who departed from the riverboat itinerary in order to fish or explore among the islands on their own.

The only other feature of the St Lawrence route ever to rival the fame of the Thousand Islands were the rapids. The Long Sault, in particular, had been known to armchair travellers for centuries, but like Niagara Falls, only recently had its violent and menacing beauty become something to be admired. Louis Hennepin, forced to go through 'these horrid currents' because his men refused to portage, had described them as 'a dreadful encounter of water that beats so furiously against these rocks ... the waters spurt up ten or twelve yards high, and appear like huge snow-balls, hail, and rain, with dreadful thunder, and a voice-like hissing and howling of fierce beasts.'[21] Tumbling waters later became part of the sublime or romantic aesthetic, but were initially recommended as something to look at rather than to be submerged in oneself. Early nineteenth-century travellers generally preferred to see the rapids from the safety of the shore, and those who passed through them while proceeding downriver often found themselves in the midst of an unwelcome adventure: 'We seemed at every moment on the point of being dashed to pieces,' shuddered Edward Wakefield.[22] Until the late 1830s or early 40s most travellers bypassed these rough passages by stagecoach if they had the choice, though a growing literature of the rapids adventure was gradually establishing this sublime experience as part of the regular tourist itinerary.

John Duncan's account of the rapids, published in 1823, may be taken as an early example of the new attitude. Duncan did not downplay their danger but in fact described their perils most graphically, while presenting the task of shooting the rapids as an aesthetic experience which an adventurous and sensitive traveller would not want to miss. His own first encounter with the Long Sault was in a Durham boat, towards the end of day, on a hot May afternoon. Like later guidebooks, his narrative recreated each stage of the experience for the reader to savour. The sun was setting as they approached the Long Sault, the air was calm, and the sail hung limp. 'Our steersman turned his head wistfully towards the falling beams – "Pull away, my lads, pull away; we are late enough."' As the rapids drew near, the tall pines 'threw a gloom' across the channel, whose waters now propelled them forwards. (The mood and imagery of his prose was suggestive of Thomas Moore's famous 'Canadian Boat Song,' discussed later in this chapter.) Soon the boat began 'to rock from side to side, and the terrible cauldron was before us,' exclaimed Duncan, and 'we were swept into the midst of the furious commotion.' Only because of the boatmen's strength and skill did their vessel survive, but the whole experience was attended by the most 'thrilling emotion,' inviting comparison with Niagara Falls for the effect that it created. 'If the sublimity of an object is to be estimated by the intensity of emotion which it produces, I doubt not that many will award the palm to the rapids,' reasoned Duncan. 'We only look at the falls, but we shoot the rapids. In the one case the spectator is in perfect safety; in the other his life is staked on the result.'[23]

Narratives such as Duncan's dared others to take the plunge, as it were, and choose a trip through the rapids as part of their travel itinerary. 'The whole voyage afforded me a great deal of amusement,' boasted William Blane in 1824, 'though when going down some of the worst rapids, I was obliged to hold my breath between fear and admiration.'[24] By the 1830s boatmen on the St Lawrence had developed a profitable business in carrying tourists. According to a later guidebook:

Parties of pleasure often chartered these boats, and, laying in a stock of provisions, choice wines, &c, procured a company of boatmen, and proceeded on their way down the river. Daylight being necessary to run the rapids, when night came, they would go on shore, and remain till morning, and then resume their journey, sometimes consuming three or four days on the trip.[25]

Although accidents were not unheard of, Richard Bonnycastle observed in 1841 that most travellers – even *women* – preferred 'going down the Rapids in the batteaux, to the more laborious and tiresome journey by coach and steam-boat.'[26]

The popularity with tourists of the whole St Lawrence excursion was one reason why steamboat owners strove to find a way of making the trip safely without bypassing the rapids. Clearly, a complete steamer service along the entire waterway would simplify the movement of goods and people travelling for all purposes, including immigration, but the importance of tourist traffic to steamer and later to rail companies should not be underestimated. Regular service through the rapids seems to have become a practical reality by the mid-1840s. Bonnycastle recorded in 1841 that Mr Hamilton of Queenston had already built 'a splendid steam-boat, called the Ontario, on purpose to pass up and down these dreadful rapids to Montreal.' After one attempt the captain and crew deemed the adventure 'too hazardous to repeat,'[27] but not long after, other steamer pilots were making their way through the south channel of the Long Sault without incident. Guidebook lore usually attributed the discovery of a safe route through the rapids to a brave pilot by the name of Baptiste, and also told how tourist demand soon dictated that steamers pass through the more tumultuous north channel in order to maximize the thrill of the experience.

An aspect of the rapids adventure which could be transferred easily from one kind of vessel to another was the image of the pilot as romantic hero. Travellers in batteaux and Durham boats knew that their safe delivery through these wild waters depended almost entirely on the skill of the pilots and other boatmen in whom they placed their trust. Their confidence in them derived partly from the boatmen's obvious skill, but was greatly enhanced by the aura of romance that surrounded these men of the woods. Most often referred to as voyageurs, the boatmen (including the early steamer pilots) engaged in the carrying trades along the St Lawrence River were, in both popular image and practical reality, heirs to a tradition now centuries old.

The voyageurs who transported explorers, traders, furs, and other goods were usually men of French-Canadian, Métis, or Iroquois descent, drawn from some of the same communities as those who worked in the carrying trades along the St Lawrence River. Many of the boatmen whom tourists encountered retained the picturesque dress of the voyageur, such as the colourful sash and the capote with peaked hood or other pointed headgear, though the style had many variations. They shared, too, the reputation for superhuman strength and endurance, primitive manners, easy dispositions, and sudden passions, and an enviable ability to live only for the pleasures of the moment. This image of the voyageur had originated in the early explorers' accounts, but was constantly reaffirmed by nineteenth-century travellers who, like Charles Lanman, chose to believe that such men belonged to a race 'entirely distinct from all others on the globe.'[28] Close encounters with boatmen along the St Lawrence gave tourists the chance to ponder this particular blend of the wild and the civilized, and they sometimes warned each other against drawing too romantic a picture. '[T]hese river men are said to drink desperately,' warned Bonnycastle, and 'the rough untutored son of nature that we are apt to imagine "*Monsieur le voyageur*" to be, with his long queue, red night-cap, and half-savage countenance,' often turned out to be a well-schooled thief and swindler, thanks to his seasons spent in the cities and towns of Lower Canada.[29]

Even when some unpleasantness threatened to undercut the romance of the river journey, the situation more often than not was rescued by the magic of the voyageurs' music. The role of the boat song in the St Lawrence River experience provides a curious study: first, of the ability of music to evoke images and associations just as powerfully in the minds of many tourists as poetry or painting might do; and second, of the extraordinary ability of tourists to displace an element of indigenous culture with an artificial one which they deemed to be more genuine, or typical. For the romantic sensibility, music might truly speak to the mysterious links between primitive humanity and nature, and yet, as we see in this study, its evocative power could deceive if its authenticity were judged solely by the intensity of feeling it produced in the listener.

Voyageur songs had fascinated explorers and fur traders from the beginning, and for tourists they were an essential feature of the St Lawrence River experience, deeply evocative of the wilderness and the primitive past, sometimes inspiring comparisons with the traditional airs of the Scottish Highlanders. James Edward Alexander, travelling in the early thirties, was enchanted by the sight of some voyageurs 'in their grey capotes and peaked hoods' poling their vessel up the rapids at Long Sault, and when they struck up 'in chorus one of those wild and plaintive boat-songs,' he was at once transported, in his words, 'to the torrents of the dark woods and silent lakes of the wilderness.' To travel on the river with a crew of singing boatmen, their voices floating over the waters and echoing in the forests, could be even more exhilarating; as John Duncan wrote of his night excursion on the St Lawrence, 'the plashing of the oars in the water, combined with the wildness of their cadences, gave a romantic character to our darksome voyage.' The minority of travellers who found the music irksome complained either that it never stopped or that its lyrics tended towards the obscene. The boat songs had diverse origins; some were old folk songs of the *ancien régime*, while others arose out of the voyageurs' own experience and preoccupations, and sometimes these seemed coarse or 'smutty' to Victorian ears. Travellers determined to set down the voyageurs' lyrics for posterity therefore confined their attention to what they called the good boat songs – those they regarded as the *real* boat songs – and in doing so assisted in isolating a Bowdlerized canon of voyageur music.[30]

But there was one song by which the beauty and romance of all the other songs were judged, and its lyrics and tune seem to have haunted the imaginations of a great many tourists who travelled down the St Lawrence River. 'The Canadian Boat Song' was in fact written by an Irish traveller and a close friend of Lord Byron, the poet Thomas Moore, who visited Canada on a North American tour in 1804. Charmed by the music of the voyageurs who rowed him from Kingston to Montreal, he wrote a poem which he set to the music of one of the voyageur's own melodies, and it quickly became a favourite drawing-room ballad in Britain:[31]

> Faintly as tolls the evening chimes,
> Our voices keep tune, and our oars keep time;
> Soon as the woods on shore look dim,
> We'll sing at St Anne's our parting hymn.
> Row, brothers, row! the stream runs fast,
> The rapids are near, and the day-light's past!
>
> Why should we our sail unfurl?
> There is not a breath the blue wave to curl;
> But when the wind blows off the shore,
> Oh! sweetly we'll rest our weary oar.
> Blow, breezes, blow! the stream runs fast,
> The rapids are near, and the day-light's past!
>
> Ottawai's tide! this trembling moon
> Shall see us float over thy surges soon.
> Saint of this green isle! hear our prayers!
> Oh! grant us cool heavens and favouring airs!
> Blow, breezes, blow! the stream runs fast,
> The rapids are near, and the day-light's past![32]

Even though its lyrics represented Moore's own romantic imaginings of the annual visit to the voyageurs' shrine at St Anne (near where the Ottawa River and the St Lawrence flow together), the poem's reputation for authenticity – for capturing, as Basil Hall said, all that was 'characteristic and pleasing in these boat-songs,' while rejecting all that might offend – was soon established.

By the 1820s most tourists, by their own testimony, knew the song by heart and recalled it when they reached the rapids, and some credited Moore with capturing the essence of the voyageur experience so perfectly that they knew what it would *feel* like before they had even arrived. Hall described this process of image formation especially well. He marvelled at the way Moore managed to combine his poetical images 'with such graphic – I had almost said geographical truth,' that they evoked feelings of intense recognition even for those who have never 'flown down the Rapids,' nor heard the 'bell of St Anne's toll its evening chime.' Thus are distant regions 'consecrated in our imagination,' he explained, and given 'a vividness of interest when viewed on the spot, of which it is difficult to say how much is due to the magic of the poetry, and how much to the beauty of the real scene.'[34]

The only problem was that, in reality, the performance of the *real* boatmen sometimes intruded upon the perfection of the image. When compared with the pure sweet sentiments of Moore's verse, ordinary voyageur songs no longer measured up; indeed, they seemed unauthentic. One traveller complained that of all the songs he heard sung none 'even approach[ed] the pathetic ballad of Moore,'[35] and his disappointment was commonplace. Travelling down the St Lawrence by batteau in the early thirties, Henry Tudor asked his boatmen to sing Moore's song, in order, he explained, 'to gratify an anticipation previously formed.' But he was sorry to have to report that their performance was so poor that they must have forgotten everything Moore had taught them.[36]

Some resorted to performing the song themselves, as did Caroline Gilman and her companions, assembled on the deck of their steamer, shortly after leaving Prescott one evening in the late 1830s. 'It was pure romance to sit by that "trembling moon,"' she mused, 'perhaps on the very spot where Moore conceived the Canadian boat song, and hear the beautiful melody swell forth on the silent air.'[37] How do we explain this universal affection for Moore's little song? Perhaps it served as a sort of romantic shorthand, an item of musical kitsch, known to all, evoking easy associations with the Canadian wilderness, making people feel as if they had been there before – as though they were *remembering* it themselves. Recounting his impressions of St Anne itself, Nathaniel Woods wrote that '[t]here is something wild, yet quiet in its rich scenery, something in the equal solemn flow of the rapids, which befits the plaintive music in which Moore has sung them, and which makes the whole scene seem not strange, but a beautiful prospect, with which you were long familiar and had long been parted from.'[38]

THE ST LAWRENCE RIVER EXCURSION

During the 1850s the expansion of steamer service and the introduction of rail travel turned the St Lawrence panorama into a mass tourist attraction, as fully codified – and by nature less open to variation in itinerary – as Niagara itself. While the linking of Toronto and Montreal via the Grand Trunk Railway was expected to lure tourist traffic away from the steamers, rail development as a whole had the opposite effect of encouraging travel, bringing great numbers of Americans north-wards, and providing convenient connections with steamers heading down the St Lawrence River.

Excursion parties came from near and far; Americans fleeing the summer heat of the southern states were drawn by the promise of cool, health-giving river breezes, and weekend holiday-makers from both sides of the border were exceedingly fond of a day's cruise downriver which promised 'to banish fatigue and ennui.'[39] It became commonplace, for example, for Montrealers to take the train upriver and enjoy the steamer trip back home. Travellers leaving Toronto could board a vessel and cross Lake Ontario during the night, transferring to a river steamer in the morning. As the Canadian habit of travel grew, the St Lawrence River excursion became, according to one *Globe* correspondent, the favourite of those who needed a short but therapeutic holiday 'to separate themselves from the many cares which environ the accustomed walks of life.' Just board the steamer, he advised, put your feet up on the rails, and feel your appetite and zest for life return. 'Ennui cannot approach you. He or she – will some one tell us the creature's sex? – seeks not to travel by a river steamer.'[40]

The Grand Trunk Railway's method of dealing with the steamers' continuing popularity was to create timetables and advertise itineraries that made the most of the river's attractions, facilitating the exchange of passengers with the Royal Mail Line of steamers and making the whole tour as attractive as possible. An 1878 brochure of the Grand Trunk Railway and Canadian Navigation Company, for example, advertised that the evening train from Toronto to Kingston offered accommodation on a Pullman Palace sleeping-car, so that passengers could repose on board until morning, when they would transfer to a steamer. They could then catch the Thousand Islands at their sunlit best, and perhaps pass through the Lachine rapids just at the very moment when 'day-light's past,' and see them through the poet's eyes.[41] Even heading upriver, a passage made easier now with canals and locks to bypass the rapids, the steamer remained the choice of many tourists: 'all is lost to those who select the railway journey,' wrote Mrs Copleston, and Duncan condemned the railways as offering 'a minimum of landscape beauties at a maximum of charge.'[42]

The St Lawrence excursion received extensive publicity in the United States as a result of the astonishing success of Burr's Moving Mirror, a 2,464-foot-long panorama executed by a group of Americans during the late 1840s and then displayed in many major cities. Inspired by the popularity of other river panoramas in the United States, such as those depicting the Mississippi, the artists walked and sketched their way from Buffalo to Lake Ontario, then boarded a specially fitted-up vessel that carried them down the St Lawrence River to Quebec. The final portion of their journey would take them up the Saguenay River north of Quebec City, a route which was beginning to rival the St Lawrence as a tourist attraction.[43] The artists' goal was to omit no scene of natural beauty, no object of historical association, no sign of advancing civilization that might be of interest to their audience. 'Upon the vast canvas,' writes one historian,

were included lakes, bays, rivers, harbors, canals and bridges; falls, rapids, islands and points; ships, rafts, steamboats and canoes; mountains, hills, plateaus, shores and capes; cities, towns, villages and residences; towers, lighthouses, churches, cathedrals, fortifications, monuments, battlefields, walls, and ruins.[44]

The panorama opened on Broadway in September 1849, and played for several months in New York City, drawing many thousands of visitors each week and receiving lavish praise in the press for its artistic merit and evocative power. It then toured other American cities with equal success, and wherever it was shown it attracted excursion parties from other centres – including large numbers of Canadians. Travel *to* Canada was also encouraged; over thirteen hundred New Englanders journeyed together by train to Montreal, for example, in the fall of 1850, and the burgeoning tourist industry along the St Lawrence clearly owed something to the Americans' fascination with Burr's Moving Mirror.

The panorama theme was duplicated in many of the guidebooks devoted to the St Lawrence which were appearing by the 1850s. These laid out an elaborate itinerary of sights, making the most of each passing view, linking natural beauty with historical association wherever possible, always stressing the theme of constant change and contrast between scenes of wilderness and human activity. One guidebook strove to duplicate the steamer excursionist's sensation of trying to keep an eye on two sides of the river at once by making a division down the middle of each page, 'representing the channel of the river, with the towns, rapids, lakes and canals placed in their relative positions' on each shore.[45] By using the present tense and often a 'Dear reader' kind of intimacy, the guidebook authors tried to create the impression that they were there, on board, with the tourist, sharing in the thrill of the rapids or the enjoyment of the Thousand Islands, though they also plagiarized freely from previous travellers' firsthand accounts. This latter habit had the effect of recycling descriptions of the journey which were no longer accurate, but the guidebooks' objective was to market the excitement of those earlier voyages while at the same time advertising all the new signs of civilization and growing wealth that tourists would discover along the St Lawrence River.

One means of fleshing out the itinerary of sights, used in Burr's panorama and all of the river guidebooks, was to retell the events of battle associated with each ruin or scene of conflict along the St Lawrence. The testimonies of tourists themselves during the 1840s and 1850s seldom failed to mention these features of the river journey. Chrysler's Farm and Fort Wellington were pointed to as reminders of the War of 1812, but more interesting to tourists was the recent Rebellion of Upper Canada, especially the events surrounding the adventures of the Patriots in 1838.[46] American travellers likely knew these stories well, as they were the subject of a number of novels and memoirs published in the United States during the 1840s and 1850s – for example, Thomas Jefferson Sutherland's *Loose Leaves from the Portfolio of a Late Patriot Prisoner in Canada* (1840) and Peter Hamilton's *The Prisoner of the Border* (1857).[47] In some American guidebooks the insurgents were treated as heroes, while Canadian and British publications were more likely to represent them as villains, at least in the years immediately following the rebellion. But as was the case with the Niagara battlefields, it was not the rights and wrongs of the conflict that mattered so much as the desperate struggle and loss of life that the once blood-soaked remains of battle signified.[48] The town of Prescott, although described by Warburton as 'a bare, bleak place, not enlivened by its association with piracy and scaffolds,' became a highly romanticized scene of battle and surrender in the guidebooks. The 'blackened and ruined houses' and the remains of the old windmill held by the Polish exile von Schultz and his American followers (depicted at sunrise in Burr's Moving Mirror) were still visible for years after the rebels' defeat, and tourists' attention was directed to these ruins as a matter of course.[49]

The romance of the Thousand Islands was heightened as well by tales of war. Even though there were no ruins for tourists to inspect, they found it easy to imagine how the islands' great numbers, as well as their labyrinthine channels, had made them 'an admirable retreat for the insurgents.' Guidebooks strove to 'give a touch of the charm of legend and adventure to these rocky mazes' by retelling the story of Bill Johnson, who was involved in the seizure and burning of the *Sir Robert Peel* in 1838, and was pursued by the British authorities. There was room for female heroism in this story, too, for Johnson 'found a safe asylum in these watery intricacies through the devotedness and courage of his daughter,' who evaded his would-be captors by 'rowing him from one place of concealment to another, under shadow of night.' As the decades passed, this story was repeated again and again, and Kate, that 'picturesque and dauntless girl' who had reputedly saved her father's life, became established as a minor romantic heroine.[50]

Further human interest was added to the St Lawrence waterway by the inclusion of the village of St Regis (Akwesasne), which straddles the Canada–U.S. border near Cornwall, in the tourist itinerary. The occupations of the several hundred Mohawks who lived at Akwesasne included hunting, farming, piloting vessels through the rapids, and making handicrafts, the latter a principal occupation of Native women along most tourist routes in the nineteenth century, and a mainstay of family income in many communities. Like the Tuscarora who lived near Niagara, the Mohawks of Akwesasne were made 'a gazing stock' by curious tourists. For example, when the steamers docked the passengers – so we are repeatedly told – amused themselves by tossing coins to the children, who dived in the water for them.[51] And like the Tuscarora village, Akwesasne was also burdened with symbolic meaning, for guidebook writers took this opportunity to pass judgment on its inhabitants level of 'civilization.' Iroquois communities aroused a particular kind of interest, for the Six Nations' former power and reputed ferocity in war had been legendary, and their now 'orderly and quiet behaviour,'[52] their reputed devotion to the Roman Catholic faith, and their unexceptional appearance were considered remarkable by contrast. George Grant and Agnes Maule Machar, for example, in their chapter in *Picturesque Canada*, seemed almost to regret that the 'little colony of Indians' at St Regis looked so 'prosaic in their ordinary civilized attire.'[53] Wild or civilized, however, the Iroquois seldom satisfied, for the appearance of domestication, even if it did not measure up to English notions of neat cottages and agricultural efficiency, was for most an obvious sign of the Indians' fall from their former 'noble savagery.'

In reality there was very little to be seen at Akwesasne from the deck of a steamer, and most guidebooks, in an attempt to work up interest in the village, retold a favourite legend which drew together the Iroquois' Christian faith and their old reputation for merciless cruelty. It told of the theft and bloody rescue of a bell, housed in the steeple of the old stone church which dominated the village, 'the tin roof of which is very distinctly seen from the steamer,' pointed out the *Ontario and St Lawrence Steamboat Company Handbook*.[54] Around the end of the seventeenth century, so the story went, the people of St Regis, under the guidance of their priest, purchased a church bell from France. It never reached them, because the ship carrying it was captured by the English. Having learned that the bell had been sold and now hung in a Protestant church at the settlement of Deerfield, the priest incited the Indians to head off 'through the then long, trackless wilderness, to Deerfield, where they attacked in the night.' The Iroquois exacted revenge by slaughtering dozens of settlers, including the pastor's ailing wife, and took many more prisoner, some of whom never returned to civilization but were absorbed into the tribe. The bell was buried at Burlington, to conceal it for the winter, and was returned to St Regis in the spring.[55] Curiously enough, the same story was told of the church bell at Caughnawaga (Kahnewake), either as a briefer, vaguer version of the tale, or in the case of Captain Mac's *Canada, from the Lakes to the Gulf*, as the same story rendered bloodier than usual through allusion to the mangled and mutilated corpses of the Iroquois' victims.[56]

In the romantic iconography of the St Lawrence panorama, the noble savage, or wild man, image survived most tenaciously in the person of the steamer pilot, who retained the status of romantic hero well beyond the middle of the nineteenth century. The passage through the rapids was, by the 1850s, regarded as quite safe, retaining 'just that sense of danger which adds zest to novelty,' as Isabella Bishop suggested, though her own description conveyed the sense of chaos that enveloped her vessel as it tumbled through the rapids: 'louder roars the flood – steeper appears the descent – earth, sky, and water seem mingled together. I involuntarily took hold of the rail – the madman attempted to jump over – the flighty lady screamed and embraced more closely her poodle-dog.'[57] Many tourist accounts and virtually all of the guidebooks continued to make much of the terrors of the rapids, implying that genuine peril must be overcome, on each passage, through the superhuman powers of the wild man at the helm.

Once steamers began to pass through the rapids as a regular practice, it became commonplace (in fact, insurance companies could require it) for such vessels to take on Iroquois pilots to see them through the roughest passages.[58] These pilots were heir to the elite tradition of the voyageur steersman, or guide, who was entrusted with the safety of both the freight and the entire crew of a canoe or bateau in rough waters. Tourists' sense of both the extreme danger of their adventure and the complete safety of their own vessel was embodied in the image of the Indian pilot, trained from childhood to this one task and assumed to possess, by virtue of his race, the essential skills and instincts.[59] Such men, in whom tourists entrusted their lives, could suddenly appear very attractive, possessed of a full range of red gifts appropriate to the task at hand, such as dexterity, strength, nerve, and resolution.

'I witnessed,' wrote clergyman John Thornton, 'all the powers and energies of the Indian character in active exercise.' He described his pilot as 'a very fine specimen of the wild man – his features quite characteristic, dark copper complexion, an eagle eye, and most athletic and muscular in person, and a physiognomy denoting "He could do or die."' By the 1850s guidebooks and many tourist accounts of the rapids followed a familiar formula, often employing a present-tense, you-are-there style of narration. First they described the 'sublime terrors' of the rapids, then they confessed that 'It makes one's heart leap' to think that one single slip on the pilot's part would mean instant death. 'A flinching eye – a mistaken signal – a wrong turn of the wheel – and before you lies a destruction quick as thought, inevitable as doom,' promised *The Canadian Tourist*. But the powers of the pilot are then evoked, the vessel is brought to safety, and the tourist's bravery is congratulated: 'Gentle reader, the danger is over – the race is run – you have performed the feat of "shooting the Long Sault."'[60]

Although the thrill of the rapids was sustained for many tourists even to the turn of the century and beyond, by the 1860s dissenting and satirical comments had begun to appear in the tourist literature. Knowing they were expected to be afraid, some tourists resisted playing the role that had been assigned to them. Nathaniel Woods's widely read account of the Prince of Wales's visit in 1860 acknowledged that while the rapids 'are among the things which tourists who visit Canada never fail "to do," ... the fact is that the terror of these Rapids exists far more in appearance than in reality.' But while Woods saw himself as an exception and was scornful of other tourists' refusal to give up the notion of their own heroism and of the ferocity of their precious rapids, the *Globe* presented the situation differently just two years later. 'The fact that the feat is successfully performed day after day, year after year, takes from it the charm of danger. The common sense of the majority looks coldly on all attempts of the enthusiast to get up a sensation.' Like so many aspects of the Niagara tour, the rapids adventure had become hackneyed. 'I hate sights,' growled a clergyman named Jones in the

1880s, and he attributed his own refusal to do the St Lawrence excursion to the self-consciousness and revulsion invoked by Montrealers repeatedly asking him, 'Have you done your rapids?'[61]

AN IMAGE TRANSFERRED

The romantic invocation of the voyageur was not confined to tourism on the St Lawrence River, however, and its employment elsewhere provides another example of the transferability of evocative imagery. Just as the rapids adventure was losing much of its poignancy, tourists became attracted to yet another incarnation of the voyageur – the raftsman or lumberman whom they saw at work on both the St Lawrence and Ottawa Rivers. 'Have you, my friend, ever been on one of our Canadian steamers, on the St Lawrence or Ottawa, and met with a raft, or perhaps a dozen of them, on their passage down to Montreal or Quebec?' queried the *British American Magazine*. '[I]f you have,' continued the author, employing a familiar rhetoric, 'you have seen the Voyageurs at work at their big paddles, like a family of Hercules' ... a class of men strangely incompatible with the rest of humanity, as brave as they are strong, as wild as they are happy.'[62] Raftsmen on the Ottawa River were likely to be French-Canadian lumbermen who had spent a season in the bush and were accompanying their own timber to its destination in Quebec, while along the St Lawrence, where rafting was a distinct trade, Iroquois boatmen were usually taken on to navigate the timber rafts through the rapids.[63] The rafts were large and carried dozens of men, and as *Hunter's Panoramic Guide* explained, the huts erected for their shelter gave them, as they passed down the river, 'the appearance of small villages.'[64] Many tourists admired the picturesque appearance of the rafts, and expressed delight at the voyageurs' exotic dress, fearless manner, and habit of singing those haunting French-Canadian songs while they worked.[65] In British and English-Canadian writings, the French Canadian was increasingly portrayed as semi-civilized or childlike, but images of Native boatmen remained the most fanciful. Peter O'Leary, for example, evoked the generic wild man image when describing his sighting of a raft in the rapids. When 'the raft got into the eddy the chief gave the word, and the red men at once – descendants possibly of those that fought under Tecumseh, the noblest of their race – were stirred into life and activity.'[66]

By the 1860s the Ottawa River was an established part of the tourist itinerary, which applied to it many of the same themes and images that had drawn travellers to the St Lawrence. The Ottawa River Navigation Company ran excursion boats between Ottawa and Montreal, and one of the highlights was a visit to the rapids and the village of St Anne, where stood *the very house* where Moore was supposed to have written his boat song.[67] Ottawa itself was becoming a popular tourist destination, with much being made of its wild, romantic setting – an ideal backdrop for the Gothic parliament buildings that rose out of the forested riverbank 'like one's idea of fairy land.'[68] The Chaudière Falls plunged 'over the precipice into a deep, dark basin,' wrote George Borrett, 'where they hiss, and boil, and seethe,' and were commonly described as second only to Niagara itself.[69]

To make the descent possible for the timber rafts, a portion of the river had been dammed and turned into a series of straight runs and small waterfalls, each involving a plunge of four or five feet. The whole course was about three-quarters of a mile long, and the main attraction of these falls for the tourist was the prospect of being transported down them on a timber shoot in the company of a team of voyageurs, portrayed as picturesque, tuneful, and devil-may-care. 'To go down the rapids of the St Lawrence is comparatively nothing,' admitted *The Canadian Handbook* in 1867, 'but to go down the rapids on a timber shoot ... and see [the waters] hissing and rushing up over the raft beneath your feet, is the most exhilarating adventure in all the repertoire [*sic*] of American travels.'[70] Again, the thrill clearly depended on the perception of danger, and *Picturesque Canada* assured readers that 'the descent is made at a pace which, with the ever-present possibility of a break-up, gives a very respectable sense of excitement to a novice.'[71] This pleasure was open to anyone just by applying 'to any of the large lumbering establishments, and judiciously disposing of a trifling "backsheesh" among the voyageurs themselves.'[72] These men aroused the usual admiration for their 'courage and contempt of death,'[73] and were pictured as true heroes of the rivers and forest. Royalty and the aristocracy travelling to Ottawa did the timber shoot as part of their essential itinerary, and thus publicized it all the more. ('I liked it extremely,' declared the Marchioness of Dufferin.)[74] One visitor pronounced the sensation equalled neither by 'balloon nor diving bells,' another declared that it 'beats the excitement and exhilaration of toboganning all to pieces,' and the first edition of Baedeker's *The Dominion of Canada* (1894) described it as 'one of the recognised items of a visit to Ottawa.'[75]

By the early twentieth century, however, the appeal of raftsmen and rapids on the Ottawa or the St Lawrence was already fading, and postwar travel literature would have little to say about such attractions. The image of the voyageur or wild man at the helm was deflated by the steamer companies' discovery that a pilot need not wrestle the boat through the rapids, where the current was strong it would of its own accord be kept from striking the rocks, leaving the captain 'quite justi-fied in sitting in his easy chair and smoking a cigarette all through it.'[76] By the turn of the century, far more tourists were choosing to travel by rail than by steamer, partly because rail travel was now so convenient and comfortable, and partly because tourists of some means were being lured farther and farther inland – to the Rockies and beyond – so that the easy choice for many was a return excursion ticket via the Canadian Pacific Railway. The St Lawrence water route remained popular, of course, with local excursion traffic, as more and more urban Canadians looked forward to quick holiday outings in the open air.[77]

FROM NATURE TO CULTURE

The Thousand Islands, too, began to lose some of their mystery by the second half of the century, and their function began to change. Like other famous tourist sights they became subject to invidious compari-sons between the promise and the reality; Isabella Trotter found them dismal, flat, and all alike, and Nathaniel Woods, perhaps trying to make his account of the prince's journey stand out from the rest, pronounced them 'a delusion and a snare,' displaying 'confusion without pictures-queness.'[78]

Such criticisms came mainly from foreigners, however, whereas post-Confederation Canadians, searching for national meaning in the land-scapes of their new country, celebrated the beauty of the Thousand Islands in art, literature, and the popular press. George Grant, in *Pic-turesque Canada*, answered the islands' detractors by insisting that one must take time to appreciate their beauty and mystery; one must sojourn among them and 'wander day after day among the hidden rocks and recesses of the island labyrinths,' and then one would dis-cover that 'in the *coup d'oeil* from any elevated point the eye uncon-sciously reads into the distant outlines the picturesque details with which it has already grown familiar.'[79] Although some painters would soon focus their attention on regions farther west, artists such as Lucius O'Brien, Daniel Fowler, and Otto Jacobi produced landscapes that portrayed the St Lawrence region in a most romantic light, and these were shown in exhibitions, reviewed in the press, reproduced in mass circulation papers such as the *Canadian Illustrated News*, and used to illustrate the new genre (in Canada) of booster travelogues such as Grant's *Ocean to Ocean* and William Withrow's *Our Own Country Canada*.[80]

Two themes emerged at once, in fact, for the burgeoning interest in Canadian nature had both patriotic and therapeutic implications. Many prose writers and poets incorporated an anti-urban message into their celebration of Ontario's beauties, and the Thousand Islands, among many other places of resort, became the subject of poetry and doggerel which dwelt on the idea of rejecting the city and returning to nature. 'Drifting – why may we not drift forever?' asked Machar, wistfully, in one of her poems, and Evan MacGill more ploddingly vowed:

> I would seek no wealth, at the cost of health,
> 'Mid the city's din and strife;
> More I love the grace of fair nature's face,
> And the calm of a woodland life;
> I would shun the road by ambition trod
> And the lore which the heart defiles; –
> Then hurrah for the land of the forests grand,
> And the Lake of the Thousand Isles![81]

By the 1880s the Thousand Islands had become a favourite place of summer resort for both Americans and Canadians. The irony of course was that, in becoming so popular, they rather quickly lost their old associations with solitude, stillness, and the Edenic paradise untouched by civilization. Situated so closely to large cities, offering so many salubrious retreats for the growing population of nature seekers, and being well-served by steamer and rail, the islands would have required very early and restrictive government protection if they were to have remained a sparsely inhabited wilderness sanctuary.

A good number of the islands had been privately owned for some time. Many of the American islands were in the hands of speculators who were selling to potential cottagers by mid-century, while on the Canadian side a more conservative government retained control and only began selling islands directly to cottagers and hotel builders in the 1870s. Among the first wealthy Americans to begin summering in the Thousand Islands was George Pullman, of Pullman Palace sleeping-car fame, and in 1872 he invited famous friends, Generals Ulysses S. Grant and William Tecumseh Sherman and their families, to visit.[82] The crowd of newspaper correspondents who reported on each picnic, each island cruise, and each fish caught gave the islands such publicity that their popularity soared, driving the price of real estate beyond the means of all but the well-to-do. Perhaps recalling lessons learned at Niagara, both governments retained or bought back land sufficient to create a public international park where the multitudes could land boats and picnic without harassment from private owners, and where no unapproved commercial development could take place.

But unlike the transformation of Niagara, a place many considered to be so sublime, so vulnerable, and so full of meaning beyond mere picturesqueness, the tourists' takeover of the Thousand Islands did not produce such anguish and soul-searching. People largely accepted, indeed promoted, the islands' development into a summer playground – a place for rest, recreation, and the recovery of health for the 'brain-fagged' victims of urban business life, a place where Mother Nature would soothe and restore rather than challenge and excite. Here a man could 'put aside all the cares and vicissitudes of life,' advised the *Canadian Magazine*, and 'study to forget for the term of his sojourn the common mercantile interests that yield him his subsistence, and, awakening from his reverie, find himself refreshed to resume his daily avocation.'[83]

By the late nineteenth century the American and Canadian islands were dotted with fashionable hotels, cottages, camp grounds, and the mansions of American millionaires. Excursionists arrived in the thousands, by rail and steamboat, from Toronto, Montreal, and many points in the United States; according to Charles Elliot, 'Wagner's palace sleeping-cars' ran from New York City to Clayton in a mere thirteen hours.[84] Different islands, and different parts of islands, took on distinct meanings in this new resort culture. Exposure to nature was carefully regulated, as was the mingling of the social classes. Alexandria Bay, 'the Saratoga of the Thousand Islands,' for some years epitomized the status-conscious summer resort; here, wrote Machar and Grant, 'one may step from the untouched wilderness of Nature's solitudes, into all the artificial development of American fashionable life.'[85] Small boats and canoes were available for hire, accommodating vacationers who wished to set out on their own and perhaps 'rusticate' for an afternoon on some small, uninhabited island.[86] Even though it was hard to venture very far from human society and comforts, true solitude was not necessary for a brief, Pauline Johnson-inspired fantasy experience. For those who believed in the restorative effect of the nature holiday but wished to ensure that their leisure had Christian meaning, there was the Thousand

Island Park, a large Methodist resort, where no boats docked and no public amusements were held on the Sabbath, and 'religion and relaxation,' according to Charles G.D. Roberts, 'are most alluringly combined.'[87] Smaller resorts were established by other denominations, originating in, if not sustaining, the spirit of the religious camp meeting.[88]

The experience of nature was, ostensibly, the main purpose of this resort culture, and yet contemporary literature, prescriptive and descriptive, illustrates how the appeal of the Thousand Islands had shifted from the infinite variety and mystery of the natural world to the intricacies of human society. Picturesque values and rhetoric still dominated, but what fascinated observers was the way that people – such large numbers of people – had adopted the islands as their lotus-land, and adorned them with all the artificial paraphernalia of their pleasure-seeking. The usual method of portraying the full range of the archipelago's charms was still the panoramic motif, with writers describing all the sights tourists would see from the palace steamers (similar to those in use on the Hudson) and other vessels that wended their way through the islands all day.[89] 'Several of the islets,' wrote Roberts admiringly, 'are built up with fantastic structures, pagodas and fairy bridges, till they look as if they had just stepped off an old blue "willow pattern" of plate.'[90] The tourist's eye was not greeted by 'castles in ruins' as along the Rhine, but by 'castellated towers in modern architecture' belonging to American celebrities. The summer dwellings of the rich and famous, a favourite subject for the tourist snapshot, were contrasted with the quaintness of the ordinary villas and 'tiny cottages which nestle here and there along the shores,' while the numerous tent villages persuaded onlookers that every one could afford a sojourn in paradise.[91] The Search Light Tour, which occurred each summer night, represented a still more curious transformation of the panorama theme, for the steamer St Lawrence, equipped with 'an electric searchlight of 1,000,000 candle power,' and loaded with sightseers, wound among the islands and cast its blinding beam of light upon campers, cottagers, and socialites disporting on the verandas and grounds of hotels and private mansions, baring every secret to the tourist gaze.[92]

Niagara, for better or worse, was always Niagara. The unity of the river panorama, on the other hand, melted away as its tapestry of romantic imagery faded. The St Lawrence River, for that matter, had never really been a *place* so much as a passage through a series of experiences –

drifting among the Thousand Islands, running the rapids, imagining past conflicts and heroic acts. The river excursion remained popular with day-trippers, but by the last quarter of the century, growing settlement along the St Lawrence River, in combination with other factors (such as the river boatmen's diminishing mystique and the disappearance of historic landmarks), meant that much of the old magic was lost. Newer tourist itineraries, meanwhile, promised to satisfy, with the additional appeal of novelty, the same aesthetic criteria which had been met along the St Lawrence route: the soothing pleasures of the picturesque, the thrill of the sublime, the bitter-sweet sensation of nostalgia, and the fascination with the primitive in its struggle against progress.

One such itinerary which was popular by the 1870s drew tourists into a far deeper wilderness than they had frequented before – through the upper lakes and to the far reaches of Lake Superior. This region was occupied mainly by its original inhabitants, and outsiders oftened assumed, however erroneously, that it was still a virgin wilderness, a 'forest primaeval.' In the usual fashion, tourists' romantic expectations were inspired by the works of earlier travellers, novelists, and artists, and more recently by the vigorous efforts of tourism promoters. In reality, of course, the entire territory had been transformed by the effects of epidemics, by the fur trade, and by other forms of European intrusion, although the largely Ojibway population retained considerable autonomy in their admittedly altered circumstances. As the following chapter shows, it was in this part of Ontario that the relationship between tourism and colonialism was particularly marked, though it might also be said that here was a region which ultimately rejected – or was rejected by? – the values of romantic tourism.

4

Native Lands

Richard Bonnycastle, author of *The Canadas in 1841*, was surprised at the way that British visitors to Canada habitually 'confine[d] their tours to the Falls of Niagara and the St Lawrence. Nature certainly exhibits her power and her grandeur on the most extensive scale in the course of that father of floods,' he admitted, but in his view 'the fresh water seas of Superior and Huron are still more extraordinary, and equally worthy of contemplation.'[1] Beyond doubt, throughout much of the nineteenth century, the greatest number of tourists contented themselves with the well-travelled waterways and multiplying railway lines of southern Ontario. But after mid-century a growing minority responded to the lure of more distant lakes and vaster, truer wildernesses. By the 1860s the far reaches of Lake Superior had been incorporated into the regular tourist itinerary, and a round-trip journey from Toronto to Fort William had become a popular choice for a sightseeing holiday.

If one image dominated the tourist experience of the upper lakes region it was that of a primitive way of life, a primordial world, doomed to disappear in the face of advancing white settlement and technology. The Native presence was the central rather than a peripheral feature of upper lakes tourism, and the beginnings of a tourist industry coincided, not accidentally, with the process of securing control over much of this vast territory from its established inhabitants. In the 1840s the Ojibway had protested vigorously against the intrusion of mining companies; their campaign (combined with the government's determination to secure control over these lands) eventually led to the signing of the Robinson Superior and Robinson Huron Treaties in 1850. The treaties created reserves and recognized the *privilege*, in the language of the treaty, to hunt and fish in ceded territories, 'except in areas that are leased or sold to individuals or companies.'[2] The imposition of a succession of Indian Acts, which dictated the numerous enterprises in which Indians could not engage, would further limit the economic viability of communities along the north shore.

Thus from mid-century onwards, British authorities, the Canadian government, and southern-Ontario expansionists cast their colonizing eyes upon the region, and dreamed of railways, mineral wealth, and the opening of the West to unlimited white settlement and agricultural potential. To them these elements of advancing civilization would 'naturally' bring a fatal disruption of Native ways of life; regrettable in some ways, conceded a few, but inevitable and desirable, most agreed, in the long run. 'The native Indian tribes still occupy portions of this colony on Lakes Superior and Huron,' read a typical traveller's guide in 1845, 'but their numbers are rapidly diminishing, and they are fast degenerating from their original spirit and character, so that the utter extinction of the race seems inevitable, as civilization advances on the wilderness.'[3]

Tourists were drawn to the upper lakes region because it satisfied many of the criteria of a wilderness paradise, and because the growth of steamer and rail services encouraged an excursion industry to develop. Many saw this tour as an opportunity to exchange the urban routine for a romantic wilderness experience, and to witness a way of life that was fast passing away – reassuring themselves as they went along that 'civilization' was a very good thing, after all. Their uncompromising outlook had been moulded by the literature they had read and the propaganda they had heard, and fleeting visits to one Ojibway community after another seldom disturbed their confidence in Victorian notions of progress and the superiority of their own race. The principal impact on Canadian and foreign opinion of the many who recorded their observations, therefore, was to bolster public enthusiasm for bringing the region fully under white control and generally to confirm established stereotypes of the Native population. Life in this 'contact zone' was indeed characterized, as Pratt says, by 'highly asymmetrical relations of domination and subordination.'[4] The historian, nevertheless, cannot represent the Ojibway response to the tourist industry as that of the merely passive and put-upon host. In communities near the lakes, in particular, Native economies and the tourist trade became intertwined during the nineteenth century, as men, women, and children found ways of making the best of a situation they had not created.

THE ICONOGRAPHY OF THE UPPER LAKES

A consistent feature of nineteenth-century tourism in Canada was the association of wilderness, as a place, with the past. For Europeans, then Americans, and finally urban Canadians themselves, the forest served as a symbol of a lost world or worlds, and the experience of the forest was partly an exercise in collective nostalgia. For the British, and the English in particular, the forest had complex associations, and meant quite different things in North America than it did at home. Living memory did not embrace the image of an *English* wilderness; 'Even in the *wilder* parts of England,' wrote Adam Hodgson, 'we have to travel back many centuries, before fancy can venture to draw even a few faint sketches of nature in her primitive dress.'[5] In their own country most wooded regions were planted and owned by aristocrats and gentry, and the semiotics of trees had as much to do with contemporary questions of class and privilege as it did with the forest as a symbol of the primordial past.[6] Among Americans, on the other hand, the idea of the forest aroused memories of their own recently subdued and decimated wildernesses, pressing home to them how far they had advanced and yet hinting at vague but deep spiritual meanings which no longer informed their lives.

For tourists, then, the Canadian forest easily served as a place to recapture the world they had lost, and during the early and middle decades of the century it was not necessary to venture far from the settled regions of Upper Canada to find oneself in its midst. Proceeding by road from Toronto to London or Guelph, for example, was for many an arresting experience, as the forest closed in around them, engulfing them in the unknown. Other visitors, staying safely in town or on the farms of friends and relatives, might set off on day-long hiking expeditions into nearby woods deliberately to experience the solitude, grandeur, and terror of the forest.

Sometimes the woods were described as a place of great danger where one might be quickly lost or set upon by wolves, but more often they were perceived as silent and empty, like a vast cathedral cast in eternal twilight. A common theme in such accounts was a sense of plunging backwards in time, to a world of mystery where nothing had changed since the beginning of creation – a feeling belied, at the same time, by the evidence of time's relentless passage and nature's unfeeling hand in the fallen, rotting trees which littered the forest floor. Sublime imagery came into play as visitors contemplated the ravages of lightning storms – the ruins of trees 'fallen before the blast, strewn about in endless confusion, and of all sizes and ages in every state of verdant life and mouldering decay.'[7] The forest thus represented an endless cycle of life and death unaffected by human agency, so tourists generally believed, until the advent of European settlement. Yet most Victorians assumed nonetheless that the Canadian wilderness would inevitably succumb to the needs of civilization, as it had done in other parts of the continent, and recognized their own culture as the agent of sudden and irrevocable change. As they contemplated the forest's antiquity, they also, with varying degrees of complacency and romantic regret, acknowledged its vulnerability.

As more and more of the Upper Canadian landscape was transformed from woodland to farmland, tourists wanting what they called a true wilderness holiday looked farther north and west. As steamers provided the quickest and most comfortable form of travel, new tourist routes followed major waterways through this otherwise alien terrain and set certain distance settlements, such as Sault Ste Marie and Fort William, as their ultimate destinations – their *Ultima Thule*, as travel writers liked to say. Once steamer services were in place, a round trip (with stops en route) to Fort William, famous as the transhipment point for the fur trade in the early nineteenth century, could easily be accomplished in ten days. There was a logic to this itinerary that would be less evident once the CPR began to lure tourists farther west.

As was true of both Niagara Falls and the St Lawrence River, tourists' understanding of the upper lakes region was governed by a mass of influences. They included the accounts of earlier explorers, ethnologists, and travellers; the works of novelists, poets, and artists; government surveyors' reports and immigration propaganda; and other promotional materials, such as guidebooks and steamer and rail company handbooks.

Throughout much of the nineteenth century, Lakes Superior, Huron and Michigan were favourite settings for tales of romance and adventure, which were widely circulated throughout Europe and North America. Washington Irving's *Astoria*, published in 1836, was one such work. In company with James Fenimore Cooper and his *Leather-stocking Tales*, Irving helped set the standard for American wilderness narratives, while endowing certain special places with great imaginative import. *Astoria*, for example, which relates the history of the fur trade empire of John Jacob Astor, included a most romantic and nostalgic picture of life at Fort William during the era of the North West Company. Irving was a great admirer of Sir Walter Scott, and shared the fascination in

Britain and America for things Scottish now that traditional Highland society was disintegrating. He made the most of that aspect of Fort William's history, comparing the North West Company partners to Highland chieftains whose company held 'a kind of feudal sway over a vast domain of lake and forest.' Their annual councils were, he said, like meetings of a feudal parliament, where 'every retainer and dependent looked up to the assemblage with awe, as to the house of lords,' and their revels he likened to 'the old feasts' which took place in Highland castles. With the disappearance of the North West Company the fort had gone into decline and acquired the appeal of a ruin, leaving plenty of scope for nostalgia. '[T]he feudal state of Fort William is at an end'; Irving concluded, 'its council-chamber is silent and deserted, its banquet-hall no longer echoes to ... the "auld world" ditty; the lords of the lakes and forests have passed away.'[8] Irving admitted that his picture of Fort William was coloured by nostalgia for his youth, when, so he claimed, he had 'sat at the hospitable boards of the mighty Northwesters' and listened to their tales of adventure. But no other description of the early days at Fort William ever achieved the fame and longevity of Irving's description, even though it was based on hearsay and flight of fancy.[9]

Charles Lanman was Irving's imitator, in turn, and shared his longing to cloak the American landscape with the romance of history. Unlike Irving, however, he had actually visited Lake Superior – fishing, exploring, and collecting material for the travel articles he wrote for various American papers.[10] Lanman spent some weeks along the shores of Lake Superior in the company of Ojibway and Métis boatmen, whom he portrayed in the most idyllic terms. While they rowed and sang, he read, sketched, and slept, 'lulled into a dreamy repose, by the measured music of the oars, mingling with the wild chanting of the voyageurs.' Lake Superior became a paradise in his eyes, lying 'in the bosom of a mountain land, where the red man yet reigns in his native freedom.' Its climate, at midsummer, was 'delightful beyond compare ... A healthier region does not exist on the earth.' The mountains and other features of this rugged landscape gained added meaning for him through legends such as that of 'Menaboujou,' which create, he explained, 'a kind of classical interest in the scenery of Lake Superior.' Lanman could lament change while praising material progress with little apparent sense of incongruity, however, and in contemplating the ultimate fate of the region and its peoples he proposed no real alternative. 'My *reason*,' he explained, 'would not stop the tide of civilization which is sweeping to the remote north and the far Pacific; but if the wishes of my heart were realised, none but the true worshippers of nature should ever be permitted to mar the solitude of the wilderness with the song of Mammon.'[11] Lanman's romantic reveries were used to embellish several guidebook descriptions of the Great Lakes during the latter half of the century, though their source was seldom acknowledged.

Poets, as well, such as William Cullen Bryant and Henry Wadsworth Longfellow, contributed to the romantic iconography of the upper lakes. A Eurocentric vision of a glorious Ojibway past was the legacy of Longfellow's *The Song of Hiawatha*, an epic poem which, like *Evangeline*, amply illustrates the cumulative effect of cultural influences and their links to tourism. Published in 1855, *Hiawatha* was inspired and informed in good part by the travelling artist George Catlin's paintings of Native North Americans, as well as by ethnologist Henry Rowe Schoolcraft's imaginative renderings of Ojibway myth, and his erroneous association of Hiawatha (who was Iroquois) with 'Manabozho.'[12] *Hiawatha*, of course, is a story of an Ojibway hero, his marriage to Minnehaha, his people's rise and decline, and ultimately the coming of 'the White Man's Foot.' As Hiawatha prepares to leave for Keewaydin, the land of the Northwest-Wind, he welcomes the missionaries who have come to their village, and instructs his people to heed and protect them. *Hiawatha* enjoyed an 'unexampled sale,' was read publicly to large audiences, was set to music and performed, and was the subject of warm praise and heated controversy.[13] Lake Superior, meanwhile, became the Land of Hiawatha, and the Ojibway themselves the object of comparison with the idealized hero and his Minnehaha. '[T]he Indian words used by Longfellow are in everyday use by these people, and to them the legend of Hiawatha is taught as soon as they can lisp,' claimed a CPR promotional brochure.[14] By the turn of the century the poem had been translated into the Ojibway language and was being publicly performed as outdoor theatre, 'in the forest primeval,' on an island near Desbarats in the North Channel, not far from the Sault. With the exception of the Black Robe, or missionary, most of the performers were Ojibway and spoke their own language, with explanations shouted in English through a megaphone when necessary. Tourists and reviewers apparently loved it, combining as it did the forest setting and the famous poem, while featuring 'real Indians' dressed for and coached in their romantic roles, finally welcoming the Black Robe as they parted in sadness from their beloved Hiawatha. 'It is impossible to describe,' sighed one reviewer, 'the sublimity of this closing scene.'[15]

The masters of romance had many imitators, and lesser works set in the upper lakes region, such as Owen Duffy's *Walter Warren, or the Adventurer of the Northern Wilds* (1854) and John Coppinger's *The Renegade: A Tale of Real Life* (1855), were proliferating by mid-century.[16] The theme of civilization versus primitivism was the focus of such works; heroes exiled themselves to the wilderness and returned, with new wisdom but also with relief and gratitude, to their familiar white, urban worlds. At the same time, popular journals such *Harper's New Monthly Magazine* took a growing interest in the back-to-nature idea and often turned their attention northward in order to capture, for eager readers, images of places which were at once a tonic for the ills of civilization and yet were bound to succumb to its relentless westward march.

The British, at the same time, had their writers of romance and their literary tourists who brought the wilderness of the Great Lakes region into the public eye. Anna Jameson's autobiographical work, *Winter Studies and Summer Rambles in Canada* (1838), attained an instant reputation as soon as it was published, and served as a point of reference for many subsequent visitors to the upper lakes. Like most pioneering tourists who left records of their travels, she was socially well placed, carried letters of introduction with her, and sallied forth with all the confidence of the English ruling class abroad. And, like most Victorian travellers to the Canadian wilderness, she had gleaned her preliminary impressions of the land and people she would see from such romanticists as Cooper, Irving, and Charles Fenno Hoffman: 'I can add nothing to these sources of information,' she modestly proclaimed, 'only bear testimony to the vigour, and liveliness, and truth of the pictures they have drawn.' Another inspiration was the earlier travel writings of explorer and trader Alexander Henry, after which she tried to pattern her own journey. 'He is the Ulysses of these parts,' explained Jameson, 'and to cruise among the shores, rocks, and islands of Lake Huron with Henry's *Travels*, were like coasting Calabria and Sicily with the Odyssey in your head or hand.'[17]

Jameson's tour was such a popular model that it is worth looking at in some detail. Her upper lakes itinerary began with her departure from Detroit by steamer to Mackinaw, where she was received by ethnologist Henry Rowe Schoolcraft and his Ojibway wife. Schoolcraft was used to literary visitors, and pronounced Jameson more sensitive – better able to see what was before her – than certain others, though he noted that her vision was not unclouded (nor was his own) by the conventions of European culture, and remarked that she looked upon 'our vast woods, and wilds, and lakes, as a magnificent panorama, a painting in oil.'[18]

As Mrs Schoolcraft was soon to leave for a visit to her family at the Sault, Jameson concluded her stay at Mackinaw by joining that expedition, and travelled for two days by batteau, rowed by five French-Canadian or Metis voyageurs. 'I cannot, I dare not, attempt to describe to you the strange sensation one has, thus thrown for a time beyond the bounds of civilized humanity,' she enthused, 'and we ... two women, differing in clime, nation, complexion, strangers to each other but a few days ago, might have fancied ourselves alone in a new-born world.'[19] Welcomed and fêted by the Johnstons at the Sault, she remained for three days, and enjoyed the distinction of being the first white woman to run the rapids of the St Mary's River in a canoe. She journeyed to Manitoulin Island by batteau, where she stayed a few days; she then went to Penetanguishene, finally returning home via Lake Simcoe in mid-August.

Throughout these travels her portrayal of the voyageurs, or boatmen, sustained the heroic image established by others' accounts. 'What [Irving] describes them to *have been*,' she testified, 'and what Henry represents them in his time, they are even now, in these regions of the upper lakes.' One young captain inspired further allusions to Ulysses 'steering away from Calypso,' while another, named Martin, struck her as a most romantic figure in his 'cotton shirt, arms bared to the shoulder, loose trowsers, a scarlet sash round his waist, richly embroidered with beads, and his long black hair waving ... [and] a paddle twice as long as the others.' As many future tourists would discover, Georgian Bay offered as remarkable a panorama of islands and channels and exotic vegetation as the St Lawrence, and Jameson's description could not have been more idyllic: 'we glided through vast fields of white water-lilies; it was perpetual variety, perpetual beauty, perpetual delight and enchantment, from hour to hour. The men sang their gay French songs, the other canoe joining in the chorus.'[20]

As she had hoped, this journey provided the opportunity to observe what mattered most to her – 'the condition of women in savage life' – and to ponder for herself the comparative merits of wilderness and civilization. As a prominent British feminist and an individual about to seek release from an unsatisfactory marriage, she had a sensitive eye for the liberties and rights of these women whose lives were so different from her own. Many aspects of their situation she found remarkable. Here was a society, she exclaimed, with no prostitution, where rape was unknown, where a woman's rights to her children were unquestioned – in contrast to England, where she had no such rights at all. She concluded that these women's lot was hard but that their status was superior, in their own culture, to that of European women in theirs. Yet she could not accept the wider meaning of such a statement: 'God forbid that I should think to disparage the blessings of civilization. I am a woman, and to the progress of civilization alone can we women look for release from many pains and penalties and liabilities which now lie heavily upon us.'[21]

Other aspects of Ojibway life, such as warfare, presented further opportunities to evaluate the differences between so-called primitivism and civilization. Jameson conceded the hypocrisy of pretending that scientific warfare conducted by Christians at a human loss in the tens of thousands was civilized, while the scalping of a few dozen captives was an act of savagery. 'I prefer the Indians on the score of consistency,' she admitted. 'They are what they profess to be, and we are *not* what we profess to be.' And yet her reasoned observations were repeatedly undermined by two factors: the sustained shock value of certain things she reported seeing (such as a warrior wearing, as decoration, 'the scalp of *long fair hair*'), and her ultimate certainty that these people could not survive what was to come. 'These attempts of a noble and a fated race,' she predicted, 'to oppose ... the rolling westward of the great tide of civilization, are like efforts to dam up the rapids of Niagara.' It was a law of nature, she maintained, that the hunter must make way for the agriculturalist, and she doubted their capacity to make the change. '[T]hey do strike me as an *untamable* race,' she wrote. '[T]here is a bar to the civilization of the Indians, and the increase or even preservation of their numbers, which no power can overleap ... I can no more conceive a city filled with industrious Mohawks and Chippewas, than I can imagine a flock of panthers browsing in a penfold.'[22]

The image of an untameable people fascinated many travellers to the upper lakes, though they were not always satisfied with what they saw. Another widely read English writer, W.H.G. Kingston, was among those who followed in Jameson's footsteps, even to the point of stopping to view a cottage at the village of Keswick, where she had stayed.[23] Kingston toured Canada with his new bride in the 1850s, and journeyed as far as the Sault in the company of an Indian agent and assorted other steamer passengers. With not much interest, unlike Jameson, in encountering real people of the region, Kingston looked for the Indians of Cooper's novels, but found himself perpetually disappointed. Plunging into the 'wild forest' after leaving Toronto by rail, he saw little evidence of any human presence apart from the odd settlers' hut, and none of the birch-bark canoes or 'Red Indians in war-paint and feathers' which, he complained, would 'have been more appropriate to the spot.' His appetite for the picturesque was better satisfied on board the steamer *Orillia*, and at Snake Island he spotted 'some tolerably rough looking specimens of the children of the wilderness on their native lands ... playing hide-and-seek among the stumps and roots of the trees which lined the shore.' Later sightings, however, convinced him that the 'Red Man' looked 'far more picturesque at a distance than near at hand,' and closer contact at Manitoulin Island led him to decide that all of these people were 'sadly inferior to the Red Warriors Cooper so beautifully described.' He felt deceived. 'People in England have a very mistaken notion of the character of Indians,' he concluded during his visit to the Sault. 'There are some fine, honourable, brave fellows; but Cooper's characters are altogether imaginative.' Derogatory and facetious by turns, Kingston was like many subsequent tourists to the upper lakes in refusing to take seriously a people whom they assumed would soon cease to exist.[24]

More straightforwardly romantic were the novels and reminiscences of Robert Michael Ballantyne, who had worked for the Hudson's Bay Company in the 1840s and then returned to Britain and a career writing juvenile fiction. He published *Hudson's Bay: or Every-day Life in the Wilds of North America* in 1847 and *The Young Fur Traders* in 1856, and to raise money for charity he took his voyageur act on tour, dressing up as a trapper, telling fur-trade stories, and singing voyageur songs. His image of the voyageurs ('men of iron nerve and strength of mind') was a romantic yet curiously sanitized one, and like Irving he looked back to North West Company times when Lake Superior was in its heyday. What must it have been like, he asked, hearing the voyageurs singing, three or four hundred strong, on their passage to Fort William? 'Alas!' he exclaimed, 'the forests no longer echo to such sounds. The passage of three or four canoes once or twice a year is all that breaks the silence of the scene; and nought, save narrow pathways over the portages, and rough wooden crosses over the graves of travellers who perished by the way, remain to mark that such things were.'[25]

Literary representations of the upper lakes thus comprised a complex variety of interrelated themes. The region was the scene of past glories because of the fur trade; it was also a place of untouched beauty and splendid (or sublimely terrifying) isolation, where one could retreat and rediscover faith in God, oneself, and one's idea of civilization. This isolation was about to be destroyed by the influx of miners, lumberers, railway builders, settlers, and tourists; this was unfortunate, yet none of these writers denied the superiority of European technology, religion, and culture which were about to engulf the region. This double vision in fact served to undercut the practical difference between the romanticists and those who openly despised the Native population of the region, since both believed in an inevitable evolution towards the triumph of white civilization.

The cultures of pre-Confederation Ontario (Canada West) and the new Dominion of Canada were imbued with a similar expansionist sensibility. Eager to portray the Canadian landscape in the most romantic light and to inspire pride and patriotism, many writers lavished praise on the beauties of a region to the west which they regarded as their own frontier. While they sometimes waxed sentimental about its Native population, at the same time they made fantastic claims about its future under white control.

Among newspapers, the *Globe* took the lead in promoting interest in the upper lakes. From the 1860s till near the turn of the century, when attention shifted elsewhere, it published a multitude of travel narratives and holiday musings, written mainly by correspondents on board Great Lakes steamers such as the *Algoma* or the *Frances Smith*. Their praise of the beauties, the health-giving properties, and the potential wealth of the region was ecstatic and exaggerated, while their descriptions of Native life in shoreline communities were more crudely dismissive than the average account. Other widely read but less ephemeral prose works, such as George Grant's *Ocean to Ocean* (which tells of his trip west with Sanford Fleming in 1871), made much of the attractions of the region while treating the future of the Native population as a serious issue for which they had no solution, except to hope for eventual assimilation. In English-Canadian literature generally, from poetry to novels to prose works dealing with the wilderness and the west, a general trend after mid-century was to regard Native peoples as members of a dying race, to ignore the existence of particular peoples in favour of the generic Indian, and to contrast their past freedom and independence with the Indian now lurking on the fringe of civilization, pictured as melancholy, passive, and dependent.[26]

Artists, meanwhile, had a double agenda as well. They portrayed the pristine beauties of the upper lakes and recorded a Native way of life now under seige, but the publicity their works achieved – through exhibitions and being reproduced as engravings in the *Canadian Illustrated News* and elsewhere – contributed to the larger process whereby Canadians laid claim to what would soon be called the New Ontario. Artist William Armstrong toured the region as both engineer and painter, and achieved recognition when his drawings of landscapes, Native people, and fur traders were published in the popular press. The widely reproduced paintings of Frances Anne Hopkins, who travelled with her husband during the last decade of Hudson's Bay Company rule, evoked the romance of canoe travel but also the trek west of the Wolseley expedition and the wistful human relics of the primeval forest.[27] Lucius O'Brien and others fished and sketched their way through northwestern Ontario, and probably at no other time in Canadian history was the simple act of touring one's country and painting it more likely to attract public interest. The Ontario Society of Artists mirrored the patriotic enthusiasms and fascination with the wilderness landscape that characterized this period of self-conscious Canadianism, and the prestigious photographic firm of William Notman and Son employed many artists to illustrate travel articles in magazines and promotional materials for the CPR. The railway often paid for artists' western travels, though some painted the upper lakes without visiting the region themselves, a practice which understandably nurtured the 'generic Indian' image still further. Frederick Verner's *Lake, North of Lake Superior*, says Dennis Reid, is little more than a 'generalized northern landscape, dressed up ... with stage-set gnarled trees, cheaply-costumed Indians, and a mechanical moose.'[28]

Publications with a frankly promotional purpose often provided, through both literary and visual representations, a sustained emphasis on the romance of the past and the prosperity of the future which virtually ignored the Native presence altogether, except for vague references to legends and odd glimpses of 'red men' in the woods. But generic Indians were at the ready in such literature, as if by magic, whenever activities requiring guides came under discussion, with no references to where these people came from or the awkwardness that this meeting of cultures often occasioned. The Canadian Pacific Railway was in the position of courting more than one audience at once through its promotional materials, and those aimed at tourists, whose economic value general manager William Cornelius Van Horne took seriously, employed art, poetry, and the testimonies of earlier travellers to the most romantic effect possible, and strove for a thoroughly idyllic and innocuous vision of this 'Land of Hiawatha.' Native people entered the landscape almost exclusively as guides – trusty servants of white tourists, or occasionally as picturesque elements of landscape where a finishing touch was needed. Pressed to say something interesting about the trip from Port Arthur to Winnipeg, for example, the author of *Summer Tours by the Canadian Pacific Railway* (1887) conjured up images of old fur trade days and wild Indians to give meaning to what tourists might think was just a tedious wilderness. Although few signs remained of the region's old associations, explained this brochure, the 'Chippewas who come out of their bark lodges, or pause in their paddling to watch the train go by, are in appearance the same wild redskins with whom Duluth treated and Marquette prayed.'[29] Literature, art, patriotic propaganda, and advertising all sprang from a culture in which Native people were seen as only marginally human; small wonder that tourists' vision was also clouded, and that most were content to keep it that way.

VICTORIAN EXCURSIONISTS

The great era of upper lakes tourism occurred during the last three or four decades of the nineteenth century. By the 1850s the Sault was already popular as a summer resort; when Lawrence Oliphant arrived he found the place full of Americans 'who make summer excursion to Lake Superior and who patronize the Sault largely as a sort of watering-place, with the advantage of sport in the shape of pigeons and trout in the neighbourhood.'[30] In 1855 the Northern Railway from Toronto to Collingwood was completed and the new American canal at the Sault allowed steamers to pass easily into Lake Superior, making the trip from Union Station to Fort William a matter of just three or four days. Depending on the desires of passengers, the need to take on fuel and other supplies, the destination of goods to be delivered, and the extent of other business to be transacted, stops would be made at various Hudson's Bay Company posts and at communities such as Killarney, Little Current, Bruce Mines, the Sault, Michipicoten, Red Rock, Prince Arthur's Landing, and Fort William. It would be misleading, however, to suppose that all the tourist traffic originated in the east; J. Ewing Ritchie, travelling from Toronto to Port Arthur in 1884, encountered on board a number of 'stalwart boys from Manitoba ... who have been enjoying a holiday in Upper Canada.'[31]

Two main varieties of tourists who frequented the upper lakes were the excursionist and the fisherman or hunter. The excursionist was usually bent on sightseeing and content with brief stops at settlements along the way, putting up at hotels or staying with acquaintances if more extended visits were made. While a certain number of overseas visitors would be included among the passengers aboard most steamers, this journey was especially popular with Americans and Canadians seeking novelty and an escape from overheated cities. Hunters and anglers, on the other hand, headed for places like Nipigon, where fish or game were abundant and where they could feel they were truly alone (under the care of their guides) in the northern wilderness. The combined costs of transportation, canoes, equipment, and guides could make this an expensive pastime, and it was especially popular with businessmen from the eastern and midwestern United States.

Many travellers, of course, had more than one reason for their journeys, and any given vessel contained a great mixture of passengers. Politicians, mining speculators, and others with an eye to personal gain combined sightseeing with more practical goals, while those who believed their health was delicate were attracted by the promise of 'ozonized air' and 'a pure bracing breeze, before which sickness must grow weak and die.'[32] Some travelled west because they were bored with eastern resorts (the 'expensive miseries' of Saratoga and Long Beach), and still others, such as the 'Botanist' on board the *Frances Smith* with George Grant and Sanford Fleming in 1872, found their greatest delight in searching for plant specimens each time their steamer docked. The very image of the Victorian naturalist at large, the botanist (who was in fact Canadian naturalist James Macoun) was always first on shore, 'scrambling over the rocks or diving into the woods, vasculum in hand, stuffing it full of mosses, ferns, lichens, liverworts, sedges, grasses, and flowers,' with such obvious enjoyment that other passengers started making collections, too.[33] Most vessels carried immigrants as well as round-trip passengers, but they were often in steerage, segregated from the cabin passengers. It was not unusual for cattle to be taken on for at least part of the journey, and descriptions of life on board such steamers often portray a scene of minor chaos. Regulations limiting the number of passengers were either nonexistent or ineffective, and over- crowding and a mad dash for cabins was usual. The unlucky ones were left to bed down on the deck as best they could: 'The scene on board the boat beggars description,' wrote Mary Fitzgibbon of her trip aboard the steamer *Manitoba*.[34]

On the other hand, a certain relaxation of the rules of polite behaviour, dictated by a forced intimacy and such social levellers as seasickness, created an atmosphere of liberation which for some became part of the attraction of the trip. It can be difficult, in fact, to equate these travellers with the more restrained middle-class Victorians with whom the historian feels most familiar, so freely did the sexes mingle, so bent were they on the pursuit of pleasure. Such excursions attracted large numbers of young unmarried passengers, including 'young ladies who are no doubt supposed at home to be "off at the seaside," [and] young gentlemen,' guessed J.H. Coyne, 'who are up here because they have nothing else to do.'[35] The time on board was passed playing cards, singing, dancing, and lounging; when the steamers docked they spent the hours before embarking again exploring, visiting waterfalls and rapids, collecting plant and mineral specimens, and purchasing souvenirs.

People made friends quickly, and saw one another in more varied circumstances than would be likely in everyday life. One young man travelling to Lake Superior in the summer of 1867 began his journey with nothing good to say in his diary about the single young women aboard the *Algoma*: 'decided nuisances on this sort of trip. I have found them so already.' He soon changed his mind. By his account, the days that followed were full of conviviality, spent in social banter, sightseeing, and evening dancing, and on shore the young women joined willingly in 'scrambling and tumbling' over rocky terrain to see the local sights. By the end of the journey his affection for them had grown, and he was reluctant to part with them for good. One of them, a Miss Withers, had given him 'permission to call on her when I go to Toronto - of which permission I shall gladly avail myself,' but there was also the young Miss Bruce: 'her face is as a book where men may read,' he sighed; 'Oh how I enjoy a conversation with her – In person she is charming to my taste … [though she] does not look so well in her bloomer costume as she does when dressed for the drawing room.'[36]

Young people sometimes assembled a party of their friends to take the excursion together, with staid society and watchful parents left far behind. In the summer of 1880, for example, a party of thirteen met at Union Station and ultimately headed west on board the *Frances Smith*. Soon the diary of their trip dropped all formalities; the travellers assumed names such as Dumpling, Honey, and The Boss. The atmosphere was one of determined levity. Rugs were spread on deck, evenings were spent singing 'Do You Know the Muffin Man' and 'playing bear (the effect of eating so many huckleberries).' A birthday was celebrated with bumps and kisses, and an attempt was made to hold a Sunday church service on a lake so rough that people were sick and laid out all over the deck.[37] The cheerful vulgarity of the young excursionist could look different through an outsider's eyes, however, and a *Globe* correspondent aboard the *Manitoba* that same summer concentrated his criticism on a flock of American passengers whose manners and speech, especially at table, he found most objectionable. They habitually shouted, he reported testily, even to friends seated twenty or thirty feet away. 'Today, for example, one of the young belles of the party called out to a youth half-way down the table:

'George, do you like cherry poie?'
'Yeas, but I got some.'
'Weall, I was going to say if you hadn't got enny you could have *my* cherry poie.'[38]

Excursionists' accounts, whether critical or approving, give the impression that small lapses in decorum were more the rule than the exception, and that the relative cheapness of the journey, its informality and inconveniences, and its overarching theme of leaving civilization behind, all encouraged these Victorian travellers to let down their hair, if only just a little.

COLONIZING EYES

The general tone of levity, combined with the cultural assumptions common to the Victorian traveller, no doubt contributed to the unequivocally bad manners that many displayed during their visits to communities along the upper lakes route. For the average excursionist, encounters with the Ojibway population were brief and mainly voyeuristic. These people were a great curiosity, a sight to be seen; their personal appearance, their demeanour, their occupations, their homes, and their children all aroused constant comment. They did not necessarily shrink from this scrutiny, however, as they had their own interest in the steamer traffic. According to various accounts it was usual for them to greet vessels on their arrival in order to receive goods being delivered to them; to market handicrafts, fish, and wild berries; and to satisfy their own curiosity about the tourists. Even at the post at La Cloche, where a two-mile shoal prevented the ship from docking, passengers might be entertained by the sight of a flotilla of 'great birchbark canoes' being paddled out to meet the steamer. One onlooker displayed his own vulgarity as he described the scene, recounting how the canoes were 'manned by Indians of every hue and degree of miscegenation ... the squaws sit in their canoes and nurse their progeny, never wincing under the scrutiny of the glasses levelled at them from the promenade deck.'[39]

At communities where the steamers docked, tourists took the opportunity to examine Native life at first hand, always superficially and sometimes intrusively. One *Globe* reporter described how, when the Orangemen of York and Simcoe reached Killarney in the summer of 1865, the 'excursionists thronged the street, ... the Indian wigwams were entered,' and conversation by means of sign language was carried on with the older women who had stayed home to mind the babies, each snug in its *tikinagan* or cradle board. 'We found the little things, shut up in boxes like Egyptian mummies, swinging from the branches of trees, or leaning up against stumps, in quiet enjoyment of life, whilst their mothers were away paddling about in a canoe, or hawking Indian wares on board the steamer.'[40] Three decades later the focus of interest was much the same, and 'Sama' told readers of the *Globe* how passengers flocked to visit a large encampment of Native people visiting Killarney 'to view the tents and wigwams and family life of the red man at close quarters.'[41]

As might be expected, the settlements were described in quite different ways by different observers. Some found them pretty or quaint, while others condemned them and their inhabitants as dirty and desolate – proof that the half-civilized Indian combined the vices of both races and was ultimately and rightly 'doomed to death.'[42] There were those who managed to see these strangers solely through the dehumanizing lens of the picturesque; James Trow found beauty in the apparent destitution he witnessed on the north shore of Manitoulin Island, and declared it 'a most romantic place. Here many poor, half-starved Indians are seen peeping through their tents.'[43] As usual, people expected to live up to a mythical ideal were apt to fall short: 'We were not very favourably impressed with the beauty and charms of these descendants of Hiawatha and Minnehaha,' wrote one traveller scornfully.[44] Tourists seldom had any notion of why poverty blighted many of the communities along the North Channel route through Georgian Bay, though a few, more well-informed travellers knew something of these people's changing circumstances. George Grant, for example, while hardly sympathetic to the idea of Native cultures' surviving, explained to readers how some inhabitants of Manitoulin Island had only recently been pressed to give up most of their territory, and were now confined to much smaller tracts of land.[45] Most, however, simply blamed the bad living conditions on some fatal flaw in the Ojibway people themselves.

The production and sale of handicrafts, while doubtless giving poor return for the skill and effort involved, provided a significant source of income in locations where older means of survival had been eroded. At some settlements women and children made a practice of going on board the steamers to display and sell their work, but tourists sought out these goods eagerly enough when exploring on shore as well. At communities such as Killarney and Little Current, stores situated near the wharf sold 'great quantities of Indian work, such as canoes and boxes made of birch-bark and adorned with porcupine quills, baskets and mats made of grass.'[46] An abundance of baskets, mats, bows and arrows, and items made of or decorated with bark, sweet grass, quills, and rushes were commonly available 'at half the prices which are charged for the same articles at Mackinaw,' another tourist observed.[47] During this period such skills as porcupine-quill embroidery, which later declined because of the forced alienation of children from their culture, still flourished throughout the upper lakes region.

The combined population of the American and Canadian villages of Sault Ste Marie comprised, for some decades, the largest settlement along the north shore route. The popularity of the Sault as a resort for American hunters and anglers, from mid-century onwards, encouraged the growth of overnight accommodation for visitors, and its attractions were such that excursionists sometimes decided to stay a day or two before boarding a later steamer to continue their journey through Lake Superior.[48] Others' visits to the Sault were fleeting, their comments supercilious: 'Arriving at the Canadian town of Sault Ste Marie,' wrote one young excursionist, 'we take thirty minutes stroll in quest of Indian work. Here we see the far-famed Shingwauk Home, where Indian children are educated and cared for. We steamed over to the Yankee Sault Ste Marie, and while waiting for our steamer to enter the canal, we walk up town to ransack the principal stores, and well-laden with candies, baskets, canoes, moccasins and papooses, we boarded the *Frances Smith*.'[49]

The Ojibway population at the Sault provided sightseers with a number of goods and services. The women manufactured souvenirs and demonstrated their responsiveness to tourists' demands as well as their own considerable talent and skill. A local shop displayed a wide variety of fine embroidery work 'in beads, porcupine quills, or silk'; Mary Fitzgibbon remarked that the women's 'imitative genius' was so great that they could 'copy anything,' and told of people who had 'had their crests and coats-of-arms embroidered upon their tobacco-pouches and belts, from an impression on paper or sealing-wax.' More commonly, however, they 'copy flowers and ferns, invent their own patterns, or what seems even more wonderful, make them by chewing a piece of bark into the form they require.'[50] An Indian agent visiting the Sault in 1889 noted that the women of the Garden River Reserve had in use 'about fourteen sewing machines,' and in combination with bark-work and mat-making, they managed to make their living.[51]

Men in the vicinity of the Sault entered into the tourist trade by combining the summer occupations of fishing, guiding tourists, and running the St Mary's rapids 'when desired by strangers.'[52] This last occupation was perhaps the most remunerative: according to Fraser Rae, who visited the Sault in 1881, 'the Indians get 2 cents a pound for the fish they catch,' but could command five dollars for a trip through the rapids.[53] Like tourists on the St Lawrence, those visiting the Sault made much of the rapids' famous perils and the great skill of the Native boatmen who 'glide down in their canoes in perfect safety.' As one appreciative visitor wrote, 'The pictures of this little "gliding act" in the old geographies always made an impression on me, but when I first made the descent myself, the impression was not only more real but more pleasant and abiding.'[54] Rae was less impressed with the procedure. 'The first step,' he wrote, 'is the payment which is enforced before-hand, the next is to spend a couple of minutes in breathless excitement, as the canoe spins down the foaming water, and to be drenched by the spray through which the canoe passes, the final conclusion being that the game is not worth the cost.'[55] But the rapids remained firmly entrenched in the upper lakes itinerary for decades, and in 1894 Baedeker was still advising that 'one of the things to "do" at the Soo is shoot the Rapids in a canoe guided by an Indian, an exciting but reasonably safe experience (enquire at hotels).'[56]

All along this route the wilderness landscape was judged according to much the same aesthetic criteria as other tourist areas in Ontario. Excursion traffic was confined to the summer months when the region was at its verdant best, but unlike Niagara or the St Lawrence its vistas were never spoiled by hordes of sightseers, beyond those travelling on one's own vessel. (Hordes of mosquitoes and blackflies, however, were an acknowledged problem.) The fact that long stretches of shoreline remained *terra incognita* for much of this period lent an enchanting mystery to the region, as did the rocky shores, fogs and mirages, and the 'sublimely' terrifying lightning storms which could occur even on the coolest summer or autumn days.

A favourite portion of the journey was the cruise through the North Channel, from Killarney to Bruce Mines. The 'picturesque, rock-bound harbours' and the 'romantic beauty and wild and variegated scenery' of its estimated 30,000 islands seemed to put even the St Lawrence route to shame.[57] There were 'islands barren, wooded, sandy, rocky, columnar, gracefully rounded, precipitous and gently sloping, wind-swept and storm-polished, large, diminutive, and infinitesimal,' wrote a correspondent in *Forest and Stream*.[58] 'The scene is enchanting beyond even the most vivid description,' exclaimed another. 'The ever-varying phases of landscape and waterscape, of land and strait, and island, and mountain, and rock, interspersed with here and there a fishing village or a rude attempt at tillage ... even the beauties of the Thousand Islands must take second rank.'[59] The habit of viewing landscape in relation to foreground, middle ground, and distance was still self-consciously paraded in some narratives of the journey in which authors strove to create word pictures in the absence of illustrations.

Upon leaving the Sault travellers entered the 'vast inland sea' of Lake Superior, where the passage might prove rough and frightening, calm and boring, or picturesque and romantic if the weather and the mood were right. Echoing Ballantyne and earlier writers many tourists liked to evoke a sense of nostalgia for a more exciting past. In 1884 John Butler resurrected, for readers of *Harper's New Monthly Magazine*, a dream world of voyageurs, missionaries, 'discoverers and traders, all in the quaint and often gay costume of the time, in never-ending and ever-renewed procession.'[60] Like many others Butler saw the region as poised between past and future – old associations passing away, new sources of incalculable wealth and growth just beginning to be exploited.

The climax of the journey through Lake Superior was the entry into Thunder Bay, around the tip of Sibley Peninsula, which was then called Thunder Cape. Here myth and poetry bodied forth in geography. The cape loomed an estimated 1,350 feet, and once the bay was entered, passengers found themselves enclosed in a vista of islands and low, brooding mountains, not infrequently shadowed by storm clouds, and dominated by Mount McKay – 'a monster, grim and grey,'[61] as one tourist saw it. From inside the bay the cape 'changed its form as if by magic, and now looked like the extended body of an enormous giant lying on his back, with arms folded on his breast, the round elevation to the north appearing to be the head.'[62] When describing the harbour, tourists often embellished their prose with garbled versions of Ojibway legend, and their most commonly expressed desire was to have 'the storm-spirit,' whether pictured as a huge bird or as Nanabijou himself, perform for them.[63] Catherine Moodie Vickers, daughter of the famous immigrant writer Susanna Moodie, was treated to a violent storm on her way around the Cape. The lightning lit up the mountains and 'ribbons of fire ran up the sky in all shapes, more like rockets and fire works, whilst the thunder leaped from mountain to mountain in a continued roar, like nothing I ever heard before,' she wrote to her mother. 'If I were an artist I would choose Thunder Bay in a storm as the grandest representation of the end of the world.'[64]

Regarding Thunder Bay's growing settlements of Port Arthur and Fort William there was less to say, though wild predictions were made regarding the future importance of the port once the railway had arrived in 1882 and western settlement had begun. The contrast between a romanticized, wilderness past and the clearly utilitarian thrust of the present was drawn most evocatively for tourists during the 1870s and early 80s, when some remains of the old fur-trading post still stood on what was to become the CPR yards. The fort was a popular attraction for excursionists stopping at Fort William, and by 1880 its appeal had become that of a ruin. Butler described how the old fort, in all its decrepitude, grew 'upon one imperceptibly as it [lay] there in the sunshine, with its quaint peaked roofs, its mossy walls full of the mellow tones of age, and the last schooner of the "trade" lying before it on the river-bank, with crumbling cordage and gaping seams.' The author recalled earlier visits, and how old voyageurs would tell stories, and how the last factor, John McIntyre, would show tourists around the fort and let them collect souvenirs. But now he, too, was gone, 'the last of the old factors, who looked like an old Scotch laird, with his ruddy face, shaggy eyebrows, and a tasselled cap that covered locks as white as the Northern snows.'[65] *Picturesque Canada's* chapter 'The Upper Lakes' recalled Irving's description, and used the fort as a symbol of the changes about to sweep across this wild territory, a transformation so inevitable that nothing could stand in its way. 'The glory of the great furtraders has departed,' wrote George Mackenzie, and 'their vast monopoly is broken up; the husbandman, true lord of the soil, is entering upon their ancient hunting-grounds. Those parallel bands of iron stretching away to the west proclaim that a mighty revolution is in progress.'[66]

Tourists' contact with the Ojibway, many of whom lived at the Fort William Reserve, was of the usual sort: they bought handicrafts and they watched and commented on the men, women, and children they saw in town and at the Roman Catholic mission on Mount McKay.[67] A few hired guides to take them up the Kaministiquia, 'an almost classic old river,' said the *Globe*, referring to its ancient role as a fur-trade route.[68] The climax of this excursion, which involved poling up twenty miles of rapids, was the spectacle of Kakabeka Falls, the famous Niagara of the North, well known to Canadians through the paintings of Lucius O'Brien and others. How wonderful, wrote Vickers, to be able to say that one had made this journey and worshipped 'at nature's shrine' before it was 'marred by the hand of man – no taverns or curiosity shops or railway, no steam whistle to bring one down to everyday life.' Anxious to convey the full emotion of the scene, she wished she 'could paint the picture for you with your fat old daughter all ragged and rumpled, looking at [the falls] with the tears streaming down her cheeks, our Indians leaning on their poles, silent and still. Do they feel as we feel about such things?'[69] The excursion to Kakabeka had become much more convenient by the mid-1880s, when passengers, canoes, and Native guides' were 'taken out by train to a point about six miles above the Falls,' where the adventure could then begin.[70]

THE ROMANCE FADES

By the late nineteenth century two processes were under way which would affect the future of the tourist industry in the upper lakes. One of these – the subject of the following chapter – was the growing habit of southern Ontario city-dwellers of seeking recreation within their own northland – in Muskoka, Temagami, Algonquin Park, and other locations which could be reached within a day. Remote communities such as Nipigon attracted hunters and fishermen, but their tourist economies grew slowly by comparison. The second process involved a shift westward of the tourist frontier, following the completion of the Canadian Pacific Railway. Steamers would continue to carry tourists through Lake Superior for decades to come, but the upper lakes were beginning to lose ground as a destination for long-distance excursion travel, as the Far West – the Rockies and the Pacific Ocean – captured more and more of the tourist traffic.[71]

In its pursuit of tourist dollars, however, the CPR let no opportunity slip by, and it did not overtly encourage tourists to abandon the Great

Lakes altogether in favour of more distant and spectacular sights farther west. The artwork it commissioned, the romantic rhetoric of its promotional materials, its special rates for hunters and fishermen, and its coordination of steamer and rail services all helped to sustain tourist interest in the upper lakes region throughout the prewar period.[72] At the same time, however, the railway promoted itself as the new 'Imperial Highway' that tied the country and the empire together, and its aggressive marketing strategies, through agents in Britain, for example, drew both travellers' and immigrants' eyes westward, where 'a whole new world has been opened up to the tourist, the invalid and the settler.'[73] The attractions of the Rocky Mountains were promoted vigorously, and tourists answered the call in large numbers, passing through or stopping just briefly at northern Ontario communities along the way. Tourists' narratives testify to the insular pleasures of travel in first-class coaches that were finished in carved mahogany, had deep plush upholstery and carpets, and gleaming brass, glass, and mirrors. The food was good, the scenery was pleasing, and tourists enjoyed the isolation from noisier, dirtier occupants of second-class and colonists' cars.[74]

Part of the romance of cross-country travel in Canada was the passengers' very separation from the wilderness through which they passed. 'Inside the Pullman all is luxury; outside is Nature in her most rugged mood,' wrote one British tourist. Another, the poet Rupert Brooke, offered this tantalizing advice: 'To taste the full deliciousness' of night travel by train, he wrote, one must 'secure a lower berth. And when you are secret and separate in your little oblong world, safe between sheets, pull up the blinds on the great window a few inches and leave them so. Thus, as you lie, you can view the dark procession of woods and hills, and mingle the broken hours of railway slumber with glimpses of a wild starlit landscape.'[75]

Despite the railway's uneven efforts to sustain interest in tourist sights all along its route to the West, the imaginative appeal of the upper lakes region began to fade as the century drew to a close. The Rockies and the scenery and settlements of coastal British Columbia were not its only competitors, either. The natural and cultural attractions of long-settled parts of the country, such as the Maritimes and Quebec, drew increasing attention from artists, writers, and tourists alike, and the prairies aroused curiosity because of their much-vaunted potential for settlement and prosperity. The New Ontario no longer seemed very new, and there was a certain sameness about travel through bush which was unrelieved by scenes of human interest beyond old mining communities, new lumbering towns, and Native communities which were losing their novelty and exotic charm now that the western provinces were opened to tourism. Much of the old forest near the shores of Lake Superior and along the railway lines was succumbing to the axe, and while white settlement was too sparse to transform the region, white resource exploitation left an atmosphere of desolation and emptiness.

Northrop Frye once wrote that Canada, being a 'colony in the mercantilist sense,' has been 'treated by others less like a society than as a place to look for things.'[76] Nowhere was this more true than in the Canadian Shield, where furs, fish, minerals, and lumber drew outsiders who depleted resources, disrupted traditional societies, and – for better or worse – built little that was new in their place. By the early twentieth century, rail travellers in particular were commenting on the tedium and gloom of the north-shore route, and were anxious to move on to more hospitable and interesting places. 'There are portions of the world which Nature reserves to herself,' wrote Stuart Cumberland; 'they, in consequence of their sterility or inaccessibleness, being unfitted for the use of man.'[77]

Waning interest in the far reaches of Lake Superior, the tourists' old *Ultima Thule*, in some respects epitomized the changes that took place. The very fact that trains travelled by land rather than water undercut the romantic power of Thunder Cape, but tourists' declining interest owed even more to the thoroughly utilitarian atmosphere that the railway helped bring to the Lakehead. Suddenly the place was turned into a transshipment point for the western grain trade, as predictions about eastern Canada's colonization of the West came true. The old fort was destroyed, the old forest receded, and grain elevators and rail yards transformed the waterfront. Mrs Howard Vincent, complaining of her five-hour wait for the westbound train, described the town of Fort William as 'a swamp laid out in streets at right angles, with wooden houses, overshadowed by some enormous grain elevators.'[78]

Some visitors entered into the prevailing spirit by touring and admiring these monstrous symbols of 'the mastery of the West,'[79] but others remarked on the way the waterfront had become inimical to human enjoyment. Thomas Wilby, who before the war performed the extraordinary feat of crossing Canada by car, reported with ironic fascination that 'a man sat all day in a kiosk' near the railway station persuading visitors that Port Arthur was the 'best place in the world,' a claim contradicted by the fact that they could not even indulge their natural urge for a stroll along the shore without danger of either falling in the water, he said, or being 'mutilated by the passing railroad trains.'[80] The reigning preoccupation was money and survival, not beauty and pleasure; nature had not prevailed but neither had culture. Don't bother with this place, the author of *Canada As It Is* warned his fellow tourists, if you 'seek for pretty towns. But go, if your soul's eye can see beyond the shanties, the miry roads, the railway tracks in chaos, the humped elevators, the snorting and evil odoured engines, all, indeed, that is revolting to aesthetic taste.'[81]

During the heyday of the upper lakes excursion, the north-shore route had been successfully packaged and promoted as yet another panorama of the picturesque and the sublime, dotted with sites of historic and nostalgic interest. This romantic way of seeing and describing landscape was still as useful for selling places to tourists in the latter part of the nineteenth century as it had been several decades before. Important to the mix of imagery in this case was the idea of 'primitive' man succumbing to the march of progress, and as this chapter has shown, the growing tourist traffic was an integral part of the colonization process that was under way by the 1860s and 70s. But the nature of that process in so-called New Ontario pitted utilitarian concerns against all notions of beauty and romance, and it was the victory of the practical over the aesthetic which drew comment from many tourists travelling west. This atmosphere, combined with the fact that northwestern Ontario remained remote from urban centres of any size, meant that tourism failed to become a major industry in this part of the north. Even though city dwellers of southern Ontario became infatuated, in the decades after Confederation, with the myth of the 'Northland' as the wellspring of individual health and racial survival, for most that wilderness fantasy would be played out among forests, rivers, and lakes much closer to home.

A Forest Scene, a romantic image of the forest primeval, by W.H. Bartlett

"WE WENT TO THE STORE AND BOUGHT SOME INDIAN WORK."

"WELL-LADEN WITH CANOES AND PAPOOSES, WE BOARDED THE FRANCES SMITH."

Shopping for souvenirs at Sault Ste Marie

Family members in front of their home on the Garden River Reserve near Sault Ste Marie in the early 1900s

A Garden River Reserve family dressed for the Hiawatha pageant, c. 1901

L.R. O'Brien's picture of a steamer passing around Thunder Cape in a storm

The Sleeping Giant, Thunder Bay, by L.R. O'Brien

L.R. O'Brien's *Kakebeka Falls*

The steamer *Frances Smith* carrying excursionists through the upper lakes

The Muskoka Club, 1866

A rest cure in a canoe: a tourist and his guide fishing on the French River

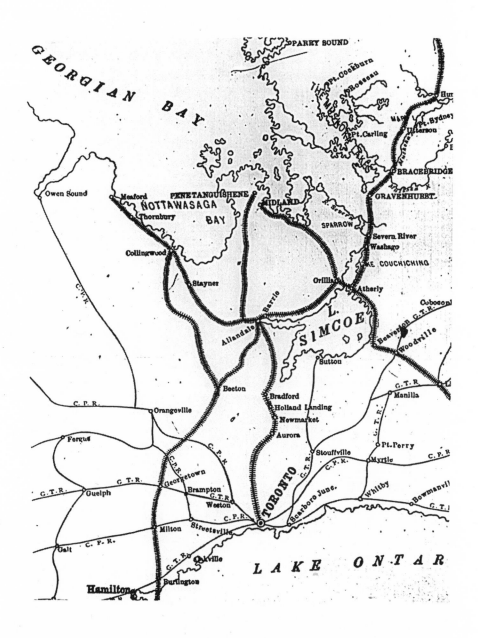

The routes north from Toronto

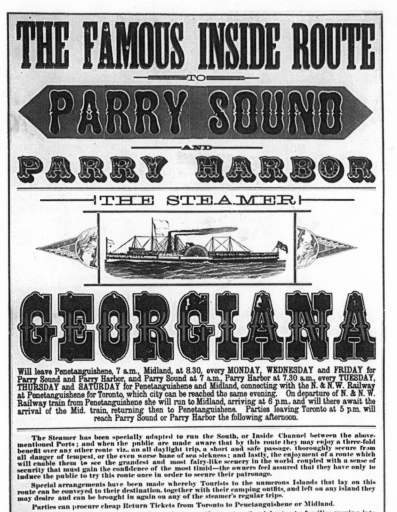

A poster advertising an excursion through Parry Sound aboard the steamer *Georgiana*: 'The grandest and most fairy-like scenery in the world.'

Boating on the Muskoka River, c. 1880

Muskoka Scenery, by Schell and Hogan

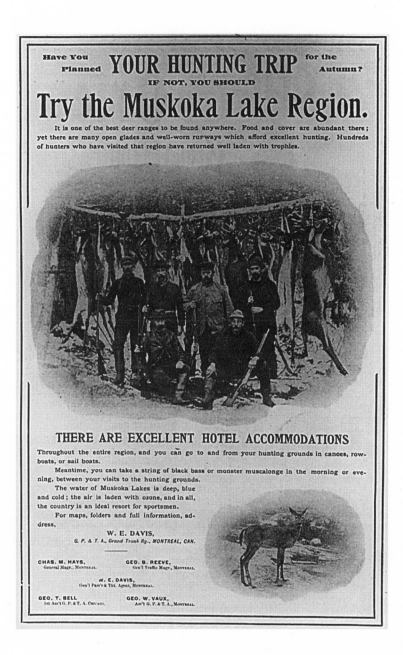

The Grand Trunk Railway advertising deer hunting in Muskoka

OUR OWN HOLIDAY PARADISE.

Family Man—NO, DAME FASHION, I'M GOING FOR REST AND
RECREATION THIS SUMMER, AND I'VE FOUND OUT WHERE TO GET IT!

A healthy, happy family resists Dame Fashion and the seaside resort in favour
of a holiday in Muskoka.

The lure of Muskoka is advertised by the Muskoka Lakes Navigation and
Hotel Company.

5

A Rest Cure in a Canoe

'*You* haven't forgotten the Stone Age,' a gun manufacturer in Wood-stock, Ontario, assured early twentieth-century readers of *Canadian Magazine.* 'That uneasy, cooped-in, office feeling ... it's your Stone Age inheritance surging in your blood.' Through a series of advertisements, the Tobin Arms Manufacturing Company of Woodstock promoted hunting as a recreation that would, they promised, bring their custom-ers nearer again to the 'original man animal – nearer physical better-ment and mental rest.' Hunting, they announced, 'is man's natural sport, and has been ever since he was a monkey. It's the best cure for brain-fag known.'[1]

During the late nineteenth century, the popularity of wilderness or back-to-nature holidays spread rapidly, especially among the urban middle classes. The growth of Canadian cities coincided with a greater tolerance for the notion of legitimate recreation, conveniently justified by growing fears about the effects of overwork and 'overcivilization' on personal and racial health. All this was also part of a new passion – or fashion – for rediscovering the wild man within oneself: in this kind of tourism, what mattered was not so much the places people visited, but the degree and quality of primitivism that could be achieved in those places. The emphasis was on creating a balance: cultivating enough exposure to wild nature, or the illusion of wild nature, to offset the debilitating effects of civilized life. All this involved manipulating, as Hayden White says, 'the fictions of artificiality and naturalness' until the desired effect was achieved.[2]

Transcendentalist Henry David Thoreau provided something of a model for this kind of endeavour. He was convinced of the need to rediscover 'the wildness ... in our brains and bowels, the primitive vigor of nature in us,' and his writings inspired generations of imitators in the United States and Canada.[3] By seeking simplicity and solitude at Walden, and by travelling deep into the wilderness as described in *The Maine Woods* and *A Yankee in Canada*, he sought to 'live deliberately' or, as he significantly put it, to 'have a better opportunity to play life.' But Thoreau, too, was seeking the right formula, and he found that, while the wilderness near Concord was rejuvenating, Maine shocked him as being 'far more grim and wild than you had imagined.'[4] Like Rousseau before and generations of tourists to come, Thoreau realized that the primitive life at which people might 'play' was a highly subjective affair, that wilderness was more a state of mind than it was objective fact.

Why and how did the back-to-nature holiday attain such vogue in Canada? The first part of this chapter looks at the impetus behind the formation of that hinterland, at why urban Canadians and Americans in such large numbers were now looking for their own opportunities to 'play life,' and at why the taking of holidays, especially northern holidays, had become such a matter of urgency. The focus then narrows to examine elements of the recreational hinterland of one city, that of Toronto, though this hinterland also served many American cities as well.

REST CURES AND RACIAL HEALTH

The rise of the wilderness holiday was closely connected to a mounting concern over the mental and physical degeneration that was common to many western industrial societies in the late nineteenth century.[5] The origins of this preoccupation were complex, and were rooted in intellectual movements as well as in social, economic, and political change. Social Darwinism was a key influence, for it encouraged people to identify all sorts of contemporary problems or phenomena as symptoms of racial decline. In Britain's case, such problems included declining industrial strength and waning imperial influence, while Americans were troubled by the disappearance of the frontier, its impact on national identity, and the perceived 'softening' of the American people. Their sense of losing ground was heightened by the contemporary obsession with racial theories and hierarchies, for it was clear that no race or nation could remain at the top of the evolutionary scale forever. If being more 'civilized' than other peoples gave a nation or class the right to rule, overcivilization, it was understood, could unfit people for the ongoing battle of life, and undermine that superiority. Proof that the 'race' (especially its middle classes) was in danger of debilitation was found in the rise of a wide range of disorders which seemed to have their common origin in 'bad nerves.' Such disorders were seen as incapacitating the very businessmen and society women who had assumed the duty of sustaining the social and economic fabric in the face of rising odds.

What Jackson Lears has aptly named 'the therapeutic world-view,'[6] which includes the compulsive search for 'wellness' as a persistent element of the modern condition, was an element of this ongoing sense of crisis which had particular significance for the tourist industry. The therapeutic holiday, in a sense, was nothing new, as the sea, the spa, and foreign travel in general had long been favoured by doctors as treatments for well-to-do patients.[7] Sea air or the taking of mineral waters restored the body, while a change of scene – the stimulation and excitement of new places and dramatic vistas – was a valued and pleasurable treatment for ennui and depression. It was understood that recovery was unlikely as long as the patient remained at home, bogged down in familiar routine and surrounded by familiar faces; Janet Oppenheim rightly points out that 'In a culture that glorified domesticity, it is striking to note the Victorian medical acknowledgement that home life could be detrimental to health.'[8] What was new in the late nineteenth century was the dramatic increase in the number of people afflicted by disorders now parcelled together under the term 'neurasthenia,' and the employment of outdoor recreation, chosen by the patient or enforced by the medical profession, as a commonplace cure and preventive measure. The idea of prevention was especially important, for most holiday-makers were not really ill, but happily confident that their pleasures had the serious purpose of stopping the symptoms of stress from overtaking their lives.

Neurasthenia was the catch-all term for a host of ailments thought to be brought on by an 'impoverishment of nervous force,' in the words of New York neurologist George Beard.[9] Some contemporaries viewed it as a peculiarly American disease, arising from the fast pace and competitive nature of commercial and urban life, but a great many Canadians found themselves afflicted as well. Daniel Clark, medical superintendent of Toronto's Asylum for the Insane, told the Ontario Medical Association in 1888 that this class of patients was already large and 'growing larger day by day in this nerve-exhausted age. The patient's mind is "centred all in self."' Symptoms encompassed dread, depression, loss of appetite, hypochondria, sexual disorders, anaemia, and hysteria; a common unifying symptom, however, was 'paralysis of the will.' According to some sources, women victims were more common, though in Clark's experience it was 'common to both sexes, but is more common in the male sex.'[10] A variety of cures were employed, including shock treatment, and many people, particularly those considered unproductive and socially redundant, were committed to asylums by doctors or family members who appreciated the fact that neurasthenia was a much more respectable diagnosis than insanity.

A kinder treatment, at least on the surface, was the rest-cure developed by Philadelphia physician S. Weir Mitchell. Elements of the rest-cure might include isolation, a bland but abundant diet, the curtailment of all responsibility and forms of stimulation, pleasant or unpleasant, and total dependence upon the administering physician. A patient might be treated at home or in a sanatorium, and success was signified by the individual's becoming calmer, fatter, and pinker of complexion. The rest-cure did not necessarily work, of course, as the absence of stimulation could induce more serious neuroses or psychoses. This was especially true, perhaps, for those women whose raw nerves originated in the boredom induced by middle-class feminine respectability and sexual repression. How much nicer to take a holiday, 'A Rest Cure in a Canoe,' as one popular Canadian magazine suggested, and drink in 'the tonic of wildness' in measured doses, to ward off physical debilitation and mental distress.[11] Beyond doubt, men and women of the late nineteenth century understood that nerves were the preoccupation of the age. As Jean Graham observed in *Canadian Magazine*, 'The papers are filled with advertisements of tonics and nerve pills, the magazines learnedly discuss "Worry: the Disease of the Age," and the doctors who are canny enough to establish rest cures are millionaires in no time.'[12] The outdoors was often prescribed as a modified rest-cure or as part of a more vigorous antidote, as the diagnosis dictated. 'No two cases can be treated alike,' Clark advised. 'If it is a case merely of brain exhaustion, then our main reliance must be upon vigorous outdoor exercises and light mental exertion. The muscular and organic life can do much through activity in bracing up the nerve centres.' His general approach was 'to divert the mind away from self-contemplation' and seek 'relief by the law of substitution' – to take a holiday, in other words. Outdoor holidays were also good for the appetite, and Clark confessed himself 'a great believer in the "gospel of fatness" – not over-feeding, but what the system can fully assimilate.'[13] There were in fact institutions that were designed to bridge the difference between places for sick and well people: St Catherine's Well, advertised in 1906 as Canada's Health Resort, offered 'the overworked businessman or tired society woman ... an antidote to the ills of modern life ... without undergoing the restraints of a Sanatorium.'[14]

The growing faith in holidays as a protection against nervous disorders permeated North American culture in a variety of ways. Physician Weir Mitchell disseminated his own belief in the links between mental health and the wilderness outing through a novel, a fishing romance, set in Canada. It was called *When All the Woods Are Green*, and in it the activities and conversations of a group of American tourist fishermen conveyed Mitchell's faith in nature's restorative value. 'In the woods, away from men and their struggles and ambitions, with the absence of need to be this or that, as duty, work, or social claims demand, we lose the resultant state of tension, of being on guard,' wrote Mitchell. This transformation is easy to see, he went on, for 'the faces of the constantly strained intellectual workers' soon lose the 'lines of care which mark the features of those on whom, in another position, the world relies to carry its burden.'[15] The close relationship between Walt Whitman, the darling of Canadian nature lovers, and Dr Maurice Bucke, who was superintendent of the London Insane Asylum and Whitman's physician/companion during his famous Northern Tour, suggests another link between the world of mental-health care and that of the wilderness tourist and nature writer.

Canadian literary culture during this period reflected the same urban anxieties as that of the United States or Britain, but to some extent it adhered to a different national agenda, that of discovering the meaning of Canadian nationhood and nationality in the alleged relationship between 'northernness' and racial health. For all those wishing 'to get closer to the primeval conditions of nature,' promised one writer, 'Canada, the future country of the world, peopled with a vigorous northern race, offers herself, disdainful of competition.'[16] In tourism literature the back-to-nature and northwoods themes were wedded to the rhetoric of nationalism, as they were in many other forms of English-Canadian cultural expression in the period after Confederation. The periodical press, such as *Canadian Magazine*, dispensed a steady stream of articles and poetry exploring this source of Canadian identity, and the interconnections among references to literature, nationalism, and the wonders of nature were pervasive. Authors might show, for example, that a place in the Canadian wilderness was special because it evoked a cherished literary scene, or literary references might provide the means by which the specialness of a place could be conveyed. If the literary passages were *Canadian* then the nationalist link was ready-made, but if they were British then this confirmed that the natural beauties of Canada could be situated within a familiar and revered cultural tradition.[17]

Specialized magazines appeared, meanwhile, which celebrated the Canadian wilderness and the back-to-nature holiday. *Rod and Gun in Canada*, as the name suggests, was devoted to the minutiae of fishing and hunting expeditions, while *Outdoors Canada* was more impressionistic than practical, and somewhat more concerned with feeling than with doing. A 1908 appeal for submissions defined its mandate: 'We want "stuff" that suggests the scent of a birch-bark canoe,' articles, poetry, and photos that capture 'the vital principle which is in Canadian soil and atmosphere.'[18]

Canada's 'serious' nature poets, such as Charles G.D. Roberts and Archibald Lampman, were also preoccupied with the menace of urban life to health, well-being, and the survival of the race itself. For them, real danger (real *wildness*, in the preromantic sense) lay in cities, not in forests. Lampman's 'The City of the End of Things,' written in 1892, expressed his vision of the industrial city of the future, 'Where no thing rests and no man is / And only fire and night hold sway / The beat, the thunder and the hiss / Cease not, and change not, night or day.' His poem 'Freedom,' on the other hand, captured the mood of escape which pervaded turn-of-the-century nature poetry: the need to flee anonymity, enfeeblement, and death for the safety of an all-caring Mother Nature. 'Out of the heat of the city begotten / Of the labour of men and their manifold hands ... Into the arms of our mother we come / Our broad strong mother, the innocent earth ...

> Here we shall commune with her and no other;
>   Care and the battle of life shall cease;
> Men, her degenerate children, behind us,
> Only the might of her beauty shall bind us,
>   Full of rest, as we gaze on the face of our mother,
>   Earth in the health and the strength of her peace.[19]

Much of the nature writing and tourist literature of the late nineteenth and early twentieth centuries adopted this therapeutic world-view, this desire to bury oneself in the bosom of the great mother who soothes away all hurts and cares. The rest-cure theme is prominent here: the individual needs to be reduced to childhood, to be committed to the care of a parent, protected from overstimulation and challenges to mind and body, so that both may be restored to health.

But so far we have only half the story, for a second and very self-consciously masculine response to the modern predicament was at least as influential in promoting the wilderness holiday movement. Lears explains how many Americans, in particular, were repulsed by the way modern life had become 'a kind of infirmary' where people reacted to stress by becoming 'paralyzed by introspection and self-doubt, obsessed with easing [their] own psychic tensions.'[20] Was this the way to ensure the survival of the fittest? Many of the key players in Nash's study of the so-called cult of the wilderness were men of Theodore Roosevelt's stamp, determined to counter the softening of America, supposedly caused by the demise of the frontier in the late nineteenth century, through a search for intense, challenging, even life-threatening wilderness adventures, where the individual could demonstrate his mastery *over* nature. Here, competing images of the Indian are very much in evidence, for a belief in their racial inferiority and inevitable extinction flourished alongside efforts to emulate their knowledge of the wilds.

This concern to revive American virility, toughness, and endurance through an idealization of the 'savage' virtues had obvious militaristic overtones; the fight against degeneracy was equated with the ability to hunt and kill for the sake of doing so, to demonstrate the vitality of one's own primitive instincts. Roosevelt's Boone and Crockett Club must have had countless imitators, as American big-game hunters poured into the wilderness – very often the Canadian wilderness – to pursue their sport. It is hard to resist borrowing a testimony from Nash's account, that of California Member of Congress William Kent, who described his sense of well-being following a kill: '... you are a barbarian,' said Kent, 'and you're glad of it. It's good to be a barbarian ... and you know that if you are a barbarian, you are at least a man.'[21] This infantile joy at rediscovering 'the wild man within' was just another aspect of the same culture of consolation, the same therapeutic world-view that it ostensibly opposed. For the tourist industry, however, it added a further dimension to the picture of the urbanite at large in the woods, seeking peace at nature's bosom or pursuing violent mastery over her world.

CLASS, GENDER, AND THE WILDERNESS HOLIDAY

If the back-to-nature holiday was of such benefit to both personal and racial health, were members of all classes invited to participate? A clear sign that workers and their families were not expected to play much part in the new leisure culture was the emphasis placed in advertising and travel writings upon the necessity of relief, not from physical fatigue but from brain exhaustion or brain-fag of the sort from which professional and business people might be expected to suffer. Perhaps the most commonly recognized cause of neurasthenia was the growing emphasis on competition. It was a characteristic of modern times, said *Canadian Magazine*, that 'as the struggle in trade, commerce, and all departments of life becomes keener,' the need for recreation and restoration becomes more widely recognized.[22] Not only were holidays essential to health, but they were good for profits as well, explained one advocate of the new leisure ethic. Thousands of businessmen, he maintained, deluded themselves into staying in their offices during the hot summer months: 'They feel that if they were to leave the office for a fortnight or a month, everything would go to smash,' but that was just 'the natural vapouring of a sick brain ... a month or more of such delightful idleness is worth more to one's business than forced labor with impaired faculties.'

In professing the need for holidays middle-class Canadians were following a trend already established in Britain, where the suppression of recreation during the Industrial Revolution had been followed by a gradual rehabilitation of the idea of enjoyment, made palatable to Victorian morality through the gospel of 'rational recreation.'[24] This meant of course that holidays, in the eyes of many, had to have a useful purpose, principally that of restoring one's powers and sense of well-being as preparation for further work. But by the late nineteenth and early twentieth centuries there was some relaxation of the Victorian moral code, and a significant portion of the middle class was allowing leisure, for its own sake, to play a more important role in their lives. They were somewhat less preoccupied with work as a source of individual identity than the previous generation, and were in fact 'cultivating play instead of merely permitting it.'[25] There remained, however, a tendency to judge leisure activities in relation to output; time 'spent' on leisure had to yield sufficient return in pleasurable experience and other benefits. The work ethic was more easily downplayed than the middle-class fear of not succeeding, and as leisure took its place as a central part of life, enjoyment became associated with personal success.

All of these developments were evident in Canada as well, although there were differences. A British traveller remarked in 1891 concerning how attitudes towards holidays had only lately been liberalized in Canada:

Recently, that is, during the last eight or ten years, Canadians have begun to take some enjoyment in life, more, at any rate, than they were wont to do. With more wealth, has come to them more desire for pleasure. The upper ten have set the example, the rest follow the fashion, as they can. Hence, the summer cottages by lake and stream.[26]

Because Canada was a newly industrialized nation which shared something of the growing American preoccupation with industrial efficiency, there remained, at least in prescriptive literature, a strong emphasis on the holiday as a means of recreating oneself for further work. At the same time a competitive concern over the quality of one's holidays was manifest as well. How thoroughly, how *quickly*, could the return to primitive vigour be achieved? The advantages and disadvantages of various holiday destinations were often discussed in terms such as these. Muskoka, for example, owed its enormous popularity not to uniqueness of place, but to the fact that it offered all of the lauded qualities of the wilderness vacation while being so easily and quickly reached by rail and steamer.

The middle-class holiday had thus become a commonplace in Canada by the late nineteenth century, and middle-class women as well as men were expected to take part. The camping and canoeing trip remained to some extent a male preserve, but women often participated, especially in fishing expeditions. Holidays at resorts and cottages, meanwhile, were usually family affairs, though women and children might stay all summer while fathers and husbands returned to the city and the demands of the office. The inclusion of servants in the holiday party ensured the maintenance of basic comforts and a life of bucolic ease: 'All day the women and children lead ideally wholesome lives out-of-doors, berrying, boating or lounging about in true summer fashion,' wrote Katherine Hughes in *Rod and Gun*. One woman columnist in the *Globe* had some concerns about the growing habit of leaving husbands behind, but there were many sides to this story. 'Farseeing men are beginning to discover that the town in summer is not wholly devoid of comfort,' observed another writer, evidently male, in the same paper, 'even if the furniture is swathed in linen and the dust lies deep on the hall heater.' While not at all put out by being left at home, they 'play the martyr and send their family out of town – with an excursion party.' He concluded that this was why there were more women at resorts than men: 'the ratio being, according to a truthful hotel clerk, as thirteen and a half to three.'[27]

Women's automatic right to holidays, however, may not have been a matter of consensus as yet. Even after the turn of the century, some writers still felt the need to emphasize that women had the same recreational needs as did the rest of the population, whether they were 'weary mothers, energetic housekeepers, brain-workers, [or] fagged-out society women.' Fathers should realize, argued one, that providing summer holidays for their children was not enough; that wives and grown daughters had the same need 'to have their mental perspective straightened out, so that, with a store of health, a refreshed mind, and a cheerful spirit, they may prepare for the coming winter.' A writer in the *Globe* scolded women who were themselves reluctant to take a break, couching her argument in the familiar Victorian rhetoric of getting and spending:

'I can't rest,' you say, 'there is so much to be done.'
   'You must,' I reply, 'for you sin when you carry your recklessness so far as to consume the capital of energy, which is earning for you an income as interest.'[28]

Women's right (and willingness) to take part in the more rugged camping holiday was linked to larger feminist concerns at the turn of the century, including the idea that women's *nature* is not fundamentally different from men's. 'Spring brings a tingle to their blood' as much as it does to that of men, Hughes pointed out, while Ella Walton maintained that the supposedly delicate female sex possesses as great a capacity for healthy nerves and an independent spirit as does the male, if only these qualities were cultivated. 'Primitive instincts are the same in a woman as in a man,' she wrote, and if a woman takes to the wilderness she will, just like her gentleman relatives and friends, 'forget to be nervous and hysterical, and gain a self-reliance and courage that years of travelling and mixing with the world cannot give.' For Mary Harvey Drummond, the extent to which women joined in the passion for wilderness holidays was a measure of their emancipation. 'We women of to-day talk much of our rights, and while our tongues wag, we are letting slip by us the very things we clamour for. In the woods of Canada, equally with our brothers and husbands awaits us, a share in the sports that give health to body and mind. But how many of us avail ourselves of such privileges?' she demanded. 'Too few indeed. The sea-side resort with its second-rate bands, euchre parties, and boundless opportunities for the display of diamonds and dress, still reigns supreme favourite of the gentler sex; proving more strongly than anything else, that the day of emancipation has not yet dawned for women.'[29]

A wilderness holiday might indeed prove liberating for women because some established elements of Victorian gender relations were more easily challenged in the woods than they were at home. In matters of clothing, for example, common sense mattered more than fashion. A writer who signed herself Wahnaptae recommended the flannel, deep-pocketed skirt, short enough to keep out of the mud (four to five inches above the ground) but still long enough to offer protection from mosquitoes. For Drummond, skirt length had meaning beyond the merely practical. 'Short skirts were the rule in camp,' she wrote, 'and I felt as I donned mine that the new woman was after all no curiosity of mushroom growth, but a clear glimpse of the true woman to come.'

Judging from these women's accounts of their wilderness holidays there was also a chance for some readjustment of gender roles with regard to duties in the woods. If guides were employed they – rather than the women – assumed the usual servants' roles of cooking and cleaning up, while women could fish, hunt, and perform heavier tasks as they saw fit. Wahnaptae described how a tump-line was used for carrying a pack, and acknowledged that 'the carrying is of course not compulsory, but if one is able and falls into the spirit of the thing, one wants to help.' Getting into the spirit of the thing while remaining feminine in appearance and manner was offered as a ideal. If something unpleasant happened, such as losing one's footing and getting a moccasin full of water, the right response was to 'remove the moccasin, pour out the water and replace it without any fuss, all the time looking pleasant,' she counselled. How one looked still mattered, and even Walton had advice to offer on matters of dress and personal embellishment. While wearing light-coloured clothing was indisputably a bad practice in the woods, she suggested brightening up dark dresses 'with some of the trifles of ribbons and lace that every woman hoards, but that are not fresh enough to be worn at home.'[30]

For both sexes, however, the essence of the wilderness holiday was the idea of discovering and freeing a part of oneself which normal civilized life restrained. The Victorian understanding of the home as the ideal sanctuary (and the wife and mother as the ministering angel) had been permanently altered; it was now understood, far more vividly than before, that not only the city and the factory but home itself was part of the treadmill existence. Women as well as men needed 'the tonic of wildness' each summer. 'The deadly monotony of the daily round,' wrote Jean Graham, 'is never such a strain as it is in the months when flowers, trees and dancing water are calling us to come out and play.'[31]

MY HEART IS IN MUSKOKA

My heart is in Muskoka, my heart is not here,
My heart is in Muskoka a chasing the deer;
Chasing the wild deer, *in dipping canoe*,
My heart is in Muskoka, wherever I go.[32]

In earlier chapters of this book the developing holiday habit among the late-nineteenth-century urban middle classes has been observed in other contexts, such as the resort culture of the Thousand Islands and the steamer excursion traffic through the upper lakes. But no part of Ontario was more thoroughly and widely affected by the growth of wilderness tourism and the therapeutic holiday during this period than the region of Muskoka and its adjacent territories. Tourists enjoyed believing that here was a true primeval wilderness, not far from civilization but very real nonetheless. 'Muskoka is no fake summer resort,' promised one promotional brochure, and a travel writer in the *Globe* observed that 'In the Thousand Islands, art seems in some places to have elbowed nature into the background, but here nature is sweet mistress.'[33]

Judging from the number of hotels and boarding houses, Muskoka at the turn of the century was by far the most popular destination in Ontario for holidays of any length, and its reputation was still growing.[34] 'Muskoka has no superior in all the beautiful districts of the Dominion,' asserted the *Globe*, and it was all the better for its *not* possessing 'the sublime grandeur of a mountainous country, if it did it would not be a good place to run up to for a few summer weeks.'[35] But Muskoka still offered all the requisite qualities of picturesqueness, a fresh, brisk climate, and accessibility, and was widely viewed as the *natural* place for Torontonians in particular to retreat to and renew themselves for the business of life. As the gateway to the vast uncharted region of northern Ontario, Muskoka (so urban Canadians believed) could absorb almost unlimited numbers of visitors and seemed to exist especially to serve this purpose. During the previous decades a series of major land surrenders had largely removed this and adjacent regions from Ojibway control, preparing the way for immigrants and tourists.[36] Frank Yeigh envisioned Muskoka as 'a land awaiting the invasion of the twentieth-century white man, awaiting him with health for his ills, with rest for his throbbing nerves, with youth for age. It is, in a word, a great open-air sanatorium.'[37]

White settlement and a tourist industry began to develop in tandem in the 1860s. At the beginning of the decade the government introduced a system of free land grants which were designed to bring about rapid settlement. These would have only limited success. 'For the most part,' admitted, G. Mercer Adams, 'it is only honest to say that the Free Grants territory is a wild region,' not easily tamed for the purposes of agriculture.[38] The lands were taken up, but many settlers found themselves disappointed in the rocky territory they were attempting to farm. The opening of Muskoka drew tourists as well, and the presence of eager but ill-equipped nature seekers gave settlers an alternative way of making a living or of supplementing their income from agriculture. They soon found themselves providing accommodation, food, camping and canoeing equipment, transportation services, and advice to growing numbers of visitors, and tourism became an integral part of the local economy.[39]

Much has been written elsewhere about the young men said to be Muskoka's first tourists, and about the early settlers who met their multifarious needs. These stories concern two university students from Toronto, John Campbell and James Watson Bain, who set off to Muskoka to explore, rusticate, and botanize in the summer of 1860.[40] The north-woods holiday became a yearly habit for them and their rather literary group of friends. Of particular assistance to them as a guide and outfitter was Thomas Robinson, a British sailor-cum-Canadian settler who took up land at Gravenhurst in 1860. This was principally a male fraternity, although they were joined in the mid-sixties by Campbell's younger sister and her friend, who were chaperoned by a Mrs Young. Canadian philosopher Paxton Young, her husband, was a member of the newly founded Muskoka Club, as was James Loudon, future president of the University of Toronto. The club eventually built its headquarters, named Ophir Lodge, on Yoho Island in Lake Joseph, which reputedly had a membership of fifty by 1870.

There are some surviving Songs of Yoho which capture its members' lasting preoccupation with leaving behind the city's 'dust and folly' to return to the 'bosom' of the pure, clean north. 'The Islemen of the North,' for example, was addressed to Lake Joseph:

> Father Joseph, O receive us!
> > We have left the haunts of men;
> And from biting care relieve us,
> > Take us to thy bosom again.

Once settlement was under way in Muskoka, the flow of tourists grew apace. In June of 1863 Robinson wrote to Bain: 'The time is approaching for parties of pleasure leaving Toronto for different places, this place among the rest, I have this opportunity of mentioning my readiness to provide boats etc. for any parties that may write and inform me.' Robinson's goal was to provide a package of services so complete that 'you will have nothing to bring from Toronto,' and at that point he was in the process of getting ready 'a large decked yacht of my own for the accommodation of parties of pleasure.'[42] For years Robinson continued acting as outfitter and guide as well as providing board and room for tourists in his home, and his response to this new economic opportunity was imitated by many other Muskokans.

In these early years, surveyors, settlers, and tourists looked to the Ojibway population for various kinds of assistance. Most often mentioned are those living at Rama, many of whom had recently moved from other localities as a result of land surrenders. With the influx of tourists, guiding would become an important source of income. Robinson made frequent reference in his correspondence to the need to include Native guides on any trek into unknown areas, and even as Native people faced growing competition from settlers who took up guiding, they continued in this occupation for decades to come. The usual rate of pay rose from one dollar a day in the 1860s to two dollars a day by the 1890s, at which time the people of Rama earned their living primarily from the industries of farming, lumbering, and the various aspects of tourism, as did white settlers.[43] Tourists had looked for souvenirs since they first began visiting Muskoka; Bain and his friends bargained for items sold by the children, trading a ring for a bow and arrow, and fifty cents for a skunk skin tobacco pouch.[44] The trade in souvenirs grew along with the rest of the tourist industry in Muskoka, and Indian agents later commented on how, while the men acted as guides to tourists, the women sold 'large quantities of fancy-work to them.' A proprietor of the Wigwassan Lodge on Tobin Island in Lake Rosseau saw the souvenir trade as an asset to his business, and he proudly advertised that 'Gaily woven baskets, balsam pillows, wood carvings, etc. may be purchased from the Indians' who called frequently at his hotel.[45]

As was the case wherever white tourists employed Native guides, the latter's utility lay not only in their practical expertise but also in their imaginative appeal. The Reverend John Todd from Massachusetts, for example, nostalgically recalled his trip to Muskoka in the summer of 1867, and especially the magic of the wilderness scene at night. The guides 'pitched a simple tent directly in front of ours,' he wrote, and made 'a fire that kept both tents dry, and threw up a light that made the trees look like the tall pillars of some great temple, with the roof made of fretted silver. Hardly anything could be more wild or beauti-ful.' They ate the fresh fish their guides had cooked, then lay down to sleep, and by candlelight Todd indulged in fantasies about 'the dusky forms' that slumbered unsuspectingly nearby. '[They] have made this their highway, time without limits,' Todd imagined, and 'have had no candle but a roll of white birch bark, no food but their game, no cloth-ing but the skins of wild animals, no hopes that reach beyond tomor-row.'[46] Of course the Ojibway of Rama had already had a long and intensive exposure to European culture and religion, and it was the well-known teacher and activist Reverend Peter Jacobs and his family who were most often mentioned by name in the early tourist literature.[47]

The growth of both settlement and tourism in Muskoka were tied, naturally enough, to the development of transportation links to major cities, between new settlements, and among the many islands which dotted the region's lakes. Significant for the tourist industry was the close association between those who promoted settlement, railways, and steam navigation, and those who saw Muskoka's brightest opportunities in the tourist industry.

When settlement first began the railway reached only to Collingwood. Beyond that point transportation depended on canoes. Within a couple of years settlers began building sailboats to carry both passengers and freight, and by the summer of 1863 the steamers *Emily May* and *Fairy* were serving communities such as Muskoka Falls and Rama.[48] The indi-vidual famed for his dedication to Muskoka's development, however, was the entrepreneur Alexander Peter Cockburn, sometimes called the Father of Muskoka Tourism, who settled in the region in 1866. He entered the lumbering business and established a stagecoach line which was soon linked to his new steamer service based at Gravenhurst. As Muskoka's first MPP (1867–71) and its first MP (1872–87), Cockburn used his political influence and the support of lumbering and farming interests to ensure that the Northern Railway reached Gravenhurst by 1875.[49] With the extension of service to the Muskoka Wharf Station, Ontario's north woods were just a few hours from Union Station and just one day's travel from 'the sizzling asphalts of New York.'[50] Barlow Cumberland, another tourism entrepreneur with considerable financial interest in Ontario's rail and steamer lines, pointed out how the transformation of Muskoka into a sort of instant north had to some degree democratized the wilderness holiday habit, for now tourists and sportsmen could get 'with comparatively little trouble to a district which has hitherto been accessible only to those with ample means and time.'[51]

Cockburn used all possible strategies to draw tourists' attention to Muskoka, including organized tours for those who could publicize it most effectively. A *Globe* correspondent accompanied a group of MPs on a tour through the region in 1880, and his report acknowledged the unlimited potential of tourism as opposed to concentrated settlement in this wild and rugged land, with 'rocks on all sides, and still more remarkable, verdant and hardy trees springing from the bowels of stone.' The entrance to the region 'must be disheartening to the intending settler,' he admitted, but Muskoka was the perfect place for the 'fagged-out cit' to retire for a month or two.[52]

Cockburn's greatest interest was in promoting the northward flow of American tourists, a goal he shared with the management of the Grand Trunk Railway. From 1881 to the end of his life he was general manager of the Muskoka Navigation Company. Its steamers met tourists arriving at Muskoka Wharf via the Grand Trunk (which had absorbed the Northern Railway by the end of the decade), and took them to their holiday destinations. The Grand Trunk, while primarily concerned with moving freight, gradually recognized the importance of passenger traffic and the value of the north-south tourist flow. Even though passenger service westward was dominated by the CPR, the Grand Trunk asserted that 'the North-West is not everything in America,' and during the 1880s and 90s turned more attention to serving the travelling public. In cooperation with the Muskoka Navigation Company it produced brochures advertising the regions north of Toronto as a veritable paradise on earth.[53] Cockburn himself was probably their author, for he wrote numerous pamphlets and press releases, and toured the United States promoting the beauty and health-restoring properties of Muskoka.[54] The Grand Trunk Railway, meanwhile, was active in publishing up-to-date information for each resort area concerning accommodation, outfitting, lists of recommended guides, and the like, based on reports submitted by company agents.[55]

The north-woods theme would take on more than one imaginative meaning in the case of Muskoka. In much of their advertising the Grand Trunk termed the whole region of Muskoka, Georgian Bay, and beyond The Highlands of Ontario, and evoked, through word and picture, images of the Scottish Highlands, a paradise of lakes, rocks, hills, and woodland, a perfect place to hunt, and fish, renew one's health, and step back in time to a simpler way of life.[56] Most pervasive, however, was the tendency on the part of the Grand Trunk and the Muskoka Navigation Company, as well as other promoters, to market this northland, or North Country, as a vaguely defined extension of the United States rather than as part of a separate country. Even *Picturesque Canada*, intended to promote the beauties of the new Dominion, was republished in Chicago in 1899 under the title *Picturesque Spots of the North*.

Some of Muskoka's best-known American tourists clearly saw their summer retreat this way. H.P. Dwight, president of the Great Northwestern Telegraph Company, and Erastus Wiman, a Canadian entrepreneur making his fortune in New York, first came to Muskoka in 1863. Wiman was famous in his lifetime for many ventures, including his commercial interest in Staten Island tourism and his advocacy of commercial union between the United States and Canada.[57] Dwight and Wiman came north annually with their friends and built a spacious log house to accommodate their Muskoka Club at Lake of Bays. In 1884 a grateful and admiring guest of the club, James Alexander Hedley, put together a detailed record of its members' activities and their attitudes towards the Canadian wilderness. Their living arrangements were conventionally civilized; evening activities included the sewing on of buttons and the perusal of stock quotations fresh from New York. Their hunting habits were, by almost any standard, barbaric, but they displayed a passion for seeing their wilderness adventures through literary eyes. 'Surely James Russell Lowell has seen our camp in one of his flights of imagination,' exclaimed Hedley, rather illogically, before quoting a piece of Lowell's poetry; and elsewhere he surmised that 'Andrew Carnegie himself – long life to him – must have been delighted with our life "under the greenwood tree."' The discovery, on their arrival, that 'Robert' had forgotten to bring the flag gave rise to sentiments concerning the close bond between Canadians and Americans: 'The union of lakes – the union of lands – / The union of hearts – the union of hands – And the flag of our Union forever.'[58]

The American presence was also felt in the early hotel business in Muskoka. The arrival of lumbermen, settlers, and tourists from the beginning of the 1860s onwards necessitated some sort of accommodation being provided, but the first resort hotel, which was Rosseau House, was not built in Muskoka until 1870. To a great extent the opening of hotels and boarding-houses of all types was a spontaneous response on the part of settlers to tourist demand, but Cockburn's links with American entrepreneurs helped to accelerate the pace of change. Rosseau House was the product of a meeting in 1869 between Cockburn and New York entrepreneur William H. Pratt, who decided, after touring Muskoka as Cockburn's guest, that a first-class hotel in the wilderness might be a profitable enterprise.[59] With rates as high as five dollars a day and a clientele drawn predominantly from the United States, Rosseau House (known also as Pratt's) ushered in a new phase of Muskoka tourism, that of the large hotel wrapped in verandas wafted by pine-scented breezes, affording every comfort, including accommodation for servants, and offering entertainments in the form of music and dancing each night. Pratt's burned down after a few years, but other hotels sprang up which offered the same sense of access to the best of both civilization and wilderness. 'A minute's walk is sufficient to pass from luxurious surroundings to pristine grandeur,' wrote E. Maurice Smith of the palatial Royal Muskoka Hotel; 'I know of no place where the two extremes are so closely allied.'[60]

Meanwhile settlers continued to augment their incomes by devoting their summer months to the tourist industry. In 1889 the *Globe* reported that most of the residents in the region of Port Cockburn 'make it a point to take in all the boarders they can make room for in the summer.'[61] What began with informal arrangements often grew into a more ambitious enterprise, as outbuildings used to house the first visitors were replaced by larger and larger hotels. Each such establishment had a story behind it; in some cases, for example, hotel-keeping offered widows and their families the means of remaining financially independent.[62] In all its aspects, the tourist industry was integrated into the local economy: produce grown on local farms appeared on hotel dining room tables and was sold to campers, and settlers continued to outfit, guide, and transport tourists as demand dictated. That the tourist-settler relationship was so harmonious probably had something to do with the fact that, unlike at Niagara, there were no principal 'sights' to be exploited, controlled, and monopolized; there were no means by which tourists could be held hostage by their longing for the ecstasies of the sublime. Contrasting his experience of the two places, an author of an 1879 atlas and guidebook wrote of Muskoka: 'Here was quiet, no swearing, no drunkenness, but such unobtrusive courtesy ... There was no guide with his monotonous droning repetition of guide-book platitudes, but on the contrary my cicerone indicated the point of view and then retired, knowing that we worship best before Nature's temple in silence.'[63]

Tourists' choice of accommodation at Muskoka reflected two sets of criteria: the social class to which they belonged, and the degree of rusticity they were attempting to achieve. The well-to-do might camp, build a cottage, or stay in the most expensive hotels, and Muskoka was in fact presented as a place where people could escape the burdens of civilization without blurring the lines of social class. Some resorts might be 'frequented by an undesirable type of tourist,' but not Muskoka; here it was safe to relax and temporarily cast off some of the more superficial signs of class distinction. Visitors could enjoy perfect freedom in matters of dress, for example, without demotion on the social scale: 'No starched shirt and no collars or cuffs,' announced the *Globe*. 'You fairly revel in the comfort of an old flannel shirt, straw hat, and a pair of last season's trousers.' To maintain the pretensions of city life, it was argued, was to ensure failure in a holiday. There was no point in heading off to some 'populous watering-place to plunge into a vortex of fashionable dissipation, where rest in its true sense is only a delusion,' advised a resident of Penetanguishene. A few weeks in the Ontario Highlands would 'remove all feeling of lassitude, and like Anteaus when he touched his mother earth,' the vacationer would return home invigorated.[64] By the 1890s Muskoka had become the favourite summer retreat for the professional and business classes of southern Ontario, and published lists of cottage owners, along with weekly reports on who was in residence at the big hotels, read like a *Who's Who* of Toronto society.[65]

Many middle-class tourists, both Canadian and American, preferred cottage life to the resort hotel. Here they could pursue the ideal of 'a lodge in some vast wilderness' (the pre-Romantic poet William Cowper was much quoted), but assume a way of life as civilized or as primitive as they might like. In the early decades, land was inexpensive and so were building costs, and lake fronts became lined with cottages belonging to those who could afford to summer away from home. Islands in the three lakes were priced at between ten and one hundred dollars, and most of these were bought by Torontonians.[66] Cottage communities thus established would become commonplace across Canada during the twentieth century. The summer correspondence of the Baldwin family, holidaying on Olive Island in Lake Rosseau during the 1880s, provides a glimpse inside the social round of the cottage owner: visiting friends, rowing from island to island – with young women enjoying the freedom of unchaperoned excursioning – and the bathing, berrying, fishing, sketching, tea-drinking, and church-going that filled their days. Respectable life was reproduced in cottage country and the same social values pertained, except that here one's primary duty was to play.[67]

Tourists of lower-income levels, on the other hand, chose between the tent and the boarding-house, where rooms could be had, according to one report, for as little as four dollars a week. 'More and more,' opined the Reverend John Potts, president of the Toronto Conference, 'these Muskoka regions will attract the toilers of our Ontario towns and cities, until every island shall be inhabited, and the busy brain and muscle workers shall be nerved both in mind and body, and better fitted to resume the earnest work of life.' But despite such wishful thinking and the promises of the Muskoka and Georgian Bay Navigation Co. that the Highlands of Ontario offered 'unsurpassed advantages for holiday outings to all classes of the community,' muscle workers without annual holidays – and these were the vast majority – were unlikely ever to experience the pleasures of Muskoka.[68]

Muskoka's rise as a tourist destination was thus intertwined with many related developments, such as settlement, the growth of railways, and the rise of the holiday habit among the urban middle classes. But why did Muskoka in particular seem to satisfy so well the requirements of the therapeutic holiday? What did Muskoka mean?

One resounding theme echoed through the Muskoka tourist literature: a magical combination of beauty, timelessness, serenity, and health. Muskoka's was a northern beauty, fresh, pure, unsullied, more likely to soothe than to excite, very different from Niagara's. As with the Thousand Islands, the language of the picturesque worked perfectly for Muskoka, and the panorama theme was commonly employed as well. An important difference, however, was that while the journey through the Thousand Islands was finite, with a predetermined beginning and end, the steamer excursion through the lakes and rivers of Muskoka gave the impression that one could drift through these wild and lovely labyrinths forever: 'life seems to be suspended,' wrote Yeigh. 'A spell seems to come over the onlooker.'

The absence of an itinerary, in fact, was the very essence of the Muskoka experience. The tourist's purpose, explained the *Hamilton Spectator*, should not be to hasten from one spot of beauty to another, but to 'linger and dream away the idle hours in one place till he becomes saturated with the beauty of his surroundings and forgets that business and worry and unlovliness have any place in the whole creation of God.' The calming and unspectacular nature of Muskoka's beauty was integral to its health-giving properties. 'The character of the whole region is peaceful and restful, rather than imposing or magnificent,' declared another testimonial. Here one could pay attention to the minute details of Nature's bounty; 'It is here one feels the heart of Nature throbbing.'[69]

The association between Muskoka and health, however, was no mere creation of the tourist industry. There are numerous accounts of settlers drawn to the region in the hope of recuperating from both nervous and respiratory ailments. One woman's account published in 1878 testified to the miraculous recovery of 'a gentleman who formed one of our little colony when we came out in 1871.' He had suffered from a 'shattered' constitution due to 'over-working his brain,' and had been ordered 'an entire change of climate and out-door occupation ... The Bush-life and the pure air worked miracles; his recovery was complete.' She believed Muskoka to be unsuitable for consumptives because of sudden atmospheric changes, but testified that 'nervous and dyspeptic invalids soon lose many of their unpleasant tendencies.' Others held that Muskoka was good for all respiratory ailments (and a sanatorium was built at Gravenhurst in 1897), but relief from hay fever, asthma, and bad nerves were mentioned most frequently.

The specific qualities of Muskoka believed to have such good effect were the altitude, the cool breezes, the freedom from damp, the 'ozonized' air, 'the peculiar softness' of the water, and the 'resinous' or 'balsamic' odour of the pine forests. Muskoka was vaunted as the 'Hay Fever Mecca' in travel literature and promotional materials ('a land of pure delight where pollen never blows'), and the Grand Trunk Railway devoted a whole publication to the subject. Testimonials from doctors and patients, real or fabricated, were collected and published: '"I've been suffering so from asthma that I could not lie down for two weeks," said a fleshy woman, "and see how well I am now!"' Another confirmed Muskoka's dual claim to cure the common ailments of the urban dweller: 'Hay Fever simply cannot exist here, and the patient driven from home by that scourge will find immediate relief without medication.' Meanwhile, 'the victim of over-work, brought to the verge of nervous prostration, will soon find himself pulling an oar with the vigor of a voyageur.'[70]

But Muskoka's meaning was not static, and during the period being considered here it changed in two important respects. Muskoka became more than ever the playground of the well-to-do, but it also became rather more domesticated than many tourists liked. Even in the late 1860s the *Globe* was informing readers of desirable destinations beyond Muskoka, such as Magnetawagan in the district of Parry Sound.[71] There, lumbering and settlement began in 1867, the area became accessible by steamer in 1879, and the Northern Railway arrived in 1886. Fishing and hunting parties started coming to the Magnetawagan in the 1870s and 1880s, and a resort culture developed during the 1890s. Throughout these decades the pattern established at Muskoka was repeated again and again in other areas, where settlers were encouraged by government to move in, transportation links were established, and tourism became part of the local economy for both Native people and newcomers.

The pressures of this pattern of advancing settlement, lumbering, and tourism prompted the rise of a conservation movement and the creation of Algonquin Provincial Park in 1894. Logging still look place, but settlement would not occur, and the park was vaunted as a northern paradise that belonged to all – 'a public park and forest reservation, fish and game preserve, health resort and pleasure ground.' Not surprisingly the creation of Algonquin Park inspired a host of articles, poems, and other tributes in the popular press. Here was true isolation, announced *Canadian Magazine*. 'Cowper could have gratified his wish for "a lodge in some vast wilderness, some boundless contiguity of shade" by erecting a log hut here, so remote is it from civilization and the haunts of men.' Another piece in the same magazine echoed a familiar theme, assuring readers that if there were any man who would not respond to the beauties of Algonquin Park, then 'mark him as one whose soul is sodden with the ease of ready-made existence, a product of over-civilization.'[72]

DAY TRIPPERS

But to those compelled to stay at home because of lack of means or time, such blandishments meant little. The last part of this chapter looks at what Torontonians, including the working classes, might find to do on a Saturday half-holiday, a Sunday afternoon, or the new Dominion Day holiday, if they wished to escape the heat of city streets and the tedium of the daily round. Toronto Island was a place of resort which would eventually cater to both middle- and working-class people, as did the daily return excursion traffic to Niagara and other attractions close by.

The only kind of holiday-making which clearly included a portion of Toronto's working class was the day trip, or the Saturday half-holiday excursion. As mentioned in chapter 1, Canadian workers had won little in the way of vacation time even by the turn of the century, the sixty-hour week was still commonplace, and even statutory holidays were ignored by some employers, although judging from contemporary accounts, Dominion Day was widely observed. Unlike in Britain, however, where the sight of working-class people 'at large' aroused considerable middle-class anxiety, descriptions of the excursioning public's activities usually did not make clear class distinctions. Workers in Canadian cities did not take over the streets on bank holiday weekends, and Toronto Island was never a Blackpool. The press certainly dwelt on questions of crowd behaviour and respectability, but with blame more often cast on the authorities who, for example, neglected the public interest by failing to enforce regulations against overcrowding on steamers. This problem brought frequent comment in the *Globe*, which pointed out in the summer of 1890 that 'the effect of the present lack of system is to give steamer traffic a wrong tone. Where everyone must fight his way through as best he may, the decorum of travelling is impossible ... The crowd becomes a mob; it cannot show respect for itself nor can it claim it from others.'[73]

For Torontonians the excursioning habit was already well established by the 1860s. Friendly societies, mechanics' institutes, Sunday schools, temperance societies, and many large employers organized outings by steamer and rail; 'Excursions are now the order of the day,' reported the *Globe* in the summer of Confederation.[74] In these years, the details of excursions were often front page news. Much was made of the way people willingly cast themselves to the elements: thunderstorms and tossing steamers, it was said, only added to the excitement of the outing. The excursion arranged by the Mechanics' Institute in July of 1866 began at the foot of Yonge Street, from whence special cars on the Northern Railway, arranged for by the Grand Trunk, took the excursionists to Lake Simcoe, where they boarded the *Emily May*. It was crowded, it rained, and the lake was rough – 'Crinoline collapsed frightfully.' The boat plunged, but the young people danced; in fact, 'the worse the boat plunged, the more vigorous the dance.' At Ross's Hotel in Orillia they sat down to ham and beef, pies and puddings, and tea and beer, finally returning to Union Station by 10 P.M. The excursionists had, concluded the *Globe* approvingly, 'for a time, [thrown] off conventional stiffness, and enjoyed themselves in a whole-soulled manner.' The Odd Fellows' excursion on the *City of Toronto* that same summer was characterized by the same sense of release, or so the *Globe* suggested. Again, the lake was choppy and people were sick: 'Some lay here, some there, on the bare floor, with that delightful *abandon* which utterly disregards the effect on snowy muslin or orthodox broadcloth.' In the meantime others on board sat, 'others rushed around, others danced, others breathed copiously of the fresh air – while all agreed in sipping brandy.'[75] These outings seemed to get larger as the years went by, and by the 1890s thousands might be involved; on one occasion, 3,500 Massey-Harris employees travelled to Niagara, and on another, four to five thousand travellers set off on the CPR picnic to Brampton, the engines of the special trains decorated with such forthright messages as 'We're out for fun.'[76] The desire to escape Toronto was keen enough, but for the majority outings were confined to special days and to excursions organized by employers.

A large portion of the excursioning public was of course composed of individuals, families, and groups of friends who decided on their own to leave the city for the day. Any summer weekend brought reports of packed steamers and chaotic scenes at Union Station, and Dominion Day, which the *Globe* in 1881 testified was growing 'in popular favour,' each year saw 'Thousands of People on the Move by Land and Water.' The appeal was the same as that of any holiday – a release from tedium and the tonic effect of the open air. As one man wrote of his Saturday steamer jaunt to Niagara: 'It not only brings the delights of the ride itself, but the notion and idea you are free.'[77]

Niagara Falls was by far the most popular destination for the steamer excursion traffic. Barlow Cumberland, who had been active in promoting tourism in the upper lakes and on the Northern Railway, brought the growing passion for day tripping and the old fascination with Niagara together into a new business venture, the Niagara Navigation Company.[78] By the late nineteenth century Niagara was particularly identified with that aspect of the tourist trade, and was spurned by many middle-class vacationers for that reason. Steamers ran from

Toronto to Niagara several times a day, and excursion parties such as the Stenographers' Moonlight Excursion in 1897 often made the trip by night.[79] The new Queen Victoria Park, Canada's contribution to reclaiming the falls for free public access, meant that excursionists could visit Niagara without incurring the high fees charged when private enterprise controlled the front, although complaints about predatory guides and hackmen were still ubiquitous. Those who had campaigned for the preservation of Niagara on both sides of the border had hoped to reverse the trend towards day tripping, and eliminate the 'second-class tourists and excursionists who are brought by the carload' and who 'like locusts ... sweep everything before them.'[80] But this was not to happen. For many excursionists the carnivalesque atmosphere of Niagara was part of its appeal, while tourists looking for fashionable resorts or grandeur of scenery now had much of the North American continent at their disposal.

Toronto Island was the city's most convenient place of resort, and was one which came to mean different things to different classes of people. For the city's middle and upper classes, it was a place of retreat close to home where the tenor of Toronto society could be duplicated, and for workers and their families it offered a quick escape to a more relaxed world of beaches and open-air amusements. Its resort era began in the 1830s, before the island(s) were completely separated from the mainland, when a hotel called The Retreat was opened. Its owner's ambition (as advertised in the newspapers of Upper Canada) was to attract 'Sportsmen, parties of pleasure, and individuals who may wish to inhale the lake breezes.'[81] By the 1850s Toronto Island's popularity was prompting more of its residents to start hotels and other services, and a decade later the *Globe* noted approvingly that excursionists were converging on the island by the hundreds. 'Our health officers strongly recommend visits to the Island as better than any drugging which can be called into requisition. The fine, fresh lake air, there to be enjoyed, and the pleasant rambling room, contribute alike to enjoyment and health.'[82] The city of Toronto soon acquired ownership of the island, and by 1880 had decided to build a public park. There was an ongoing controversy, however, over city council's adminstration of the island and the amount of land it leased to private cottage-builders and speculators. Contradictory opinions expressed in the *Mail* captured the inherent class dilemma. One report agreed with those who argued for a larger park because it 'belongs to the people,' while another saw the benefits of private ownership: 'it is a great advantage to have a good class of residents on the Island,' reasoned this author; 'it keeps money in the City; and it gives busy people, who would find it difficult to go away, the opportunity of summer relaxation.'[83]

For those with cottages Toronto Island represented a closer and tamer version of what Muskoka meant to the late nineteenth-century vacationer. 'The pomp and fashion of most watering places' was said to be 'conspicuous by its absence at the Island,' and while hardly a wilderness, it offered something of a return to nature, with beaches, trees, fresh air, and freedom from certain urban conventions. Young women who would dress fashionably in Toronto could wander the island freely without their shoes and stockings, 'laying up a store of good, robust health.'[84] A great advantage for the middle-class family was its closeness to Toronto, for businessmen could repair to the island each evening and benefit from its healthy atmosphere. Moreover, despite its appeal to different classes of people, health and relaxation could be sought without fear of undesirable social mixing. One knew who was there, for example, for lists of prominent residents were printed regularly in the papers. And in any case, 'social lines are closer drawn on the Island than at ordinary summering places,' as the *Globe* remarked in 1893, and 'The people are all from Toronto, and there is no necessity to take anyone on trust. Social interchanges, which might be embarrassing when the summer was over and they had all returned across the bay to the city, are not indulged in. They are not anywhere, of course, only the difference is that on the Island there is less danger of mistakes being made.'[85]

The lower middle- and working-class presence was not discouraged everywhere on the island, merely segregated and contained. Local residents, ferry companies, and other entrepreneurs provided amusements for the masses in growing profusion, and the carnivalesque atmosphere of Niagara was in good part reproduced at Hanlan's Point. There were bowling alleys, rides, shooting galleries, a dog circus, and 'a museum of living curiosities' which included a 'wild girl' from South America and 'a real live Zulu with an Irish accent.' Erastus Wiman built two Free Floating Swimming Baths patterned after an existing attraction in New York, and a ferry transported Toronto people who would not otherwise be able to afford a swim. Temperance advocates kept the island more or less dry for some years, and promoted its development as a morally safe haven for working-class enjoyment. Crowded campgrounds caused some concern after the turn of the century, for here questions of order and social control arose; but the land shortage came to the city's rescue, for the competition for leases meant that campgrounds increasingly lost out.[86]

Despite the class distinctions that prevailed, the rise of Toronto Island and the excursion industry in general brought the occasional outing within reach of a good many city dwellers. But many more were yet excluded. For the poor, any sort of outing required some income that could be spared from the necessities of food and shelter, and any unaffordable pleasures caused deprivations elsewhere. As B.S. Rowntree would say of England's unskilled workers and their lack of recreation in the early twentieth century, the casual observer simply could not realize that 'every penny devoted to luxury or amusements by poor families' was in itself 'a tax on health.'[87] In Toronto the concern on the part of young social reformer J.J. Kelso over the health of poor children resulted in the creation of a Fresh Air Fund to take mothers and children for outings on the lake, to provide 'an exemption, however brief, from care and toil.' For him the summer excursion program was an inexpensive means to fight not only physical but moral degeneracy.

The Globe praised such efforts while stolidly refusing to see the plight of Toronto's poor as anything other than a stroke of fate. Readers were asked to think about how they would feel if they could find no respite from the heat and confinement of their own homes in mid-summer, and then to imagine what it must be like 'in the small, stuffy, clap-boarded, next-to-the-roof rooms of the poor.' How could such a situation exist? The Globe had no answer, but asked for help in creating 'a brief elysium' for some poor child, in sending 'a holiday to some eager fellow-creature in whose scheme of life holidays for some inscrutable reason have otherwise been omitted.'[88]

The slow acceptance of the workers' need for holidays reflected some basic assumptions on the part of the employing classes. As they saw it, the pressures of modern life and business were such that they themselves must learn to seek respite, and sooner rather than later, if they were to avoid the debilitating consequences of overwork and the failure to nourish their inner resources. The value placed upon the wilderness holiday was connected to their image of themselves and their class: their role in society was vital, but their efficiency could only be sustained through a careful budgeting of psychic and physical resources. Holidays for workers, on the other hand, were a threat to efficiency of another sort in this so-called age of competition and scientific management. Few employers were willing to endure that amount of lost time, or to accept that the need for holidays, for a bit of time to cultivate 'the notion and idea you are free,' was now part of the modern urban condition.

Recreational tourism of the sort discussed in this chapter was not motivated by the desire for new places and new experiences. It was motivated by a desire to recover something that was lost – 'the wildness,' as Thoreau said, 'in our brains and bowels.' In the selling of Muskoka and other destinations in Toronto's recreational hinterland, the well-worn rhetoric of the picturesque, a language understood by all, was used to evoke images of a northerly Eden with all familiar features in place: shimmering waters, labyrinthine channels, rocky shores, resinous and womb-like forests. These aesthetic pleasures were not offered as ends in themselves, but as part of a package of health-giving and health-restoring properties that belonged to the wilderness, or rather to the images of wilderness embraced by the late Victorian middle class.

The great advantage of Muskoka, for example, was that a quick jaunt by rail and steamer could produce, so its many advocates claimed, the sensation of journeying inwards to rediscover the primitive self, and back to a time when 'the race' as a whole was more vigorous, more self-reliant, more alive to its place in nature. The myth of the wild man had not lost its utility, but it had been internalized and 'despatialized,' as Hayden White has argued. Put another way, in this kind of tourism the appeal of looking at 'real Indians' gave way to the romance of feeling, temporarily, like an 'Indian' oneself. But as the following chapter shows, there was one aspect of the wilderness holiday experience, namely the guide-tourist relationship, which required tourists to come face-to-face with the very people they sought to displace, in both real and imaginative terms, in Ontario's north.

A party of men and women camp out on 'Yohocucoba,' at Lake Joseph, Muskoka, c. 1880.

The Beaumaris Hotel touts its advantages for hay-fever sufferers.

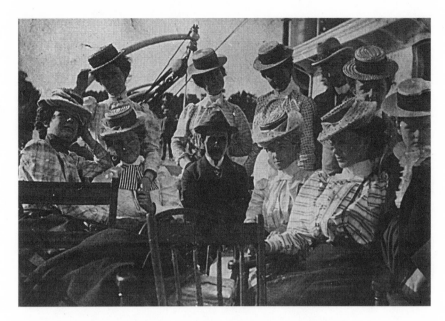

Excursionists returning from a picnic at Niagara, c. 1898

A cottage living room on Chief's Island, Muskoka, in 1914

The *S.S. Luella* discharges passengers at Toronto Island.

Toronto from the Island, by Schell and Hogan

Hanlan's Hotel at Hanlan's Point, Toronto Island, c. 1905

'Bella Villa' cottage on Hanlan's Point, Toronto Island, c. 1900

Forster's Hunt Club in Muskoka District, 1904

Fisherman and guides at Nipigon, August 1887

Duck Shooting at Lake Rosseau

The Hudson's Bay post at Red Rock on the Nipigon River

A guide and his family at Temagami, c. 1905

An Ojibway guide and his family at Fort Matachuwan, c. 1906

Temagami guide Bill Friday and companions

The Grand Trunk Railway advertises the 'wild and magnificent'
Temagami region.

'A vacation *without* a Kodak is a vacation wasted.'

A CPR sleeping-car by day

6

Close Encounters

In no aspect of Ontario tourism did ideas about civilization and the primitive come under more sustained scrutiny than in the relations between white tourists and Native guides. People who spent their holidays fishing, hunting, and camping in the wilderness relied on guides not only to avoid getting lost, but because they needed their services as oarsmen, packers, hunters, cooks, and companions. And for many, the value of Native guides went far beyond the practical, for close contact with men who lived so close to nature added another dimension to the romance of their wilderness holidays. This chapter examines the experience of travellers who spent periods of a few days to several weeks in the woods with their guides and, at least in their own minds, got to know their Native hosts on an intimate basis. Their writings reveal a host of ambiguities, born of contesting notions about the meaning and virtue of life in the wilds and the curious nature of the guide-tourist relationship.

WHITE TOURISTS AND NATIVE GUIDES

What is being examined here, of course, is the Euro-Canadian interpretation of these encounters, gleaned mainly from hunting and fishing narratives written by the tourists themselves. They are largely the product of men's experiences, for women's published narratives are a sparse commodity by comparison, though sisters and wives were often present on such trips. In such stories, the extent to which the guide himself is an active agent varies considerably. There is even a literature of the invisible guide, in which the *we* of the narrative includes a Native companion who is merely regarded as part of the outfit and is only mentioned if he steps into the foreground in some unusual incident. There are many other narratives, by contrast, in which the guide is very much part of the story, and in these the hunting or fishing adventure tale has a subtext in which the relationship with the guide unfolds.

But as one would expect, even when guides are the focus of attention, tourists' descriptions of their appearance, skills, and behaviour often say more about Euro-Canadian beliefs, desires, and intentions than they do about anything else. The evidence is further skewed by the fact that those who published their experiences generally believed that there was something unusual or authoritative about them; they were often trying to sell the wilderness adventure to their readers, or to evoke the atmosphere and pleasures of the wilds. And of course there were always at least two versions of the encounter. The guides' own stories, told at home and among friends, if they could be retrieved through oral histories, would reveal another world of interpretation.[1]

In the context of late nineteenth-century ideas about progress, civilization, and the fate of nations and races, the tourist-guide relationship is an especially interesting one. In northern and northwestern Ontario, Native people's role in the tourist industry blossomed during a period when Euro-Canadian society's recognition of and regard for their traditional skills and knowledge were disappearing. With the War of 1812 far behind them, the fur trade in decline, and much of the province already explored and surveyed, the cooperation of Native people was not needed as it had been before. This was the era of 'scientific racism,' the Indian Act, aggressive white settlement, and a thoroughgoing assault upon Native cultures and economies.

But those out for a wilderness holiday might see things in a slightly different light. When tourist and guide were alone in the woods, the so-called savage attributes regained their value, for what counted then were the knowledge and skills of the wilderness, just as they had mattered in earlier times, when explorers, traders, missionaries, and soldiers had relied upon Native expertise. Notions about the eventual demise of the 'Indian race' or its inevitable assimilation were, in this setting, quite often beside the point; what mattered was survival in the here and now. The guide's value to the tourist, however, extended beyond mere practical matters of comfort, safety, and a successful hunt. What many also paid for was a carefully managed exposure to the mysteries and romance of the wilderness, and a chance to ponder, at close hand, the differences between their own race and one they regarded as distinctly 'other.'

Such distinctions were of course muddied by the fact that many guides, perhaps a majority, were of mixed descent. Some were distinctly identified as Métis and others were not, but it was generally true that while Victorian travellers might be otherwise disdainful of the effects of what they called miscegenation, mixed blood was considered no crime against nature or culture where the ideal guide was concerned. A Métis guide might possess all of the 'red gifts' Cooper described, but have a more reassuringly European-looking countenance and greater fluency in English than his more 'racially pure' counterpart. Many favourite guides were in fact former Hudson's Bay Company employees, who were often Métis. They had a reputation for being knowledgeable, responsible, and respectful, with a lifetime's experience in the fine points of serving their employers. 'Our Indians had travelled with the factor, and they had learned the art of pleasing the canoeist and camper almost to perfection,' said one writer of his vacation in Temagami.[2] With the Metis guide, the romance of being alone in the bush with 'a real Indian' was still available. In other words, the guide of mixed descent gave tourists the opportunity to choose when and when not to regard him as exotic or alien.

In many locations the Hudson's Bay Company served as the intermediary between guides and tourists, though outfitters' took over this role in areas close to advancing white settlement. White settlers were often drawn into the guiding business themselves, though not always to good effect; C.C. Farr was probably referring to these neophytes when he complained of the number of 'pseudo-guides' who should 'stay at home and hoe potatoes [rather than] pass themselves off as guides.'[3] Published lists of guides suggest a growing degree of white competition in some areas but not in others, and where white guides were not available, Native expertise was most highly valued. An Ontario Guides' Association, formed early in the twentieth century to protect wages, regulate the profession, and serve the functions of a friendly society, may well have had as part of its agenda the exclusion of Native guides (or at least those so defined by the Indian Act), for it placed great emphasis on the notion of 'citizenship,' the possession of a permanent residence in the province, and the honouring of provincial game laws among the guides themselves.[4]

Guiding remained, nonetheless, an important element of Native economic survival in many parts of Ontario, as it is today. Many men evidently preferred guiding to other nontraditional occupations, for it often paid better and was more congenial in other respects. The men of

Rama on Georgian Bay, for example, could earn one dollar a day as farm labourers in 1889, but as Indian agent D.J. McPhee noted the following year, 'as guides to tourists and pleasure-seekers' they received 'as much as sixty dollars per month.'[5] (As a point of comparison, wages paid in railway construction at Fort William in the early 1880s began at 1.50 a day, rising to $2.50 to $3.00 for carpenters, and higher for other skilled trades.[6]) The rate of $2.00 a day for head guides was typical throughout Ontario during the 1880s and 1890s, sometimes rising as high as $3.00 in popular areas such as Nipigon and Temagami. Additional sums were charged for the use of canoes. A Hudson's Bay Company employee at Red Rock wrote that he was 'very glad to see that those parties who go up the river give the Indians about here lucrative employment at a time when they cannot hunt,' for it 'helps very much to tide them over until they can begin their fall work.'[7]

The economic value of this occupation did not always impress agents of the Department of Indian Affairs, and they sometimes complained that guiding distracted the men from their primary duties as farmers. Unlike the production of handicrafts, which women undertook in winter, guiding and farming both made their claims upon men and boys in the summer months. Agents visiting Nipigon rejoiced when the potato crop seemed to be receiving sufficient attention, but despaired when the more compatible occupations of hunting and guiding – and the more traditional habits of life that went with them – regained ascendency.[8] As Hugh Brody says, in a culture which saw agriculture as 'the very starting point of civilization ... hunters were beyond the pale.'[9]

There is no question that tourism brought ready cash to these communities, but it also reintroduced the curses of European civilization – especially alcohol and contagious disease – which had devastated Native populations in earlier periods. 'I may say there is more intemperance in this band than in any other in my agency,' said Indian superintendent R.W. Ross, writing of the Red Rock reserve in 1896, and he saw tourists as the source of the problem.[10] More dangerous still, in all probability, was the steady exposure to disease brought by tourists from so many different places.[11] Canadians, Americans, and Europeans in ill-health might see the northern wilderness as a great open-air sanatorium, but they easily passed on their illnesses to the people they employed as guides. And at Native communities situated at the heart of a wilderness tourist industry, such as Lake Temagami, venereal diseases, including syphilis, also became more prevalent.

UP THE NIPIGON

Of the favourite fishing and hunting regions of Ontario, Nipigon (or Nepigon), presented rather a singular case. The Nipigon River was famous throughout North America for its speckled trout, and despite its remoteness, from the 1850s through to the twentieth century it was a destination favoured by wealthy Americans looking for a true wilderness holiday. Steamer and rail company promotional literature lavished attention on the wonders of the Nipigon, and timetables were arranged so as to make stopovers as convenient as possible.[13] In the early decades tourists were always advised to book guides in advance through the Hudson's Bay post at Red Rock, where 'Indians, canoes, tents, bedding, clothing and rough cooking materials' were available, as well as 'all ordinary supplies and camping requisites.'[14] Because the post was not very profitable, the company welcomed the business, yet had difficulty predicting demand and ensuring that enough guides were available. Sometimes reinforcements had to be recruited from as far away as the Sault. 'Tourists are as thick here as the flies,' complained a Hudson's Bay Company employee one summer, as he struggled to cope with the pressure placed on the small post's facilities.[15] Another admitted that he had let down '40 Gentlemen Fishing Tourists, as I had promised to supply them with Every thing necessary ... they were rather annoyed that I had them not, I don't think it likely they will rely on me again.'[16] The lessening reliance on steamers caused by the railway reduced the importance of Red Rock, and by the early twentieth century the outfitting business was centred up the river at Nipigon. It remained necessary to arrange well ahead for guides, however, 'particularly during the months of July and August, when the season is in full blast.'[17]

As they were in demand, Native guides at Red Rock and Nipigon had some degree of control over the circumstances of their employment. A Hudson's Bay Company employee went so far as to complain in the summer of 1888 that, finding themselves in a seller's market, 'our Nepigon guides have lately been acting rather ugly with the tourists, and gentlemen visiting the river, demanding excessive wages for very little work, $2 1/2 and $3 day is now commonly asked by them.'[18] In published testimonials, however, the guides of Nipigon came in for a good deal of praise. Tourists were always impressed with their physical strength, shown in their willingness to carry enormous weights on their backs, and they also described them as 'smart, clean and civil,' and 'superb examples of their craft, excellent cooks and delightful companions.'[19] The government fishery overseer at Nipigon confirmed that the men employed as guides were invariably 'intelligent and desirous of giving satisfaction to their employers, doing all the packing over portages, putting up tents, making comfortable beds, and attending to the cooking – in fact are ever on the alert for their employers' comfort.'[20]

Certain guides became known as favourites. There was Andrew Laxie, 'six feet four,' raved one tourist, 'the handsomest Indian I have ever seen, Mayor of the little town of Red Rock, and one of the most innately refined and cultured companions any man could ask.'[21] An article in the *Globe* reported Esquimalt Joe to be 'the most distinguished cook on the river,' and Louis Bouchard was highly regarded for his skills as a cook and guide as well.[22] The Bouchards, a Métis family, were active as guides for decades. In 1913, reported one tourist, 'Old Johnny' Bouchard, '82 years of age, still makes trips on the river as cook and carries his share of the duffle.'[23]

Of course, tourists' narratives were not simple tales of racial stereotypes exploding as heart-warming friendships blossomed in the solitary woods. From the tourists' point of view, guides were their employees and also members of a race seldom conceded full equality, and these factors influenced their interpretations of events. They usually expected to exert a certain amount of control over such men, and were sometimes frustrated, offended, and annoyed when full cooperation was not forthcoming.

One of the functions of the guidebook and wilderness narrative was to provide a forum for advice on the matter of handling guides. A point in favour of those at Nipigon was that they had not been 'spoiled yet by too great familiarity with the ways of the cities,' and tourists realized that it was to their long-term advantage that this not change. Such narratives alerted other tourists to the kinds of problems that might arise, how they could be prevented, and how to avoid 'spoiling' guides or rendering them overly sophisticated about the ways of white folk. Should drink, for example, be shared? The author of *Nipegon Trout* said no, counselling tourists who carried alcohol to keep it entirely for private use. Otherwise, he warned, expectations would develop among the guides, and 'if you are known to have a supply and fail or refuse to circulate it, look out for sulks or spills.'[24] Overpaying, on the other hand, might set a standard which future tourists would be pressured to meet. 'No Indian,' another writer predicted darkly, 'will ever work again for less than he has once received. The next employer, be he a man of moderate means or better judgement, is regarded as poor white trash.'[25]

Then there was the unfortunate matter of guides learning how to fool or manipulate tourists, and thus avoid work. One correspondent, whose 'Ten Days on the Nipigon' appeared as a series in the *Globe* during the summer of 1884, brought readers into seemingly intimate contact with the ways and wiles of the Bouchards, including the young Antoine's habit of disappearing into the bush on his visits 'of pure friendship' to young women. The writer's main frustration, however, arose over his guides' unwillingness to work as hard as he thought they should. According to his report, to avoid the labour of paddling his guides tried, with dismal effect, to hoist a red blanket as a sail: 'Such is the nature of a Nipigon Metis, that he prefers a mile an hour under sail than four miles with the paddle.' Later on he and his companions encountered a group of tourists virtually immobilized on the river because their guides had persuaded them that paddling was impossible because of strong winds. You must never lose control of the situation like this, the writer insisted. 'They are good, civil men, and responsive to courteous treatment, as all decent men are. Still, there is a freakish streak in these men of the wilds, and when their employer puts his foot down on reasonable grounds, he must keep it down lest they get the control.'[26] What could be more frustrating, however, than the Indian who refused to be employed at all? Douglas Sladen, an English journalist who made a tour of Canada by rail, told how one group of anglers, having reached the station at Nipigon, could not obtain guides. When they arrived

the Indians were hay-making, and, after their haymaking was done, felt too lazy to do any more work. And the particularly aggravating part of the matter was that they had pitched their teepes (*sic*) in the township close to Mr Mac———'s store, and were hanging about all day. Even Mr Mac———, who had far more influence with them than the Hudson's Bay agent, could do absolutely nothing.[27]

From the tourists' point of view, they had a right to the services of guides, and the Indians had a duty to oblige them.

In remote regions of Ontario, Native guides maintained a level of autonomy which was difficult to preserve in more settled areas. This is not to suggest that the guide-tourist relationship was one of equality in any part of Canada, for Native communities had not invited the influx of tourists and were, in a sense, drawing the best economic advantage from a potentially dangerous situation. On the other hand, guiding was an occupation in which those so employed could retain a good deal of personal dignity and control. Said one Ojibway elder, looking back on his long career as a guide in the Fort Frances area in our own century, 'I loved working as a guide because, once I left camp, I was the boss. The tourists had to depend on me, on what I knew about fishing, about not getting lost, and about surviving in the bush if anything went wrong.'[28]

TEMAGAMI AND BEYOND

The great majority of hunters and fishing tourists did not travel as far as Nipigon for their holidays, but looked to the regions north of Toronto instead. As Muskoka became populated, other areas, in a widening arc, were opened to wilderness tourism: the French River, the Maganetawagan River, the Montreal River, Lake Nipissing, Lake Temagami, Lake Temiskaming, and Temagami, which became a forest reserve at the turn of the century, received the most lavish publicity, for it was promoted by both the Grand Trunk and Canadian Pacific Railways and was written about in glowing terms in the sporting press. Here was a 'primeval' wilderness, supposedly devoted to the joys of fishing, hunting, and camping. 'You who are tired of the old worn trails may have your first peep into this new sportsman's paradise,' urged an anonymous author in *Rod and Gun*. 'Civilization is shoving the wild things farther and farther north. But you who are lucky enough to live today may hurry to these last fastnesses.'[29] Temagami was also a favourite place for the founding of organized camps, such as youth camps, which were part of the pre–First World War movement in Canada, the United States, and Britain aimed at countering the alleged effects of urban life and racial decline on these nations' youth. As one magazine wrote, praising an American wilderness canoe-tripping program based at Temagami, 'Self-reliance, resource, and independence are brought out as much as possible, so that the boy may become a true white Indian.' The boys' models included Ernest Thompson Seton's *Two Little Savages* and other such writings, but also their real Native guides – and one pseudo-Indian in the person of Archie Belaney (or Grey Owl) – who were employed by Camp Keewaydin.[31]

Like Muskoka, Temagami after the turn of the century, for city dwellers, came to stand for the restoration of health to mind and body. Temagami's 'primitive' connotations remained more intact, however, making it easier for visitors to fall under the transforming influence of the wilderness. 'With each mile breath came freer,' wrote two satisfied campers fresh back from holiday, 'with each hour we grew delightfully more savage.'[32] As rail links to remote areas continued to multiply, the theme of the easy-to-reach North Country could still apply; it was just a twenty-four hour journey from New York to Mattawa, for example, where a wilderness trip to one of the lakes could begin. An American tourist remembered happily how he had arrived on the platform, and within moments was 'listening to the greeting of white and Indian and half-breed guides, and discussing with them questions of duffle and the portage. These men carry with them the unmistakeable flavour of the forest.'[33]

The circumstances of employment for Native guides varied considerably throughout this region. In some places the Hudson's Bay Company remained actively involved in serving tourists, and in others, white outfitting companies took over much of this role. Some guides were from remote communities, and they combined catering to tourists with more traditional means of subsistence. Others, meanwhile, lived close to or summered at centres of tourist and lumbering activity, and their economic and social lives were more quickly and deeply affected by the influx of outsiders. At Temagami the Ojibway of Bear Island had no reserve, and rather abruptly found their lands and livelihoods threatened by encroaching tourism.[34]

As at Nipigon, certain individuals and families became well known as guides and appeared repeatedly in the sporting press. Men by the name of Paulson (and Polson) were highly recommended, with their qualities of strength, skill, reliability, and good manners being emphasized most. 'Our own men were a splendid lot of fellows,' wrote a Temagami tourist. 'One of them carried seven bags of flour on his back at one time over a portage. He was six feet two in height, stout in proportion, and as intelligent and modest as he was big. Readers when you come this way ask for the Indian Willy Paulson.'[35] Most frequently mentioned were the Fridays, a family of Cree descent who had moved south and eventually ran their own tourist lodge.[36] 'An integral part of Lake Temagami – Canada's newest and greatest and loveliest holiday land – is the Friday family,' gushed Frank Yeigh in 1906, 'a worthy family with Indian blood.' The wise tourist, he advised, 'will close a contract with one of the Friday boys to be his guide, philosopher, friend, fisherman, canoeist, cook and tentmate.' Yeigh's party employed Bill Friday, 'a swarthy young giant' (guides were quite commonly represented as huge), who made Temagami reveal all its 'beauty haunts' to them. He intrigued them all the more because he was said to be in love, 'and the same charge brought with it a smile of such expansiveness and so instinct [sic] with happiness and good-nature as to make of Big Bill a charming fellow-voyageur.'[37]

Frank Carrell and his companions engaged the young George Friday, who not only acted as guide but social convenor as well. Temagami's Bear Island, where there was a Hudson's Bay Post, was the scene of frequent dances (Yeigh attended one as well), and on one occasion Carrell and friends urged Friday to find a house where they could hold such an entertainment. Carrell recounted the curious story of how, while searching for a suitable spot, they found themselves peering in a window and seeing an elderly man and woman listening to 'The Old Folks at Home' on their gramophone. They secured the house, though the gramophone was carefully packed away and replaced by a fiddler, and as George Friday 'had sent messengers around and gathered in all the young Indian girls ... in a short time we had two full sets going it at a lively gait.'[38] The tourist literature is understandably silent on the subject of prostitution at wilderness resorts.

Wherever tourists encountered Native people they were usually interested in the progress-of-civilization question, and such close encounters at Temagami provided ample opportunity. Carrell was moved to remark on how quickly the Ojibway of Temagami were changing; they spoke English well, though with a Scots accent, and the young tended to imitate tourists' dress. Perhaps with mock naivete, he marvelled at 'the extraordinary white features and appearance of many of the young Indian girls' who worked in the hotels, and he was generally impressed with 'the advanced state of civilization of the members of the tribe around this Post.' That of course did not make them Carrell's equals, and he was critical of his hotel-keeper for allowing guides to eat and drink with the guests, thus eroding the proper distance between master and servant. Most annoying in this regard was a man named Charley, a spoiled guide, as Carrell called him, who was 'inclined to too much familiarity with his patrons, and not sufficiently disciplined as to his place at all times. He thought nothing of drawing up a chair on the verandah of the hotel [and] making himself one of our group ... with as much freedom as if he were one of ourselves.'[39] At Nipigon, Temagami, and at tourist spots throughout the North, Native guides were valued by their employers, but relations between them were frequently characterized by a subtle – or sometimes overt – contest for control.

THE POLITICS OF RACE

A closer look at the tone and content of the hunting and fishing narratives published in magazines such as *Rod and Gun* can tell us much about the ways in which turn-of-the-century racial attitudes influenced the guide-tourist relationship. Some tourists, in keeping with their romantic understanding of the entire wilderness adventure, idealized their guides and wrote about them in a tone of awe-filled respect. But many others, however infatuated they were with the Canadian North, exempted their guides from such praise. Their accounts tended to be patronizing and often laced with wry humour, perhaps suggesting a need to establish a competitive masculine edge over these men, despite their own ignorance of the woods and the ways of animals. And finally there was the 'expert' who wrote for such magazines on a regular basis, and cultivated a certain knowingness with respect to the ways of the Indian guide. One such writer was C.C. Farr, an Englishman who came to Canada in 1870 and spent a decade and a half working for the Hudson's Bay Company. He then bought land on Lake Temiskaming, which he named Haileybury, and spent many years promoting agricultural settlement and railway building in the area.[40] In the pages of *Rod and Gun*, his years with the HBC and his continued participation in the wilderness life allowed him to assume a voice of authority, offering guidance and inside knowledge to the novice hunter and camper.

Much attention in the sporting press was focused on the question of the guides' special abilities and 'instincts,' which made outsiders feel safe with them in the wildest surroundings and circumstances. In the woods, tourists themselves became figures in an alien landscape, one they no longer controlled through the familiar patterns of perception they employed as sightseers. Engaging a guide and venturing outside the bounds of civilization meant entering into his way of seeing and understanding the land, or at least trusting in his accumulated and intuitive knowledge and allowing him to assume control. Many tourists, at least when they told their stories publicly, were content to marvel at how their guides could read the forest – discerning paths through the wilderness where there seemed to be none, and detecting the presence of animals when they themselves saw and heard nothing. Sometimes they picked up tidbits of their guides' knowledge and passed them on to readers: 'See the pond-lily leaves snipped off, leaving the stem standing up: That is the work of the moose. If bitten off recently, the end will be fresh; if longer, it will have dried ... There are "signs" for everything,' wrote H. Barnard, 'to discover the whereabouts and habits of animals.'[41] Few writers went as far as one who called himself St Croix, author of a piece called 'Second Sight and the Indian,' who hinted in a patronizing manner at some sort of special powers possessed by such people, and C.C. Farr himself sometimes played a debunking role. In 'Indians and the Weather,' for example, he tried to account for why Native guides seemed able to predict the weather from the habits of animals. One's guides merely know what to look for, he explained. 'The Indian is inductive in his methods of his treatment of the seen world, for he builds his theories on known facts, and is always ready to make all allowance for the modifications of conditions.'[42]

It was of course understood that while the guide's expertise in the wilderness was beyond question, he was less capable and perhaps thoroughly dysfunctional in any environment except the wilderness. Farr recalled how, in town while waiting to leave, his guides appeared 'somewhat ungainly, and incongruous, so that I was obliged to extend a kind of protectional aegis over their ignorance of surrounding conditions.' Once they entered the wilderness, however, 'the relative positions were reversed ... It was I who was at sea, and they were completely at home.' For St Croix, any special qualities the Native guide showed in the wilderness were bound to be offset by his deficiencies elsewhere, and this writer managed to bring into question the whole nature of intelligence as it pertained to Native people. 'The more one sees of the thoroughly wild and unspoiled Indian,' he wrote, 'the more one realizes what a strange being he is – in many respects wonderfully gifted, and in others perfectly idiotic, from our point of view.' If one of these 'men of the woods' is introduced to civilization, St Croix continued, 'his intelligence seems far below that of a child, but in his own wilderness he is a different creature, and pitted against him, we are forced to acknowledge his infinite superiority.'[44]

If guides often found themselves in the company of tourists with St Croix's sensibilities, it is easy to imagine how some might have sought as little social intercourse with their employers as possible. The demeanour of many guides was described as friendly, but the personalities of others were often an enigma to tourists, who found them withdrawn and silent, showing little emotion, 'whether they are happy, pleased or discontented, their countenances give no sign.'[45] The barrier of language only added to their confusion. Guides were often referred to as taciturn: Aleck Longevin (another 'giant' at six foot five) was as 'taciturn as they are made,' according to one writer, and had even acquired a reputation, perhaps undeserved, for abruptly abandoning tourists in the woods when they displeased him.

But Farr tried to explain to readers that Native people's real personalities and their behaviour before strangers were quite different things. After a trip north with his wife, during which an entire family acted as their guides, he described how the 'light and happy good humor' they display with each other is 'suppressed by shyness before strangers, and hence the white man's idea of the silent, smoky Indian.'[47] But good humour in a guide was not to be taken at face value, either. Farr's partial knowledge of Ojibway put him more in the know than most tourists could hope to be, and elsewhere he explained that a guide's laughter and seeming friendliness might mask quite different emotions. Guides like to play jokes, 'and little does the inexperienced sportsman know how he is criticized by his apparently obsequious Indian guide. It was not until I had learnt the Indian language that I knew this myself,' confided Farr. 'He is not the grinning imbecile that he often gets credit for being, and when the inexperienced white man is thinking that the Indian is laughing with him he is often really laughing at him and thinking what a fool he is.'[48]

Tourists who spent several days travelling with their guides often had glimpses into Native ways of life that no other kind of travel would afford. They visited summer camping grounds where guides had business to conduct or friends to see, or sometimes they just viewed them in passing. G.M. Richards, on his way to Fort Metagami with Aleck Longevin, saw numerous camps and had the chance to examine closely the remains of one that had been deserted. The highlight of this stop was the discovery of a message, written in syllabics on a piece of birchbark and placed in a cleft stick by the remains of the campfire. Aleck translated into English:

Sam Chicken, I am writing to you
We saw your snares
We ate two rabbits
We fixed them again
We saw six snares
We trimmed two new snares
Sam Chicken we thank you for the snares.
                    My name is
                            Jos. Moore

'Courtesy is not entirely lacking in the North,' concluded Richards lamely.[49]

What often fascinated tourists, in fact, were signs that Native people had a social life not so dissimilar, in its basic elements, from that of their own 'civilization.' Like Bill Friday they fell in love, and sometimes love letters were to be found in the woods as well.[50] They had a wide circle of friends and acquaintances, and planned or chance meetings were the occasion for an exchange of gossip and affectionate banter. If tourists travelled with a guide and his family, though this was an exceptional practice, the interaction between spouses, parents, and children could also be observed. Only when such intimate contact was possible, in a setting far from the influence of Euro-Canadian communities, could the position of women in Native society, for example, be better understood by tourists. Farr's observations on Native family life might have been superficial by the standards of an ethnologist, but he imparted little details to ordinary readers which were not the usual stuff of prewar popular journalism, such as his comments on the women's activities during his 'Trip to Matachuan.' One day, he recalled, 'I saw the old woman gathering a plant having a white flower, and carefully stowing it away with her other treasures. I asked her what she did with it; she said that it was a good medicine for weak lungs, and that it was somewhat rare.'[51]

An aspect of Native life to which tourists did not give much thought was their beliefs about the practice of hunting itself. Nineteenth-century tourists, like twentieth-century historians, displayed little understanding of Native beliefs about and attitudes towards the natural world, and seldom referred to this cultural gulf between themselves and their guides in their narratives. As earlier explorers had done, tourists sometimes commented on Native men's passion for killing, though such observations are difficult to interpret. An American woman in Barnard's company, for example, showed her skill with a gun in shooting a duck, and a group of men looking on from another canoe were clearly impressed. 'This is the only time that I saw Indians demonstrative,' wrote Barnard, 'and I believe the only thing to stir them to this pitch is to kill. To take life is part of their nature, and to see it done in an artistic manner commends itself to their admiration.'[52]

But other instances were reported of guides appearing at times to divert tourists' attention away from nearby animals to avoid having them killed, and when a bear, for example, was shot, guides sometimes performed acts of respect or mourning. 'There is an affinity between the bear and the Indian,' Farr attempted to explain. 'The latter always looks upon the bear as his friend, and a good hunter will always shake hands with a dead bear saying "Meegeutch shoomis nias ka mijian." "Thank you, old man, for the meat you have given me." This is etiquette and must be observed by those who would kill more.'

Farr's Ojibway was less than perfect, as no doubt was his understanding of this ritual, but he was open to the possibility that the bear had special significance in the Ojibway belief system. And his remarks were somewhat less patronizing than those offered by the author of *Nepigon Trout*. Whitcher described his keen exasperation when the beliefs of his guide, Kenise, seemingly interfered with the catching of fish. The tone of this narrative works against its being taken too seriously. According to Whitcher, he and Kenise were fishing in Hamilton's pool in the Nipigon, a tangle of whirlpools which spun their canoe dangerously. Kenise suddenly scrambled for shore – convinced that Whitcher had hooked 'the spirit trout, declaring that he had felt her underneath trying to upset the canoe.' The trout thus got away, 'the empty frying-pan cried aloud for fish,' and Whitcher was determined to try again. Whitcher taunted Kenise for showing his fear, 'whereupon he shot at me an arrowy look of barbarian contempt and walked away, muttering in native gibberish some sarcasm equivalent to "Fools rush in where angels fear to tread."' But Whitcher got his fish, he and his companions ate it, then persuaded a second guide to relax his 'Ojibwa taciturnity' and tell them the story of the enchanted pool. Whitcher finally concluded, with a curious, ethnocentric twist, that the story was not of Ojibway origin, it being much too close in general theme to a poem he knew of Goethe's. 'Where does the untutored savage get fast hold of such slippery tales?' he asked. 'They are neither original or aboriginal, but taste of common origin and smell of civilized manufacture.'[54]

Tourists' accounts of such experiences are rare and hardly trustworthy, but it is probably safe to assume that they would show little patience with any belief system that might curtail their sport. Guides wishing not to violate their own traditional practices, therefore, probably used tactics not revealed to their employers. But it is also likely that guiding tourists was a practice, often dictated by economic necessity, about which some guides and their families held very ambivalent views.

The whole question of Native hunting rights was another issue often addressed in the pages of *Rod and Gun*. Guides were sometimes accused of cooperating with tourists in hunting out of season, but were themselves equally criticized for overhunting and causing the depletion of fish and game. Their critics, however, often lacked a sense of priorities, and placed the future of sport hunting and fishing above people's right to make necessary preparations for winter. One writer explained how the Nipigon trout (then heavily exploited by commercial fishing) were threatened by Native people's use of them for winter food.[55] But as the Native population at Nipigon was not increasing at that point, their habit of smoking fish for winter use and piling them up 'like cord wood' could not have been the source of a growing problem.

At the bottom of the controversy was a question that probed deeply into the politics of identity. Whose wilderness was this? In an article called 'The Old and the New,' Farr approached this issue in a circuitous manner, beginning with a story about an encounter he had observed many years ago between a Métis canoeman and an 'innocent young man.' On the surface, this story simply seems to mock the type of traveller whose only experience of Native people had been through fiction 'of the Fennimore Cooper type,' and who eventually became aware of his folly:

Johnny McDonald was the name of the Indian who was steering, and my young friend gazed in rapt admiration, for here, at last, was before his very eyes, a dusky denizen of the forest, a modern Osceola, in baggy pants.

Then he asked. 'Can you speak English?' 'Of course,' answered Johnny.

'Are you happy doing this kind of work?'

'What do you mean?' asked Johnny.

'I mean work like this, steering boats for the pale-faces.' Johnny grinned and said that he guessed that he was all right.

'Would you not sooner be hunting the wild deer with your people?' asked the innocent.

'What do you mean?' again asked Johnny.

'I mean, would you not sooner be dwelling with your own tribe?'

Johnny became somewhat mystified at this, and knew not how to answer. Then the young man again came to the charge, and asked:

'What tribe do you belong to?'

'What?' asked Johnny, still more mystified.

'What nation do you belong to; what are you?'

Johnny looked at him with ineffable scorn, and answered with a ring of national pride in his tone.

'D———n it man, I'm a Scotchman.'[56]

But Farr's purpose in telling this story was not just to ponder the ambiguities of race. Johnny had unwittingly given 'the innocent' a lesson on 'the Indian question and its anomalies,' and that was the author's goal as well. The problem in Farr's mind boiled down to the fact that Indians defined as such under the Indian Act claimed certain privileges on racial grounds, and yet in practice could choose, according to Farr, when to identify themselves as Indians and when to claim the same rights as 'whites.' The grievances he outlined were quite specific. He resented the existence of Indian reserves unavailable for white exploitation, and the creation of game laws which allowed only Indians to hunt out of season. If an Indian wanted a glass of whisky, complained Farr, he announced himself a Scotchman or an Englishman, but if he wanted to kill a moose his defence was 'Indian me.'[57] Farr grossly overestimated the right of self-definition possessed by people governed by the Indian Act, but he rightly singled out the exercise of Native hunting rights as a common complaint of white tourists.

The relationship between white tourists and their Native guides was one of the many stages on which the politics of race were played out in the late nineteenth and early twentieth centuries. In some respects the tourists' position was unique, in that they came into contact with Native people fleetingly and by choice, drawing insofar as they wished to upon romantic images of such encounters to enhance their experience. These encounters were unusual in another respect, in that they required tourists to trust and obey individuals to whom, in the normal run of affairs, they would accord no power or control, and who were defined by law as wards of the state.

And yet tourists' very presence in the wilderness also identified them as members of an intruding race, opening up more and more areas to tourism and laying claim to their beauty and wealth. C.C. Farr's many roles – as a former HBC employee, as a settler, as a local booster, and as a sportsman in his free time who took on the role of counselling other tourists – captured the dynamics of wilderness tourism on the larger colonial stage. 'I miss my Indians,' wrote Farr, plaintively, on his return from Matachewan, but it was the geographical advance of his own civilization, which he pursued so assiduously in daily life, that made it necessary for him to go farther and farther north to find them.[58]

Conclusion

When William Varley outlined the tourist attractions of Ontario for the Canadian reading public at the beginning of the twentieth century, he said almost nothing of cities and industries, but portrayed the province still as a wild and watery wonderland:

A land of lakes and rivers ... rivers that have their source in the cool northern forest, and flow, now swift, now peaceful, till they join those vast inland seas, Superior, Huron, Erie, Ontario, whose waters are in turn borne by the broad St Lawrence to the ocean.

Varley urged tourists to follow the now familiar routes: to Niagara, through the Thousand Islands and the rapids, along the Ottawa River (Moore's 'Canadian Boat Song' did service again here), up to Muskoka, north to Temiskaming, and through the upper lakes to Thunder Cape, 'the Giant Asleep.' The usual romantic allusions came into play – Ontario's north was a 'fairyland,' Ottawa's lumbermen were 'devil-may-care' voyageurs, and tourists were invited to engage Indian guides who would take them camping in the wilderness so that they could see 'the forest as it looked when only the red man held sway.'[1]

The aesthetics of tourism had changed little from the beginning of the nineteenth century to its end, if the continuing importance of romantic imagery in marketing and interpreting the tourists' world can be taken as evidence. The notion of the 'sublime' may have fallen somewhat out of fashion, though it survived in hackneyed descriptions of Niagara, but the language of the picturesque, of romantic concepts of history, nationhood, and the so-called primitive past, remained the staple fare of the travel narrative and the tourist brochure. Infused with literary references, this was a language that spoke particularly to the middle and upper classes, though in diluted form it had become the universal and mindless lingo of the tourist trade. It was as if they had 'got it right' in the beginning, not only for Ontario or for North America as a whole, but also for any place in the world where a tourist industry was to develop.

The structure of romantic values which informed nineteenth-century tourism was closely related to the values of a wider consumerism. Since the beginnings of the Industrial Revolution the marketing of goods and services increasingly depended on creating new 'needs,' fuelled by appeals to the imagination and promises of individual fulfilment. Those who could afford to respond were largely of the propertied classes, and as the century progressed, the 'right' to holidays and travel, for example, became an established element of middle-class identity. For this process to occur, however, the Victorian middle-class bias against self-indulgent pleasures had to be partially overcome, and here, too, the romantic legacy played a part as notions of individual fulfilment and freedom gained a broader currency. But even the work ethic could now justify the taking of holidays, for as the desire for release from the tedium of daily life grew so did the mounting obsession with the health of the body, the mind, and society at large. People no longer simply desired holidays, a change of scene, and the excitement of exotic places, they *needed* them, felt they deserved them, and felt virtuous in taking them.

The relationship between tourism and personal freedom created special opportunities for women, for it raised questions of identity related to gender as well as to class. Although they were subjected to constraints and criticisms, women did travel, and for many of the same purposes as men. Examples drawn from tourist practices in Ontario have illustrated this point. At Niagara early in the nineteenth century men and women were drawn by the new fashion for wild places, and both hoped for an experience of the sublime that was as wonderful, passionate, and liberating as those they had read about. At other tourist destinations the evidence suggests the ready participation of women in most activities, although the pride they sometimes displayed in certain achievements (such as running rapids), along with the need felt by some men to comment on their presence, imply that certain restraints were being consciously challenged. What we know of the excursioning public in the nineteenth century clearly shows that women were well represented, both on day trips (and on moonlight runs to Niagara) and on much longer journeys, such as steamer trips through the upper lakes, where usual standards of Victorian decorum sometimes lapsed in the face of determined levity and close contact. Women's participation in wilderness camping and cottaging also represented a bid for greater freedom. Reproducing domesticity on a simpler scale at the cottage, finding amusement in berry-picking, going barefoot, and paddling in canoes, was reminiscent of Rousseau's notion of the natural woman, but spending several days in the bush in the company of men or with other women was more suggestive of the New Woman's claim to true equality. But what did that mean? Women's advice to one another about what to wear when camping, what duties they should perform, and how they should behave under situations of duress were all part of an attempt to redefine identity in this new middle-class role of 'playing' at the primitive life.

The history of tourism in any nation or region is related to another aspect of travellers' perceptions of themselves; that is, their identity as citizens of a nation. In places which were subjected to the forces of colonization, this aspect of tourism had particular significance. The growth of the tourist industry in Canada paralleled the founding of a country, the exploitation of its resources, and the arrival of millions of immigrants. The tourist industry was an ally of many forms of economic development in the nineteenth century, such as the growth of railways and steamer companies, and all of these industries were intimately associated with the gospel of expansionism, whereby the fate of the 'unsettled' regions of Canada was identified with the interests of the metropolis. The tourists themselves had an important role to play. On the one hand, the seemingly boundless regions of northern Ontario were an ideal place for city dwellers to indulge their passion for wild places and to act out their dreams of the primitive life. But their mere presence in this 'contact zone' meant assuming a right to be there, and even the mixture of ways in which they described their personal experiences and perceptions had much broader implications. A seemingly benign romantic reverie about the beauties of Lake Superior took on new meaning when the tragic demise of the Native population was predicted, or when it gave way to dreams of progress and the westward march of civilizing forces. Tourists who described their journeys to others, through whatever means they chose, passed on information and confirmed prejudices which would be of great service to the expansionist cause.

What changes would the twentieth century bring to the structure of values underlying the tourist industry? Did the romantic sensibility survive the Great War? It is commonly understood that the devastation caused by the First World War brought about a reaction against the cultural values of the nineteenth century – against 'heroic' history, against notions of progress, against beliefs about meaning in human affairs in general.[2] Did this movement undermine tourism's links to romanticism? There is little evidence that it did. The reason may lie in the fact that *modernism*, if that term is still precise enough to be meaningful, was a reaction of the few against the many; 'serious' art and literature, for example, were transformed, but at the cost of further alienation from the culture of the majority. In mass culture, certainly in all aspects of culture in which advertising played a central role, the facile manipulation of romantic imagery was too useful a tool (or too seductive a pleasure) to be abandoned. This was certainly the case with tourism, which developed after the war into a truly mass industry due to the introduction of the automobile, the granting of annual holidays to workers, and the entry of all levels of government into the tourist business.

It is not difficult, in fact, to trace the continuity in romantic values from the last century through the present one. While the word *sublime* is seldom heard in the present day, its legacy persists in the importance many tourists still place on dramatic encounters with the natural world, and in their search for transcendent experience through the illusion (or carefully controlled reality) of personal danger. Uses of the picturesque are omnipresent and much more obvious, for it is these aesthetic criteria which still guide our sense of beauty in landscape and cityscape, and which we try to satisfy when we take photographs as tourists. The use of nostalgia is also common fare in the marketing of tourist attractions, and the economic value of historic sites is almost completely dependent on romanticizing the past and appealing to tourists' sense of national, regional, or ethnic pride. And finally, the renewed tourist interest in Native cultures in Canada and in the rest of North America again reflects, if only in part, the continuing power of images created centuries ago.

Notes

CHAPTER 1 Introduction: Nature, Culture, and Tourism

1 James Buzard, *The Beaten Track: European Tourism, Literature, and the Ways to 'Culture' 1800–1918* (Oxford: Clarendon Press, 1993), 1.
2 Paul Fussell, *Abroad: British Literary Traveling between the Wars* (Oxford: Oxford University Press 1980), 42; and see Daniel Boorstin, *The Image: A Guide to Pseudo-Events in America* (New York: Atheneum 1972): 77–117.
3 Jonathan Culler, 'The Semiotics of Tourism,' in *Framing the Sign: Criticism and Its Institutions* (Oxford: Basil Blackwell 1988), 156.
4 Ibid., 155–7.
5 Dean MacCannell, *The Tourist: A New Theory of the Leisure Class* (New York: Schocken Books 1976), 194n9.
6 See Buzard, *Beaten Track*; Ian Ousby, *The Englishman's England: Taste, Travel, and the Rise of Tourism* (Cambridge: Cambridge University Press 1990).
7 Standard works on English romanticism include Anthony Thorlby, ed., *The Romantic Movement* (London 1966), and M.H. Abrams, *Natural Supernaturalism: Tradition and Revolution in Romantic Literature* (New York: W.W. Norton 1971).
8 On the sublime, see Marjorie Hope Nicolson, *Mountain Gloom and Mountain Glory: The Development of the Aesthetics of the Infinite* (Ithaca: Cornell University Press 1959); S.H. Monk, *The Sublime: A Study of Critical Theories in Eighteenth-Century England* (first pub., 1935, repr. Ann Arbor: University of Michigan 1960); Thomas Weiskel, *The Romantic Sublime: Studies in the Structure and Psychology of Transcendence* (Baltimore: Johns Hopkins University Press 1976); and Elizabeth McKinsey, *Niagara Falls: Icon of the American Sublime* (New York: Cambridge University Press 1985).

9 Quoted in Malcolm Andrews, *The Search for the Picturesque: Landscape Aesthetics and Tourism in Britain, 1760–1800* (Stanford: Stanford University Press 1989), 44.

10 Ibid., citing Nicolson's analysis in *Mountain Gloom and Mountain Glory*.

11 Longinus, *Dionysius Longinus on the Sublime*, trans. William Smith, 4th ed. (London 1770), quoted in McKinsey, *Niagara Falls*, 31.

12 See note 9 above.

13 On the popularity of country houses and gardens as tourist attractions in the eighteenth century, see Esther Moir, *The Discovery of Britain: The English Tourists, 1540–1840* (London: Routledge and Kegan Paul 1964).

14 On the picturesque, see Andrews, *Search for the Picturesque*; Alexander Ross, *The Imprint of the Picturesque on Nineteenth Century British Fiction* (Waterloo: Wilfrid Laurier University Press, 1986); Moir, *Discovery of Britain*; and Monk, *Sublime*, 204–28.

15 Roland Barthes, 'The *Blue Guide*,' in *Mythologies* (London: Penguin 1973), 74.

16 See John Barrell, *The Idea of Landscape and the Sense of Place, 1730–1840* (Cambridge: Cambridge University Press 1972).

17 Quoted in Andrews, *Search for the Picturesque*, 39.

18 Denis Cosgrove and Stephen Daniels, in 'Introduction: Iconography and Landscape,' *The Iconography of Landscape* (Cambridge: Cambridge University Press 1988), 1.

19 On the nature and use of these instruments, see Don Gifford, *The Farther Shore: A Natural History of Perception* (New York: Atlantic Monthly Press 1990), 18–20.

20 McKinsey, *Niagara Falls*, 58.

21 Moir, *Discovery of Britain*, 148. On early English tourism, see Ousby, *Englishman's England*.

22 See Ross, *Imprint of the Picturesque*, 11–21; also Michel Baridon, 'Ruins as a Mental Construct,' *Journal of Garden History* 5, no. 1, 84–96.

23 On Britain, see Patrick Wright, *On Living in an Old Country: The National Past in Contemporary Britain* (London: Verso 1985). On the uses of history in Maritime Canada, see Ian McKay, 'Twilight at Peggy's Cove: Towards a Genealogy of Maritimicity in Nova Scotia,' *Border/Lines* 12 (summer 1988), 28–37; 'Among the Fisherfolk: J.F.B. Livesay and the Invention of Peggy's Cove,' *Journal of Canadian Studies* 23 (spring 1988), 23–45; 'History and the Tourist Gaze: The Politics of Commemoration in Nova Scotia, 1935–64,' *Acadiensis* 22, no. 2 (spring 1993), 102–38; and Michael Boudreau, '"A Rare and Unusual Treat of Historical Significance": The 1923 Hector Celebration and the Political Economy of the Past,' *Journal of Canadian Studies* 28, no. 4 (winter 1993–4), 28–48.

24 On Highlands tourism, see T.C. Smout, 'Tours in the Scottish Highlands from the Eighteenth to the Twentieth Centuries,' *Northern Scotland* 5 (1983), 99–121.

25 *Collected Letters of Samuel Taylor Coleridge*, quoted in Keith Thomas, *Man and the Natural World: Changing Attitudes in England, 1500–1800* (London: Penguin Books 1984), 91.

26 Buzard, *Beaten Track*, 121.

27 Denis Cosgrove, *Social Formation and Symbolic Landscape* (London: Croom Helm 1984), 58.

28 On the tourist as pilgrim, see John Sears, *Sacred Places: American Tourist Attractions in the Nineteenth Century* (New York: Oxford University Press 1989); Donald Horne, *The Great Museum: The Representation of History* (London: Pluto Press 1984); Nelson H.H. Graburn, 'Tourism: The Sacred Journey,' in Valene L. Smith, *Hosts and Guests: The Anthropology of Tourism* 2d ed. (Philadelphia: University of Pennsylvania Press 1989), 21–35; Eric Cohen, 'A Phenomenology of Tourist Experiences,' *Sociology* 13, no. 2 (1979), 179–201; Patrick McGreevy, 'Niagara as Jerusalem,' *Landscape* 28, no. 2 (1985).

29 See note 23 above.

30 Culler, 'Semiotics of Tourism,' 160.

31 Roderick Nash, *Wilderness and the American Mind* 3d ed. (New Haven: Yale University Press 1982), 3.

32 See Nash, *Wilderness*; Hayden White, 'The Forms of Wildness: The Archaeology of an Idea,' in *Tropics of Discourse: Essays in Cultural Criticism* (Baltimore: Johns Hopkins University Press 1978), 150–82.

33 Thomas, *Natural World*, 17–50.

34 See Thomas, *Natural World*, 92–142; Nash, *Wilderness*; Olive Patricia Dickason, *The Myth of the Savage and the Beginnings of French Colonialism in the Americas* (Edmonton: University of Alberta Press 1984); Maximillian Novak, 'The Wild Man Comes to Tea,' in Edward Dudley and Maximillian Novak, eds., *The Wild Man Within: An Image in Western Thought from the Renaissance to Romanticism* (Pittsburg: University of Pittsburg Press 1972), 183–222; Hayden White, 'The Noble Savage Theme as Fetish,' in White, *Tropics of Discourse*, 183–96.

35 Nash, *Wilderness*, 48.

36 On Rousseau's recycling of the wild man image, see Geoffrey Symcox, 'The Enclosed Vision of Rousseau's *Discourses*,' in Dudley and Novak, *Wild Man Within*, 223–47.

37 White, 'Forms of Wildness,' 33–6.

38 Edward W. Said, *Culture and Imperialism* (New York: Alfred A. Knopf 1993), xxi.

39 Mary Louise Pratt, *Imperial Eyes: Travel Writing and Transculturation* (London: Routledge 1992), 5.

40 Marianna Torgovnick, *Gone Primitive: Savage Intellects, Modern Lives* (Chicago: University of Chicago Press 1990).

41 W.J.T. Mitchell, *Iconology: Image, Text, Ideology* (Chicago 1986), 2; quoted in Cosgrove and Daniels, *Iconography of Landscape*, 7.

42 Pratt, *Imperial Eyes*, 6.

43 See, for example, Terry Goldie, *Fear and Temptation: The Image of the Indigene in Canadian, Australian, and New Zealand Literature* (Montreal: McGill-Queen's University Press 1989); Robert F. Berkhofer, *The White Man's Indian* (New York: Random House 1979); Daniel Francis, *The Imaginary Indian: The Image of the Indian in Canadian Culture* (Vancouver: Arsenal Pulp Press 1992).

44 On American literature and stereotypes of Native peoples, see Louise K. Barnett, *The Ignoble Savage: American Literary Racism, 1790–1890*, rev. ed. (London: Methuen 1987); Richard Slotkin, *Regeneration through Violence: The Mythology of the American Frontier, 1600–1860* (Middletown, Conn.: Wesleyan University Press 1973); Wynette L. Hamilton, 'The Correlation between Societal Attitudes and those of American Authors in the Depiction of American Indians, 1607–1860,' *American Indian Quarterly* 1, no. 1 (1974): 1–26; Barrie Hayne, '*Ossian*, Scott, and Cooper's Indians,' *Journal of American Studies* 3 (July 1969): 73–87; Robert L. Hough, 'Washington Irving, Indians, and the West,' *South Dakota Review* 6 (winter 1968–9): 27–39.

45 Quoted in Barnett, *Ignoble Savage*, 72.

46 James Fenimore Cooper, 'Preface to the *Leather-Stocking Tales*' in *The Deerslayer*, quoted in Hayne, '*Ossian*, Scott, and Cooper's Indians,' 80.

47 White, 'Forms of Wildness,' 168.

48 Reginald Horseman, 'Scientific Racism and the American Indian in the Mid-Nineteenth Century,' *American Quarterly* 27, no. 2 (1975), 152–68; Robert E. Bieder, *Science Encounters the Indian, 1820–1880* (Norman, Okla.: University of Oklahoma Press 1985).

49 Helen Harris, 'Mark Twain's Response to the Native American,' *American Literature* 46, no. 4 (1975): 495–505; and see Louise K. Barnett, 'Nineteenth-Century Indian-Hater Fiction: A Paradigm for Racism,' *South Atlantic Quarterly* 74, no. 2 (1975), 224–36.

50 White, 'Forms of Wildness,' 178–80.

51 On the wilderness movement, see Nash, *Wilderness*; Jonas Frykman and Orvar Lofgren, *Culture Builders: A Historical Anthropology of Middle Class Life* (New Brunswick 1987); George Altmeyer, 'Three Ideas of Nature in

Canada, 1893–1914,' *Journal of Canadian Studies* 11, no. 3 (August 1976), 21–36.

52 White, 'Forms of Wildness,' 178.

53 On middle-class identity and patterns of consumption in the nineteenth century, see Stuart M. Blumin, *The Emergence of the Middle Class: Social Experience in the American City, 1760–1900* (Cambridge: Cambridge University Press 1989).

54 See Peter Bailey, *Leisure and Class in Victorian England* 2nd ed. (London: Methuen 1987); J.A.R. Pimlott, *The Englishman's Holiday* (London 1947; repr. Harvester Press 1976); J.K. Walton, 'The Demand for Working-Class Seaside Holidays in Victorian England,' *Economic History Review* 34, 249–65; Tony Bennett, 'Hegemony, Ideology, Pleasure: Blackpool,' in Tony Bennett, Colin Mercer, and Janet Woollacott, eds., *Popular Culture and Social Relations* (Open University Press 1986), 135–54.

55 Michael J. Piva, *The Condition of the Working Class in Toronto, 1900–1921* (Ottawa: University of Ottawa Press 1979), 89.

56 See Greg Kealey, ed., *Canada Investigates Industrialism* (Toronto: University of Toronto Press 1973), 182, 267, 296–8, 321–2.

57 Greg Kealey, *Working Class Toronto at the Turn of the Century* (Toronto: New Hogtown Press 1973), 16.

58 Eric Leed, *The Mind of the Traveler* (New York: Basic Books 1991).

59 Buzard, *Beaten Track*.

60 See Dea Birkett, *Spinsters Abroad: Victorian Lady Explorers* (Oxford: Blackwell 1989); Leo Hamelin, ed., *Ladies on the Loose: Women Travellers of the Eighteenth and Nineteenth Centuries* (New York: Dodd, Mead 1981). Such women were not necessarily, or even usually, feminists. See Eva-Marie Kröller, 'First Impressions: Rhetorical Strategies in Travel Writing by Victorian Women,' *Ariel* 21, no. 4 (October 1990): 87–99.

61 Sears, *Sacred Places*, 8.

62 Sara Mills, *Discourses of Difference: An Analysis of Women's Travel Writings and Colonialism* (London: Routledge 1991), 6.

63 Bina Friewald, '"Femininely Speaking": Anna Jameson's *Winter Studies and Summer Rambles in Canada*,' in Shirley Neuman and Smaro Kamboureli, eds., *A Mazing Space: Writing Canadian Women Writing* (Edmonton: Longspoon/NeWest 1986), 61–73.

64 'Lady Travellers,' *Quarterly Review* 76 (1845), 117–18. And see 'Spinsterhood Abroad,' *Dublin University Magazine* 43 (1854), 267–74.

65 On women as travellers, also see Marni L. Stanley, 'Travellers' Tales: Showing and Telling, Slamming and Questing,' in Neuman and Kamboureli, eds. *A Mazing Space*, 51–60; Susan Greenstein, 'Sarah Lee:

The Woman Traveller and the Literature of Empire,' in David F. Dorsey et al., *Design and Intent in African Literature* (Washington: Three Continents Press 1982), 133–7; Janet Gilthrow, 'North American Travel Writing' (Ph.D. diss., Simon Fraser University, 1980); Joan Corwin, 'Identity in the Victorian Travel Narrative' (Ph.D. diss., Indiana University, 1987).

66 Andrew Hassam, '"As I Write": Narrative Occasions and the Quest for Self-Presence in the Travel Diary,' *Ariel* 21, no. 4 (October 1990): 45–6. Citing Annette Kolodny, 'Honing a Habitable Languagescape: Women's Images for the New World Frontier,' in *Women and Language in Literature and Society*, ed. Sally McConnell-Coinet, Ruth Barker, and Nelly Furman (New York, Praeger 1980), 188–204.

67 See Heather Murray, 'Women in the Wilderness,' in Neuman and Kamboureli, eds., *A Mazing Space*, 74–83.

68 Susanna Moodie, *Roughing It in the Bush* (New York 1852), 2: 26, 83.

69 Mrs Edward Copleston, *Canada: Why We Live in It and Why We Like It* (London 1861), 59.

70 Cosgrove, *Social Formation*, 15.

71 Paul Carter, *The Road to Botany Bay: An Exploration of Landscape and History* (New York: Knopf 1988), 168; Cosgrove, *Social Formation*, 19.

72 Corwin, 'Victorian Travel Narrative,' 5; Carter, *Road to Botany Bay*, xxii.

73 Carter, *Road to Botany Bay*, xxii.

74 Robert A. Fothergill, *Private Chronicle: A Study of English Diaries* (London: Oxford University Press 1974), 50; quoted by Corwin, 'Victorian Travel Narratives,' 5.

75 See Gilthrow, Introduction to 'North American Travel Writing,' in Hassam, 'As I Write.'

76 Simon Pugh, *Garden, Nature, Language* (Manchester: Manchester University Press 1988), vii.

CHAPTER 2 Taming Niagara

1 McKinsey, *Niagara Falls*, 127.

2 Weiskel, *Romantic Sublime*, 3.

3 Popular histories include Gordon Donaldson, *Niagara! The Eternal Circus* (Toronto: Doubleday Canada 1979); Pierre Berton, *Niagara: A History of the Falls* (Toronto: McClelland and Stewart 1992). For scholarly studies of Niagara see McKinsey, *Niagara Falls*; Sears, *Sacred Places*; Rob Shields, *Places on the Margin: Alternative Geographies of Modernity* (London: Routledge 1991).

4 Johann Georg Kohl, *Travels in Canada and through the United States*, trans. J. Sinett (London 1861), 132.

5 McKinsey, *Niagara Falls*, 14–15.

6 Francois Gendron (1644–5), in Charles Mason Dow, *Anthology and Bibliography of Niagara Falls* (Albany 1921), 1:20, quoted by McKinsey, *Niagara Falls*, 8.

7 McKinsey, *Niagara Falls*, 8–17. Hennepin's description of Niagara is from his *A New Discovery of a Vast Country in America*, 1697.

8 Charles Prentice's Journal, ms., Baldwin Room, Toronto Metropolitan Reference Library.

9 McKinsey describes how the poet Alexander Wilson compared Niagara to Mecca, and how other visitors felt that at Niagara they 'must adore the Supreme Being' in *Niagara Falls*. Also see Sears, *Sacred Places*, 13; McGreevy, 'Niagara as Jerusalem'; Shields, *Places on the Margin*, 121–2.

10 Moore is quoted in Donaldson, *Niagara!*, 86; John Melish, *Travels through the United States of America in the Years 1806 and 1807, and 1809, 1810 and 1811 ... and Travels through Various Parts of Britain, Ireland, and Canada, with Corrections and Improvements till 1815* (Belfast 1816), 491; Priscilla Wakefield, *Excursions in North America; Described in Letters from a Gentleman and His Young Companion ...* (London 1806), 314.

11 Isaac Weld, Jr, *Travels through the States of North America and the Provinces of Upper and Lower Canada during the Years 1795, 1796, and 1797* (London 1800), 2: 128; George Heriot, *Travels through the Canadas, Containing a Description of the Picturesque Scenery on Some of the Rivers and Lakes* (London 1807), 159. See also Patrick Campbell, *Travels in the Interior Inhabited Parts of North America in the Years 1791 and 1792* (Edinburgh 1793), 174; Duke de la Rochefoucault-Liancourt, *Travels through the United States of North America, the Country of the Iroquois, and Upper Canada, in the Years 1795, 1796, and 1797* (London 1799), 218–20.

12 Timothy Bigelow, *Journal of a Tour to Niagara Falls in the Year 1805* (Boston 1876), 62; Wakefield, *Excursions*, 316; Heriot, *Travels*, 161; Christian Schultz, *Travels on an Inland Voyage* (New York 1810), 78–9; T.C., 'A Ride to Niagara,' in Dow, *Anthology*, 1196–98.

13 See the numerous editions of G.M. Davidson's *The Fashionable Tour: A Guide to Travellers Visiting the Middle and Northern States, and the Provinces of Canada* (Saratoga Springs), first pub. 1821.

14 Anon., *A Summer Month; or Recollections of a Visit to the Falls of Niagara and the Lakes* (Philadelphia 1823), 2.

15 John M. Duncan, *Travels through the United States and Canada in 1818 and 1819* (Glasgow 1823), 2: 38.

16 *Richard Barrett's Journal: New York and Canada, 1816*, ed. Thomas Brott and Philip Kelley (Winfield, Kansas 1983), 39; William Blane, *An Excursion through the United States and Canada during the Years 1822–23* (London 1824), 397; Edward Allen Talbot, *Five Years' Residence in the Canadas: Including a Tour through Part of the United States* (London 1824), 1: 123–31.

17 Robert Gourlay, *Statistical Account of Upper Canada* (London 1822), 1: 61–76.

18 John Galt, *Bogle Corbet; or, The Emigrants* (London 1831?), 217–25.

19 William Darby, *A Tour from the City of New York to Detroit in the Michigan Territory, Made between the Second of May and the Twenty-Second of September, 1818* (New York 1819), 167.

20 Robert L. Fraser, 'William Forsyth,' *Dictionary of Canadian Biography*, 7 (Toronto 1988), 311–12.

21 Ibid., 312; *Richard Barrett's Journal*, 40–4

22 Thomas Fowler, *The Journal of a Tour through British America to the Falls of Niagara* (Aberdeen 1832), 214; Blane, *An Excursion*, 402; Talbot, *Five Years' Residence*, 128; John Goldie, *Diary of a Journey through Upper Canada and Some of the New England States* (1819, pub. Toronto 1897), 27.

23 Blane, *An Excursion*, 402.

24 Forsyth's own testimony, quoted in Fraser, 'William Forsyth,' 313.

25 M. Smith, *A Geographical View of the Province of Upper Canada ... Containing a Complete Description of Niagara Falls* (Hartford 1813), 76–7, quoted in McKinsey, *Niagara Falls*, 44; Francis Hall, *Travels in Canada and the United States in 1816 and 1817* (London 1819), 183.

26 John Howison, *Sketches of Upper Canada, Domestic, Local, and Characteristic* (Edinburgh 1821), 75

27 Ibid., 76.

28 Goldie, *Diary of a Journey*, 23; E.T. Coke, *A Subaltern's Furlough: Descriptive of Scenes in Various Parts of the United States, Upper and Lower Canada, New Brunswick, and Nova Scotia* (New York 1833), 44; J.W. Orr, *A Pictorial Guide to the Falls of Niagara: A Manual for Visitors Giving an Account of This Stupendous Natural Wonder; and All the Objects of Curiosity in Its Vicinity, with Every Historical Incident of Interest* (Buffalo 1842), 182; Donald Horne, *The Great Museum: The Representation of History* (London 1984), 10.

29 [Mrs William Minot], 'Sketches of Scenery on Niagara River,' *North American Review* 2 (March 1816), 321. This reference was gleaned from McKinsey.

30 Ibid., 320–1; MacCannell, *The Tourist*, 128–9.

31 *Richard Barrett's Journal*, 48; William Dalton, *Travels in the United States of America and Part of Upper Canada* (Appleby, the author, 1821), 162, 184–5;

P. Stansbury, *A Pedestrian Tour of Two Thousand Three Hundred Miles in North America* (New York 1822), 122–8.

32 Goldie, *Diary of a Journey*, 23–4; Howison, *Sketches of Upper Canada*, 73–4.

33 Stansbury, *Pedestrian Tour*, 122–3; Minot, 'Sketches of Scenery,' 327–8.

34 Minot, 'Sketches of Scenery,' 327–8.

35 See, for example, Davidson, *The Fashionable Tour*, 4th ed. (Saratoga Springs 1930), 266; Fowler, *Journal* 233; Caroline Gilman, *The Poetry of Travelling in the United States* (New York 1838; repr. New York 1970), 111; Henry Tudor, *Narrative of a Tour of North America* (London 1834), 1: 263–4; James, *Niagara Falls: A Poem in Three Cantos* (Toronto 1843).

36 Dalton, *Travels*, 184; Donaldson, *Niagara!*, 115.

37 See McKinsey, *Niagara Falls*, 20–26.

38 Wakefield, *Excursions*, 318; Duncan. *Travels*, 2: 83ff.

39 Anon., *A Summer Month*, 20–5. He admits he is indebted for this information to Frances Wright's *Views of Society and Manners in America* (New York 1821).

40 Dalton, *Travels*, 152–3; Elizabeth Harvey to George F. Barlow, 8 Sept. 1820, MU 4563, no. 19, Archives of Ontario.

41 See McKinsey, *Niagara Falls*; Ernest Green, 'The Niagara Portage Road,' *Ontario History* 23 (1926), 260–311.

42 Eliot Warburton, *Hochelaga, or England in the New World* (London 1846), 235–6.

43 John Hope Franklin, *A Southern Odyssey: Travelers in the Antebellum North* (Baton Rouge: Louisiana State University 1976); Davidson, *The Traveller's Guide* (Saratoga Springs 1833), 17.

44 Roger Haydon, *Upstate Travels: British Views of Nineteenth Century New York* (Syracuse: Syracuse University Press 1982), 6–10; Horatio A. Parsons, *The Book of Niagara Falls* (Buffalo 1836), 91.

45 The poster advertising the event is reproduced in Ralph Greenhill and Thomas D. Mahoney, *Niagara* (Toronto: University of Toronto Press 1969), 90.

46 William L. Mackenzie, *Sketches of Canada and the United States* (London 1833), 94–7.

47 Kohl, *Travels*, 176.

48 On Niagara poetry, see Dow, *Anthology*, vol. 2. This stanza is from a poem by A.N.C., first published in 1836.

49 For some accounts of the experience, see F. Fitzgerald de Roos, *Personal Narrative of Travels in the United States and Canada in 1826* (London 1827), 170–7; Gilman, *Poetry of Travelling*, 106; Edward Strutt Abdy, *Journal of a Residence and Tour of the United States of North America* (London 1835),

287–8; Tudor, *Narrative of a Tour*, 1: 235–6; Thomas Hamilton, *Men and Manners in America* (Edinburgh 1833), 2: 316–27; Warburton, *Hochalega*, 234–6; Lady Emmeline Stuart-Wortley, *Tours in the United States etc. during 1849 and 1850* (New York 1851), 21–31.

50 Anna Jameson, *Winter Studies and Summer Rambles in Canada* (London 1838), 1: 82–3.

51 On the history of the industry, see Fraser, 'William Forsyth,' 312–15; George A. Seibel, *Ontario's Niagara Parks: 100 Years* (Niagara Falls 1985); and Greenhill and Mahoney, *Niagara*. On the bloody rivalries of the 1870s, see Berton, *Niagara*, 162–72.

52 Charles Latrobe, *The Rambler in North America* (London 1835), 73–4; Isabella L. Bishop, *The Englishwoman in America* (London 1856), 218–20.

53 McKinsey, *Niagara Falls*, 140; Bishop, *Englishwoman in America*, 228; Abdy, *Journal*, 293.

54 Latrobe, *Rambler*, 73–4. For comment in the press, see 'Niagara with Improvements,' *Globe* (2 August 1848), 1; *Globe* (18 August 1849), 23.

55 For descriptions of hotels, see Fowler, *Journal*, 214; Robert J. Vanderwater, *The Tourist: or Pocket Manual for Travellers ... to Niagara Falls* (New York 1835), 73; James Taylor, *Narrative of a Voyage* (Hull 1846), 56.

56 *The Canadian Journal of Alfred Domett*, ed. E.A. Horseman and L.R. Denson (London, Ont. 1955), 30; James Edward Alexander, *Transatlantic Sketches* (London 1833), 143.

57 Gilman, *The Poetry of Travelling*, 110, Captain Basil Hall, *Travels in North America in the Years 1827 and 1828* (Edinburgh 1830), 187–8; O'Brien Journal, ms 199, reel 2, Journal no. 64, Archives of Ontario; William H.G. Kingston, *Western Wanderings: or A Pleasure Tour in the Canadas* (London 1856), 270–1.

58 Warburton, *Hochalega*, 235.

59 Parsons, *Book of Niagara Falls*, 13–17.

60 Bishop, *Englishwoman in America*, 120; Francis Duncan, *Our Garrisons in the West* (London 1864), 206.

61 *Canadian Tourist* (Montreal 1856), 8–9.

62 Warburton, *Hochalega*, 236.

63 William Fleming, *Four Days at the Falls of Niagara* (Manchester 1835), 8.

64 Warburton, *Hochalega*, 236; Fleming, *Four Days*, 8; Fowler, *Journal*, 216; Alexander Dunlop, *The New World Journals of Alexander Graham Dunlop (1845)*, ed. D. Sinclair and G. Warkentin (Toronto: Dundurn Press 1976), 48–9. For a different description, see *Canadian Journal of Alfred Domett*, 28. One woman's experience is recounted in the O'Brien Journal, Archives of Ontario.

65 Isabella Trotter, *First Impressions of the New World* (London 1859), 54–5; Parsons, *Book of Niagara Falls*, 73–4.

66 Trotter, *First Impressions*, 55; William Cullen Bryant, *Picturesque America, or the Land We Live In* (New York c. 1872), 442; Kohl, *Travels*, 156; Robert Playfair, *Recollections of a Visit to the United States and British Provinces of North America in the Years 1847, 1848, and 1849* (London 1856), 59.

67 Kohl, *Travels*, 156

68 Playfair, *Recollections*, 59.

69 Kohl, *Travels*, 158.

70 Lieutenant Levinge, *Echoes in the Backwoods*, quoted by Greenhill and Mahoney, *Niagara*, 112.

71 See Stuart Ewen, *All Consuming Images: The Politics of Style in Contemporary Culture* (New York: Basic Books 1988), 24–6; McKinsey, *Niagara Falls*, 147.

72 O.L. Holley, *The Picturesque Tourist: Being a Guide through the Northern and Eastern States and Canada* (New York 1844), 213.

73 Orr, *Pictorial Guide*, 43, 69; Holley, *Picturesque Tourist*, 216.

74 Coke, *Subaltern's Furlough*, 24; Orr, *Pictorial Guide*, 194.

75 Kingston, *Western Wanderings*, 269, 296.

76 *Traveller's Guide* (1840), 206.

77 MacCannell, *The Tourist*, 123.

78 Jesse Walker, *Queenston, a Tale of the Niagara Frontier* (Buffalo 1845), 107.

79 Fowler, *Journal*, 211. For other responses to the Brock Monument, see Hall, *Travels*, 257–8; James Thomas Horton, *Rambles in the United States and Canada during the Year 1845* (London 1846), 87–8; Taylor, *Narrative*, 54; Joseph Pickering, *Inquiries of an Emigrant* (London 1831), 94; Andrew Picken, *The Canadas* (London 1832), 2: 183: Gilman, *Poetry of Travelling*, 110–11; David Wilkie, *Sketches of a Summer Trip to New York and the Canadas* (Edinburgh 1837), 150; Coke, *Subaltern's Furlough*, 43–5; Patrick Shirreff, *A Tour through North America* (Edinburgh 1835), 88; Abdy, *Journal*, 1: 299.

80 Kohl, *Travels*, 134.

81 William Burr, *Burr's Moving Mirror of the Lakes, the Niagara, St Lawrence, and Saguenay Rivers* (Boston 1850), 13–14.

82 Stuart Wortley, *Tours*, 25.

83 Ibid, 23.

84 Dunlop, *New World Journals*, 46.

85 Kohol, *Travels*, 134.

CHAPTER 3 Wilderness Panorama

1 Norman Lacey, *Wordsworth's View of Nature and Its Ethical Consequences* (Hamden, Conn.: Archon Books 1965), 85.

2 Henry David Thoreau, *The Maine Woods* (1864; New York: Harper & Row 1987), 5.

3 C.D. Arfwedson, *The United States and Canada in 1832, 1833, 1834* (London 1834), 320. For the itinerary, see Davidson, ed., *The Fasionable Tour,* 4th ed., 282–3; on the development of navigation on the St Lawrence River, see Edwin C. Guillet, ed., *Pioneer Travel in Upper Canada* (University of Toronto Press 1972).

4 Talbot, *Five Years' Residence,* 1: 95.

5 Florence Marsh, *Wordsworth's Imagery: A Study in Poetic Vision* (New Haven: Yale University Press 1952), 91.

6 See Charles Norton Coe, *Wordsworth and the Literature of Travel* (New York: Bookman Associates 1953); Russell Noyes, *Wordswoth and the Art of Landscape* (Bloomington: Indiana University Press 1968). Also see Frederic S. Coldwell, *Rivermen: A Romantic Iconography of the River and the Source* (Kingston and Montreal: McGill-Queen's University Press 1989). On the Romantics' differing interpretations of water, see David Perkins, *The Quest for Permanence: the Symbolism of Wordsworth, Shelley, and Keats* (Cambridge, Mass.: Harvard University Press 1959).

7 Andres, *Search for the Picturesque,* 89.

8 Rev. Gilpin, quoted in Andrews, *Search for the Picturesque,* 89.

9 Sears, *Sacred Places,* 47–91.

10 Alexander von Humboldt, *Cosmos* (London 1849–58), 2: 457, quoted in Sears, *Sacred Places,* 51. On the panorama, see Sears, 50–2; McKinsey, *Niagara Falls,* 65–7.

11 Talbot, *Five Years' Residence in Canada,* 1: 95.

12 *The New World Journals of Alexander Dunlop* (1845), ed. David Sinclair and Germaine Warkentin (Toronto: Dundern Press 1976), 57; Tudor, *Narrative of a Tour,* 296; Richard Bonnycastle, *The Canadas in 1841* (London 1841), 1: 104.

13 Warburton, *Hochelaga,* 217.

14 *Canadian Journal of Alfred Domett,* 21.

15 Tudor, *Narrative of a Tour,* 295.

16 Rollo Campbell, *Two Lectures on Canada* (Greenock, 1857), 28; Tudor, *Narrative of a Tour,* 295; *Canadian Journal of Alfred Domett;* Bishop, *Englishwoman in America,* 243; George Tuthill Borrett, *Out West: A Series of Letters from Canada* (London 1866), 49; Duncan, *Garrisons,* 182; James Booty, *Three Months in Canada and the United States* (London 1862), 62.

17 James Dixon, *Personal Narrative of a Tour through Part of the United States and Canada* (New York 1849), 138; Gilman, *Poetry of Travelling,* 117; [A.W.M. Rose], *Pioneer of the Wilderness: The Emigrant Churchman in Canada*

(London 1849), 57–8; T.D.L., *A Peep at the Western World* (New York 1860), 114–15; Copleston, *Canada*, 23.

18 *A Summer Month*, 106; Taylor, *Narrative of a Voyage*, 16–17; Dixon, *Personal Narrative*, 138.

19 Arfwedson, *United States and Canada*, 2: 330; Copleston, *Canada*, 23.

20 Tudor, *Narrative of a Tour*, 295.

21 Quoted in Bonnycastle, *Canadas in 1841*, 1: 90–2.

22 Wakefield, *Excursion*, 297.

23 Duncan, *Travels*, 2: 124–38.

24 Blane, *An Excursion*, 438.

25 *Ontario and St Lawrence Steamboat Company Handbook for Travellers to Niagara Falls, Montreal, ...* (Buffalo 1858), 109.

26 Bonnycastle, *Canadas in 1841*, 1: 93.

27 Ibid., 1: 93. And see James Croil, *Steam Navigation and Its Relation to the Commerce of Canada and the United States* (Toronto 1898), 326.

28 Charles Lanman, *Adventures in the Wilds of the United States and British American Provinces* (Philadelphia 1856), 114. Also see Bonnycastle, *Canadas in 1841*, 1: 93. Explorers' and others' accounts containing descriptions of voyageurs include those of Alexander Henry, Nicholas Garry, Gabriel Franchere, Daniel William Harmon, George Heriot, Alexander Mackenzie, and Thomas McKenney.

29 Bonnycastle, *Canadas in 1841*, 1: 94–5.

30 Alexander, *Transatlantic Sketches*, 174; Duncan, *Travels*, 2: 121–3; Talbot, *Five Years' Residence*, 1: 254–5.

31 Norah Story, *Oxford Companion to Canadian History and Literature* (Toronto 1967), 146.

32 'The Canadian Boat Song,' as reprinted in Talbot, *Five Years' Residence*, 1: 85.

33 Hall, *Travels*, 382–3.

34 Ibid.; and see *Canadian Journal of Alfred Domett*, 19; Taylor, *Narrative*, 15–16; Dixon, *Personal Narrative*, 139.

35 Bonnycastle, *Canadas in 1841*, 2: 28.

36 Tudor, *Narrative of a Tour*, 299.

37 Gilman, *Poetry of Travelling*, 118.

38 N.A. Woods, *The Prince of Wales in Canada and the United States* (London 1861), 150.

39 John Thornton, *Diary of a Tour through the Northern States of the Union and of Canada* (London 1850), 57; Warburton, *Hochelega*, 213; T.D.L., *A Peep*, 63; William Chambers, *Things As They Are in America* (London 1854), 97–8; J. Churchill, *The United States and Canada* (London 1862), 91.

40 'Down the St. Lawrence,' *Globe* (10 August 1863).
41 *Handbook of Canadian Excursion Routes via Grand Trunk Railway and Canadian Navigation Company* (1878).
42 Copleston, *Canada*, 17; Duncan, *Garrisons*, 171.
43 *Globe* (2 July 1847), 2; and see Patricia Vervoort, 'Sunrise on the Saguenay: Popular Literature and the Sublime,' *Mosaic* 21 (spring 1988), 123–38.
44 Joseph Earl Arrington, 'William Burr's Moving Panorama of the Great Lakes, the Niagara, St Lawrence and Saguenay Rivers,' *Ontario History* 51 (1959), 141–62. The panorama was destroyed long ago, but for a description of the scenes depicted, see *Descriptive and Historical View of Burr's Moving Mirror of the Lakes, the Niagara, St Lawrence, and Saguenay Rivers* (Boston 1850).
45 *The River St Lawrence in One Panoramic View, from Niagara Falls to Quebec* (New York 185?).
46 For example, see Bonnycastle, *Canadas in 1841*, 1: 96–101; Warburton, *Hochelega*, 216; Bishop, *Englishwoman*, 245; J.C. Myers, *Sketches on a Tour through the Northern States, the Canadas, and Nova Scotia* (Virginia 1849), 188; George Moore, *Journal of a Voyage Across the Atlantic* (London 1845), 53.
47 James Doyle, *North of America: Images of Canada in the Literature of the United States* (Toronto: ECW Press 1983).
48 See Davidson, *Fashionable Tour* (1840), 245; Holley, *Picturesque Tourist* (1844), 228–9; *River St Lawrence*, 27; *The Canadian Tourist*, 48–9; *Hunter's Panoramic Guide from Niagara to Quebec* (Cleveland 1857), 29–30; *Ontario and St Lawrence Steamboat Company Handbook* (Buffalo 1858) 109; *The Canadian Handbook and Tourist's Guide* (Montreal 1867); 115–16, Bishop, *Englishwoman*, 245; Moore, *Journal of a Voyage*, 53.
49 Warburton, *Hochelega*, 216; *The Canadian Tourist*, 49; Arrington, 'William Burr's Moving Panorama,' 150.
50 George Monro Grant and Agnes Maule Machar, 'Eastern Ontario,' in Grant, ed. *Picturesque Canada: The Country As It Was and Is* (Toronto 1882), 2, 671; *Hunter's Panoramic Guide*, 27; Charles G.D. Roberts, *The Canadian Guidebook: The Tourists's and Sportsman's Guide to Eastern Canada and Newfoundland* (New York 1891), 44.
51 Holley, *Picturesque Tourist*, 230; John Disturnell, *A Trip through the Lakes of North America* (New York 1857), 263.
52 *Canadian Handbook*, 120.
53 Grant and Machar, 'Eastern Ontario,' 673.
54 *Steamboat Company Handbook*, 114; *Hunter's Panoramic Guide*, 36.
55 *Hunter's Panoramic Guide*, 36–7; *Canadian Handbook*, 118; *Steamboat Company Handbook*, 114–15.

56 *Canadian Handbook*, 120; Captain Mac, *Canada, from the Lakes to the Gulf* (Montreal 1881), 50–57. Also see Gardner B. Chapin, 'The Church Bell of Caughnawaga,' *Tales of the St Lawrence* (Rouse's Point 1873), 139–52.

57 Bishop, *Englishwoman*, 245.

58 A.S. *A Summer Trip to Canada* (London 1885), 104.

59 *Canadian Tourist*, 46–7; *Hunter's Panoramic Guide*, 30; Borrett, *Out West*, 47; Charles Mackay, *Life and Liberty in America, or Sketches of a Tour in the United States and Canada in 1857–8* (London 1859), 306; *New World in 1859*, (New York 1959) 44–5.

60 *Canadian Tourist*, 46–7; W.H. Withrow, *Our Own Country Canada: Scenic and Descriptive* (Toronto 1889), 266–70.

61 Woods, *Prince of Wales*, 137–8; 'Down the St Lawrence'; Rev. H. Jones, *Railway Notes in the North West, or the Dominion of Canada* (London 1884), 40.

62 W. George Beers, 'The "Voyageurs" of Canada,' *British American Magazine* (1863), 472–4.

63 D.D. Calvin, 'Rafting on the St Lawrence,' *Canadian Geographical Journal* (October 1931), 271; Adam Shortt, 'Down the St Lawrence on a Timber Raft,' *Queen's Quarterly*, 10 (July 1902), 16–34.

64 *Hunter's Panoramic Guide*, 28.

65 William Varley, 'Tourist Attractions in Ontario,' *Travel* 15 (1900), 27–8; Frank Yeigh, *Through the Heart of Canada* (London 1892), 145–7; Roberts, *Canadian Guidebook*, 54–5. Roberts quotes Archibald Lampman's 'Between the Rapids' in full.

66 Peter O'Leary, *Travels and Experiences in Canada, the Red River Territory, and the United States* (London 1876), 64.

67 *Canadian Handbook*, 21; J.D. Borthwick, *The Tourist's Pleasure Book* (Montreal 1874), 12; 'A Trip on the Ottawa,' *Harper's New Monthly Magazine* (August 1885), 340–1; G. Mercer Adam, *Canada: Historical and Descriptive* (Toronto 1888), 20; J.B. Loudon, *A Tour through Canada and the United States of America* (Coventry 1879), 112; Douglas Sladen, *On the Cars and Off* (London 1895), 124–6.

68 O'Leary, *Travels and Experiences*, 288; Captain Mac, *Canada, from the Lakes to the Gulf* (Montreal 1881), 24–7.

69 Borrett, *Out West*, 42; and see Amelia Murray, *Letters from the United States, Cuba, and Canada* (New York 1856), 93–4; *Canadian Handbook*, 101–2; Mackay, *Life and Liberty*, 291–2.

70 *Canadian Handbook*, 103.

71 F.A. Dixon, 'Ottawa,' in Grant, ed. *Picturesque Canada*, 1: 176.

72 *Canadian Handbook*, 102–4.

73 Kohl, *Travels in Canada*, 1: 220.

74 Lady Dufferin, *My Canadian Journal, 1872–78*, ed. Gladys Chantler Walker (Don Mills 1969), 6–7. And see Woods, *Prince of Wales*, 163–5; Roberts, *Canadian Guidebook*, 52.

75 Woods, *Prince of Wales*, 165; *Across the Canadian Prairies: A Two Month Holiday in the Dominion* (London 1895), 19; Karl Baedeker, *The Dominion of Canada with Newfoundland and an Excursion to Alaska* (Leipsic 1894), 147.

76 Sladen, *On the Cars and Off*, 132.

77 See *The Excursionists' Hand-book and Saturday Half-Holiday Guide to Places within Easy distance of Montreal by Rail and River* (1886).

78 Trotter, *First Impressions*, 57–8; Woods, *Prince of Wales*, 139.

79 Grant and Machar, 'Eastern Ontario,' 668–9.

80 See Russell J. Harper, *Painting in Canada: A History* (Toronto: University of Toronto Press 1977), 17; Dennis Reid, *'Our Own Country Canada': Being an Account of the National Aspirations of the Principal Landscape Artists in Montreal and Toronto, 1860–90* (Ottawa: National Gallery of Canada 1979).

81 Agnes Maule Machar, 'Drifting among the Thousand Islands,' in *Lays of the 'True North,' and Other Canadian Poems* (London 1902), 62–3; Evan Macgill, *Poems and Songs* (Toronto 1883), 192.

82 'President Grant in the Thousand Islands,' *Globe* (3 August 1872), 1.

83 Frederic W. Falls, 'The Thousand Islands,' *Canadian Magazine* (December 1894), 153.

84 Charles Elliot, *A Trip to Canada and the Far North-West* (London 1887), 53; William Smith, *A Yorkshireman's Trip to the United States and Canada* (London 1892), 268.

85 Roberts, *Canadian Guidebook*, 45; Grant and Machar, 'Eastern Canada,' 671; Argyll, *Canadian Pictures: Drawn with Pen and Pencil* (London 1885), 76; *Globe* (10 August 1895).

86 Alfred William Cutler, 'A Vacation amongst the Thousand Islands,' *The Travel Magazine* (June 1908), 396–9; Clifton Johnson, *The Picturesque St Lawrence* (New York 1910), 30.

87 Roberts, *Canadian Guidebook*, 45.

88 Grant and Machar, 'Eastern Ontario,' 671; Elliot, *Trip to Canada*, 53; *Hints for Pleasure Seekers: The Thousand Islands, the Summer Paradise of the St Lawrence River, By One Who Has Been There* (Watertown, New York 1885).

89 *Chrisholm's All Around Route and Panoramic Guide of the St Lawrence* (Montreal 1872); *Earth's Grandest River, the St Lawrence* (Watertown, New York 1895); *The Routes Pursued by the Excursion Steamers upon the St Lawrence River* (Albany 1895); *Craig's A.B.C. Key to the River St Lawrence* (Toronto 1901); Clifton Johnson, *The Picturesque St Lawrence* (New York: Macmillan 1910).

90 Roberts, *Canadian Guidebook*, 44.

91 *Gateway of Tourist Travel* (Toronto, 1897), 25; Baedeker, *Dominion of Canada*, 185; Johnson, *Picturesque St Lawrence*, 30.

92 'The Summer Girl,' *Globe* (10 August 1895); *Routes*, 26; Cutler, 'Vacation amongst the Thousand Islands.'

CHAPTER 4 Native Lands

1 Bonnycastle, *The Canadas in 1841*, 2: 7–8.

2 On the Robinson Superior Treaty, see Dennis H. McPherson and J. Douglas Rabb, *Indian from the Inside: A Study in Ethno-Metaphysics*. Lakehead University Centre from Northern Studies, Occasional Paper no. 14 (Thunder Bay 1993), 36–8.

3 H.S. Tanner, *The Traveller's Hand Book for the State of New York, the Provinces of Canada, and Parts of the Adjoining States* (New York 1845), 113.

4 Pratt, *Imperial Eyes*, 4.

5 Adam Hodgson, *Letters from North America* (London 1824), 340.

6 See Stephen Daniels, 'The Political Iconography of Woodland in Later Georgian England,' in Cosgrove and Daniels, eds., *The Iconography of Landscape*, 43–82.

7 Thornton, *Diary of a Tour*, 41; and see Taylor, *Narrative*, 111–13; Chambers, *Things As they Are*, 123; William Brown, *America: A Four Years' Residence* (Leeds 1849), 81; *Canadian Journal of Alfred Domett*, 23; Howison, *Sketches of Upper Canada*, 165–6.

8 *Works of Washington Irving*, vol. 3, *Astoria* (New York: G.P. Putnam's Sons 1949), 45–8.

9 George A. Mackenzie, 'The Upper Lakes,' in *Picturesque Canada*, 274–6; G. Mercer Adam, *The Canadian North West: Its History and Its Troubles* (Toronto 1885), 35–7.

10 These were collected and published in Lanman's *Adventures in the Wilds of the United States and British North American Provinces* (1856). See Lanman's 'Preface,' and James Doyle, *North America: Images of Canada in the Literature of the United States, 1775–1900* (Toronto: ECW Press 1983), 88.

11 Lanman, *Adventures in the Wilds*, 1: 100–17. Menaboujou refers to the same entity as the more commonly used names *Nanabijou* or *Nanabozho*. A wide variety of spellings are used, and there are many different stories concerning Nanabijou. For some examples, see Selwyn Dewdney, *The Sacred Scrolls of the Sourthern Ojibway* (Toronto: University of Toronto Press for the Glenbow-Alberta Institute 1975), 40–3.

12 See Douglas Leechman, 'Longfellow's Hiawatha,' *Queen's Quarterly* 45 (1944). Schoolcraft was an ethnologist, geologist, and U.S. superintendent of Indian Affairs at Sault Ste Marie.

13 *The Complete Works of Henry Wadsworth Longfellow*, Cambridge ed. (London: George Routledge 1895), 113.

14 For example, see Canadian Pacific Railway, *Summer Tours to the Upper Lakes* (1902).

15 I.M. Slusser, 'Hiawath Land,' *Rod and Gun* (July 1903), 57–62; and see 'The Hiawatha Drama – Performed by Ojibway Indians,' *Rod and Gun* (September 1900), 321.

16 See Doyle, *North of America*, 85–7.

17 Jameson, *Winter Studies*.

18 Schoolcraft quoted in Clara Thomas, *Love and Work Enough: The Life of Anna Jameson* (Toronto: University of Toronto Press 1967), 135.

19 Jameson, *Winter Studies*, 444.

20 Ibid., 439–441, 521–7.

21 Ibid., 469.

22 Ibid., 459, 510, 305, 322.

23 Kingston, *Western Wanderings*, 134. Kingston wrote young people's adventure stories, many of which were published by the Society for Promoting Christian Knowledge, and was secretary of a colonization society. He published *The Log House: A Tale of Canada* in 1864.

24 Kingston, *Western Wanderings*, 131, 135–7, 151, 219, 169.

25 Robert Michael Ballantyne, *Hudson's Bay: Or Every-day Life in the Wilds of North America* (Nelson ed. 1912), 223–4.

26 On literary representations of Native people, see Mary Lu MacDonald, 'Red and White Men: Black, White and Grey Hats,' *Canadian Literature* (spring–summer 1990), 92–111; Goldie, *Fear and Temptation*; Ronald G. Haycock, *The Image of the Indian* (Waterloo: Wilfrid Laurier University Press 1971); Thomas King et al., *The Native in Literature* (Oakville, Ont.: ECW Press 1987); Leslie Monkman, *A Native Heritage: Images of the Indian in English-Canadian Literature* (Toronto: University of Toronto Press 1981).

27 Henry C. Campbell, *Early Days on the Great Lakes: The Art of William Armstrong* (Toronto: McClelland and Stewart 1971); Janet E. Clark and Robert Stacey, *Frances Anne Hopkins, 1838–1919: Canadian Scenery / Le Paysage Canadien* (Thunder Bay: Thunder Bay Art Gallery 1990).

28 Reid, *'Our Own Country Canada,'* 209–10.

29 *Summer Tours by the Canadian Pacific Railway* (1887), 75–6. *Chippewa* is another term for *Ojibway*, more commonly used in the United States.

30 Lawrence Oliphant, *Minnesota and the Far West* (Edinburgh 1855), 93–4.

31 J. Ewing Ritchie, *To Canada with Emmigrants: A Record of Actual Experiences* (London 1885), 114, reprinted in Thunder Bay Historical Museum Society *Papers and Records* (1977), 13. Port Arthur (formerly Prince Arthur's Landing) and Fort William (orginally a fur-trade post) were the principal settlements at the Lakehead. The name Thunder Bay is centuries old, and was used to describe the location and its settlements throughout this period.

32 Advertisement for the *Algoma*, *Globe* (15 August 1866).

33 *Globe* (19 August 1867); Grant, *Ocean to Ocean*, 30.

34 Mary Fitzgibbon, *A Trip to Manitoba, or Roughing It on the Line* (Toronto 1880), 15. Fitzgibbon was Susanna Moodie's granddaughter.

35 J.H. Coyne, 'Across Georgian Bay in 1871,' reprinted in Ontario Historical Society *Papers and Records* 28 (1932), 26.

36 Anonymous, 'Trip to Fort William on Lake Superior, August 1, 1867,' Thunder Bay Historical Museum Society Archives, A 3/1/1.

37 *A Pleasure Trip, Toronto to Duluth, July 1880* (Toronto 1880), privately printed, Baldwin Room, Toronto Metropolitan Library.

38 'Up the Lakes,' *Globe* (30 July 1880).

39 George Wyatt, *Traveller's and Sportsman's Guide* (Liverpool 1880), 20.

40 'To Fort William and Back,' *Globe* (25 July 1865).

41 'Summer Holiday: Sama Continues Her Wanderings on the Lakes,' *Globe* (18 August 1894).

42 'Trip to Fort William,' *Globe* (19 August 1867).

43 James Trow, *A Trip to Manitoba* (Quebec 1875), 6.

44 Coyne, 'Across Georgian Bay,' 28.

45 George Grant, *Ocean to Ocean* (Toronto 1873), 34.

46 Coyne, 'Across Georgian Bay,' 26–7; Fraser W. Rae, *Newfoundland to Manitoba* (New York 1881), 144.

47 'In the North Channel,' *Globe* (8 July 1884).

48 Oliphant, *Minnesota and the Far West* 92–4; Kingston, *Western Wanderings*, 1: 194–5.

49 Anon., *Pleasure Trip*, 7.

50 Fitzgibbon, *Trip to Manitoba*, 25.

51 Canada, Sessional Papers, Department of Indian Affairs, 1889.

52 Anon. *Pleasure Trip*, 7: *Canadian Handbook*, 147–8.

53 Rae, *Newfoundland to Manitoba*, 150.

54 'A Trip Up the Lakes,' *Globe* (12 August 1887).

55 Rae, *Newfoundland to Manitoba*, 150.

56 Baedeker, *Dominion of Canada* (1894); Canadian Pacific Railway, *Summer Tours to the Upper Lakes* (1902), 14.

57 *Globe* (25 July 1865); (19 August 1867); (8 July 1884); (12 August 1887).
58 Quoted in Barlow Cumberland, ed., *The Northern Lakes of Canada* (Toronto 1886), 171.
59 'Trip up the Lakes.'
60 John A. Butler, 'The North Shore,' *Harper's New Monthly Magazine* 69/409 (1884), 105.
61 'Trip up the Lakes.'
62 J.H. Coyne, 'A Week on Lake Superior,' first published in the *St Thomas Journal* (July 1871), reprinted in Thunder Bay Historical Museum Society, *18th and 19th Annual Reports and Papers* (127–8), 131.
63 Bryant, *Picturesque America*, 408; *Handbook for the Dominion* (Montreal 1888); Anon., *Pleasure Trip*, 15; Rae, *Newfoundland to Manitoba* 163; 'Trip up the Lakes'; Alfred Pegler, *A Visit to Canada and the United States* (Southampton 1884), 21; Walpole Roland, *Algoma West: Its Mines Scenery, and Industrial Resources* (Toronto 1887), 17–18; Cumberland, ed., *The Northern Lakes*, 179.
64 'Thunder Bay and the Kaministiquia Half a Century Ago: A Letter from Catherine Moodie Vickers to Her Mother, Susanna Moodie' (August 31 1873), Thunder Bay Historical Society, *Sixteenth and Seventeenth Annual Reports and Papers* (1925–6), 53.
65 Butler, 'The North Shore,' 113; Annie E. McIntyre, 'John McIntyre,' Thunder Bay Historical Society *Eighteenth and Nineteenth Annual Reports* (1927–8), 78.
66 Mackenzie, 'The Upper Lakes,' 274–6; and see Sanford Fleming, *England and Canada: A Summer Tour between Old and New Westminster, with Historical Notes* (Montreal 1884), 165–70.
67 Butler, 'The North Shore,' 112–13.
68 'Trip up the Lakes.'
69 Thunder Bay and the Kaministiquia,' 57.
70 Cumberland, *Northern Lakes*, 182.
71 See E.J. Hart, *The Selling of Canada: The CPR and the Beginnings of Canadian Tourism* (Banff: Altitude Press 1983); Esther Fraser, *The Canadian Rockies: Early Travels and Explorations* (Edmonton: M.G. Hurtig 1969).
72 See *Along the Line of the Canadian Pacific Railway*, 2, no. 12, tourist ed. (London July 1885); *Summer Tours by the CPR* (1887); *Fishing Resorts along the Canadian Pacific Railway* (Montreal 1887); W.O. Armstrong, *A Canoe Trip through Temagaming the Peerless in the Land of Hiawatha* (1900); *Summer Tours to the Upper Lakes* (1902).
73 P.H. Bryce, *Health Resorts and Climates of Canada* (1897). And see CPR, *By the West to the East* (London 1885); *The New Highway to the Orient: Around the World* (1900).

74 For example, see 'Toronto to Winnipeg: Marguerite's Experiences on a Railway Train,' *Globe* (July 4 1891).

75 Clive Phillipps-Wolley, *A Sportsman's Eden* (London 1888), 32–3; Rupert Brooke, *Letters from America* (London: Sidgewick and Jackson 1916), 101; Edward Roper, *By Track or Trail: A Journey through Canada* (London 1891), 29; *A Holiday Trip: Montreal to Victoria and Return via the Canadian Pacific Railway* (Montreal 1888).

76 Northrop Frye, 'Conclusion to a *Literary History of Canada*,' in *The Bush Garden: Essays on the Canadian Imagination* (House of Anansi 1971), 221.

77 Stuart Cumberland, *The Queen's Highway from Ocean to Ocean* (London 1897), 302.

78 Mrs Howard Vincent, *Newfoundland to Cochin China* (London 1892), 39.

79 John Foster Fraser, *Canada As It Is* (London 1905), 90.

80 For example, see John W.C. Haldane, *3,800 Miles across Canada* (London 1900), 79–83; Thomas W. Wilby, *A Motor Tour through Canada* (London 1914), 147; Sir Henry Edward, *A Two Months' Tour in Canada and the United States* (London 1889).

81 Fraser, *Canada As It Is*, 99.

CHAPTER 5 A Rest Cure in a Canoe

1 *Canadian Magazine Advertiser* throughout 1912.

2 White 'Forms of Wildness,' 33.

3 On the popularity of Thoreau in Canada, see George Stewart, 'Henry David Thoreau,' *Canadian Magazine* (December 1894).

4 Nash, *Wilderness and the American Mind*. On *Walden*'s popularity in Canada, see 'Henry David Thoreau,' *Canadian Magazine* (December 1894), 101–9.

5 See Daniel Pick, *The Faces of Degeneration* (New York: Cambridge University Press 1989); Samuel Hynes, *The Edwardian Turn of Mind* (Princeton: Princeton University Press 1968); Nash, *Wilderness and the American Mind*; Peter J. Schmitt, *Back to Nature: The Arcadian Myth in Urban America* (New York 1969).

6 Jackson Lears, *No Place of Grace: Antimodernism and the Transformation of American Culture, 1880–1920* (New York: Pantheon 1981).

7 See Phyllis Hembry, *The English Spa 1560–1815* (London: Athlone Press 1989); 'The Romance of Travel,' *Quarterly Review* 149 (1880), 225.

8 Janet Oppenheim, *Shattered Nerves: Doctors, Patients, and Depression in Victorian England* (New York: Oxford University Press 1991), 124.

9 George M. Beard, *Sexual Neurasthenia*, quoted by Barbara Sicherman, 'The Uses of a Diagnosis: Doctors, Patients, and Neurasthenia,' in Judith

Walzer Leavitt and Ronald L. Numbers, eds., *Sickness and Health in America: Readings in the History of Medicine and Public Health* (University of Wisconsin Press 1978), 25. Also see Lears, *No Place of Grace*, 47–58.

10 Daniel Clark, *Neurasthenia* (Toronto 1888).

11 'A Rest Cure in a Canoe,' *Rod and Gun in Canada* (October 1910), 619.

12 Jean Graham, 'Camping Out,' *Canadian Magazine* (July 1912), 272.

13 Clark, *Neurasthenia*, 8–9.

14 *Canadian Magazine Advertiser* (April 1906), 63.

15 Weir Mitchell, *When All the Woods Are Green* (New York 1894), quoted in Doyle, *North of America*, 117–19.

16 Robert Owen, 'The Coming North,' *Rod and Gun* (December 1903), 379.

17 For examples of how these themes were brought together, see John Hague, 'Aspects of Lake Ontario,' *Canadian Magazine* (June 1893), 261–3; Arnold Haultain, *Two Country Walks in Canada* (Toronto: George N. Morang 1903); *Canada: Painted by T. Mower Martin, Described by Wilfred Campbell* (London: A. & C. Black 1907).

18 *Outdoor Canada* (September 1908), 75.

19 *The Poems of Archibald Lampman* (Toronto: University of Toronto Press 1974), 179, 17.

20 Lears, *No Place of Grace*, 56.

21 Kent Family Papers, Yale University Library, quoted by Nash, *Wilderness*, 153.

22 Thomas W. Gibson, 'Algonquin National Park,' *Canadian Magazine* (1894), 543.

23 W.A. Craik, 'Summer Holidays and Where to Spend Them,' *Rod and Gun* (June 1911), 20–7.

24 Peter Bailey, *Leisure and Class in Victorian England: Rational Recreation and the Contest for Control, 1830–1885* (London: Routledge and Kegan Paul 1978).

25 See Kenneth Roberts, 'A Society of Leisure,' in J.F. Murphy, ed., *Concepts of Leisure: Philosophical Implications* (Englewood Cliffs, N.J. 1974); Patricia Jasen, 'Attitudes to Leisure in Edwardian England' (M.A. thesis, University of Manitoba, 1980).

26 Roper, *By Track and Trail*, 423.

27 Katherine Hughes, 'The Canadian Summer Girl,' *Rod and Gun* (August 1904), 120; 'Women's Work and Ways,' *Globe* (25 July 1891); 'Tide of American Travel,' *Globe* (18 July 1890).

28 Ella Walton, 'A Woman's Views on Camping Out,' *Rod and Gun* (September 1899), 72; Craik, 'Summer Holidays,' 22; 'Women's Work and Ways.'

29 Hughes, 'Canadian Summer Girl,' 121; 'Women's Views,' 72; Mary Harvey Drummond, 'A Woman's Trip to the Laurentides,' *Rod and Gun* (December 1900), 389.

30 Wahnaptae, 'A Woman on the Mississaga,' *Rod and Gun* (October 1904), 218–21; Drummond, 'Woman's Trip,' 388; Walton, 'Woman's Views,' 73.
31 Graham, 'Camping Out,' 272.
32 Chas. H. Tinker, in James Alexander Hedley, *Notes of a Hunting Trip with the Dwight-Wiman Club in the Muskoka District, Canada, October 1884* (Toronto n.d.), 74. Tinker's inspiration was Robert Burns's 'My Heart's in the Highlands.'
33 Grand Trunk Railway and Muskoka Navigation Company, *A Paradise for Anglers* (1895); *Globe* (2 July 1890).
34 Barbaranne Boyer, *Muskoka's Grand Hotels and Resorts* (Boston Mills 1987), 161, citing the *Canada Summer Resort Guide* (1910).
35 'Muskoka: Lovely Scenery within a Few Hours' Ride of Toronto,' *Globe* (2 July 1884).
36 See Peter S. Schmalz, *The Ojibwa of Southern Ontario* (Toronto: University of Toronto Press 1991)
37 Frank Yeigh, *Through the Heart of Canada* (Toronto 1911), 139.
38 G. Mercer Adams, 'Georgian Bay and the Muskoka Lakes,' in *Picturesque Canada*, 2: 604.
39 See Roy I. Wolfe, 'The Summer Resorts of Ontario in the Nineteenth Century,' *Ontario History* 54 (September, 1962), 153–5; D.H.C. Mason, *Muskoka: The First Islanders* (Bracebridge: Herald-Gazette Press 1957); Florence B. Murray, ed., *Muskoka and Haliburton 1615–1875: A Collection of Documents* (Toronto: The Champlain Society 1963); Joe Cookson, *Tattletales of Muskoka* (Bracebridge: Herald-Gazette Press 1976).
40 Most histories of Muskoka date the beginnings of tourism from Bain and Campbell's first visit, and rely on accounts included in the James Watson Bain Collection of journals, reminiscences, and letters concerning Muskoka, ca. 1860–80, Baldwin Room, Toronto Metropolitan Library.
41 'Songs of Yoho,' Bain Collection.
42 Robinson to Bain, 9 June, 1863, Bain Collection.
43 Correspondence between Robinson and Bain, Bain Collection; Barlow Cumberland, ed., *Muskoka and the Northern Lakes of Canada* 2d ed. (Toronto 1886), 128; Canada, Sessional Papers, Department of Indian Affairs, 1897; Schmalz, *The Ojibwa of Southern Ontario*, 176–8.
44 'Expedition Number Two – Journal,' Bain Collection.
45 Canada, Sessional Papers, Department of Indian Affairs, 1897; advertisement reprinted in Boyer, *Muskoka's Grand Hotels*, 85.
46 John Todd, 'A Trip to Muskoka Lakes,' *New Dominion Monthly* (March 1868), 361–3.
47 Ibid. See also 'Brown, Jones, and Robinson's Narrative of their

Adventures in the Far North,' Bain Collection; 'Up the Muskoka and Down the Trent,' *Globe* (4 October 1865).

48 Redmond Thomas, 'The Beginning of Navigation and the Tourist Industry in Muskoka,' *Ontario History* 72 (April 1950), 101–5. Thomas writes that the first steamer was launched in 1866, but there are earlier advertisements for steamer services in Muskoka in the *Globe* (1 July 1863, 20 August 1863).

49 Boyer, *Muskoka's Grand Hotels*, 15–19.

50 Craik, 'Summer Holidays,' 23.

51 Cumberland, ed., *The Northern Lakes of Canada*, 152. On Cumberland's career in the tourist industry, see 'Friends of the Great Travelling Public,' *Globe* (5 August 1893).

52 'An Excursion of Members of Parliament to the Lake Country,' *Globe* (17 August 1880).

53 Grand Trunk Railway of Canada, *Verbatim Report of the President's Speech at the Ordinary General Meeting of the Company* (26 April 1887), 6–8. See Grand Trunk Railway and Muskoka Navigation Co. publications such as *A Paradise for Anglers; Picturesque Muskoka Lakes; To the Highlands and Lakes of Northern Ontario*.

54 Boyer, *Muskoka's Grand Hotels*, 19; Richard Tatley, *Steamboating in Muskoka* (Bracebridge: Muskoka Litho. 1972), 35–9.

55 See the *Guide to the Fishing and Hunting Resorts in the Vicinity of the Grand Trunk Railway of Canada*, published annually.

56 *To the Highlands and Lakes of Northern Ontario*; and see advertisements in the *Canadian Magazine* at the turn of the century.

57 Webster McKay, *The Macmillan Dictionary of Canadian Biography*, 4th ed. (Toronto: Macmillan 1978), 898; *Who's Who in America, vol. 1 (1897–1942)* (Chicago: A.N. Marquis 1943); Elgin Myers, 'A Canadian in New York,' *Canadian Magazine* (1893), 435–43.

58 James Alexander Hedley, *Notes of a Hunting Trip with the Dwight-Wiman Club in the Muskoka District, Canada, Ontario, 1884*, Toronto, n.d.

59 Boyer, *Muskoka's Grand Hotels*.

60 E. Maurice Smith, 'Muskoka: The Summer Playground of Canada,' *Canadian Magazine* (May 1903), 37.

61 'Holiday Experiences in the Muskoka Country,' *Globe* (20 July 1889).

62 Boyer, *Muskoka's Grand Hotels*.

63 John Rogers et al., eds., *Guide Book and Atlas of Muskoka and Parry Sound Districts* (1879), 2d offset ed. (Port Elgin: Ontario Atlas Reprints 1972), 43.

64 Craik, 'Summer Holidays,' 22; 'In the North: Holiday Experiences in the Muskoka Country,' *Globe* (20 July 1889); E.W.M., testimonial in Muskoka and Nipissing Navigation Co., *Guide to Muskoka Lakes*, 47.

65 Cumberland, *Northern Lakes*, 191–5; *Globe* (4 July 1891, 17 August 1895).

66 Geoffrey Wall, 'Recreational Land Use in Muskoka,' *Ontario Geography* 11 (1977), 19–20.

67 Baldwin Family Papers, L14, Baldwin Room, Toronto Metropolitan Library; and see 'Our Summer Resorts: Muskoka,' *Globe* (17 August 1895).

68 See advertisements in Grand Trunk Railway, *Pen and Sunlight Sketches of Scenery Reached by the Grand Trunk Railway and Connections* (1892). Pott's testimonial appeared in Muskoka and Nipissing Navigation Co., *Guide to Muskoka Lakes*, 19.

69 *Guide to Muskoka Lakes*, testimonial by Frank Yeigh, 43; 'Aldermanic Trip to Burk's Falls,' reprinted in *Guide to Muskoka Lakes*, 25–8; H.J. Menzies, in the *Week* (25 August 1887), reprinted in *Guide to Muskoka Lakes*, 29; Smith, 'Muskoka,' 37.

70 Mrs H.B. King, *Letters from Muskoka by an Emigrant Lady* (London 1878), 260–70; Edith Ward Sherman, 'Muskoka – The Hay Fever Mecca,' *Rod and Gun* (December 1906), 586; *Muskoka: Land of Health and Pleasure* (Toronto 1896), 6.

71 'Beyond Muskoka – the Land of the Magnetawagan,' *Globe* (20 August 1868).

72 Thomas W. Gibson, 'Algonquin Provincial Park,' quoting 'the Act of the Legislature establishing the Algonquin National Park,' *Canadian Magazine* (1894), 543–5; J. Harry Smith, 'September in Algonquin Park,' *Canadian Magazine* (May 1911), 28.

73 'Passenger Steamers,' *Globe* (16 August 1890).

74 *Globe* (9 August 1867).

75 'Mechanics' Institute Excursion on Lake Simcoe,' *Globe* (19 July 1866); 'Odd-Fellows' Excursion to St Chatherine's,' *Globe* (11 August 1866).

76 *Globe* (22 July 1897; 1 August 1892).

77 'Dominion Day,' *Globe* (2 July 1881); C.C. Stone, 'The Trip to Old Niagara,' *Outdoor Canada* (August 1907).

78 'Friends of the Great Travelling Public,' *Globe* (5 August 1893).

79 Advertisements in the *Canadian Magazine* (July 1905), *Globe* (25 July 1897).

80 Henry Norman, *The Preservation of Niagara Falls* (New York 1881), 10–11; Sears, *Sacred Places*, 182–208.

81 *Courier of Upper Canada* (4 October 1833), *Canadian Freeman* (3 October 1833), quoted by Sarah Gibson, *More Than Just an Island: A History of the Toronto Island* (Toronto: Clarke, Irwin 1984), 38.

82 'The Island,' *Globe* (29 August 1866).

83 *Mail* (October 1893 and August 1894), quoted in Gibson, *More Than Just an Island*, 110.

84 *Globe* (18 July 1893; 5 July 1888).

85 'Summering at the Island,' *Globe* (12 August 1893). And see 'Summer Homes among the Cool Breezes on Old Ontario: Where Some of Our People Go,' *Globe* (8 July 1889); *Toronto Island Guide: Where to Go and What to See – an Explanatory Overture* (Toronto 1894).

86 Gibson, *More Than Just an Island*, 96, 26–9.

87 B.S. Rowntree, 'The Industrial Unrest,' *Contemporary Review* 100 (1911), 455.

88 'Children Made Happy,' *Globe* (29 July 1891); 'Fresh Air for Babies,' *Globe* (13 July 1897); and see John Bullen, 'J.J. Kelso and the "New" Child-Savers: The Genesis of the Children's Aid Movement in Ontario,' *Ontario History* 92/2 (June 1990), 111.

CHAPTER 6 Close Encounters

1 The pursuit of a balanced interpretation of the tourist-guide relationship, which is beyond the scope of this book, will require that an extensive oral history project be undertaken. Interviews conducted for another paper on this subject revealed how different the guides' experiences of these relationships were. See P. Jasen, 'Who's the Boss?: Native Guides and White Tourists in the Canadian Wilderness, 1850–1914.' Paper read at the Canadian Historical Association Conference, Ottawa, June 1993.

2 Canadian Pacific Railway, *A Canoe Trip through Temagaming the Peerless* (1900), 8.

3 C.C. Farr, 'In the Woods with Indian Guides,' *Rod and Gun* (October 1906), 327.

4 'A Fine Tourist Region,' *Rod and Gun* (April 1907), 99–100.

5 Canada, Sessional Papers, Department of Indian Affairs, 1889, 1890.

6 Alfred Pegler, *A Visit to Canada and the United States in Connection with the Meetings of the British Association Held at Montreal in 1884* (Southampton 1884), 22. On wages in the early 1870s, see Marshall, *Canadian Dominion*, 224.

7 Provincial Archives of Manitoba, B. 134/c/147, fo. 453, cited in Arthurs, 'Some References to Tourism North of Lake Superior.'

8 Canada, Sessional papers, DIA, annually from 1889. For an analysis of the Canadian government's contradictory policies regarding Ojibway agriculture, see Leo G. Waisberg and Tim E. Holzkamm, 'A Tendency to Discourage Them from Cultivating: Agricultre and Indian Affairs Administration in Northwestern Ontario,' *Ethnohistory*, 40, no. 2 (spring 1993), 175–211.

9 Hugh Brody, *Maps and Dreams* (Penguin Books 1983), 51.

10 Canada, Sessional Papers, DIA, 1897.

11 Consumption is mentioned as a problem by Indian agents; see Sessional Papers, DIA, 1890. Also see Scott Hamilton and C.F. Ritchie, *Rediscovering Red Rock House: The 1984 Test Evacuations*, Ontario Conservation Archaeology Report, 23.

12 Bruce W. Hodgins and Jamie Benidickson, *The Temagami Experience: Recreation, Resources, and Aboriginal Rights in the Northern Ontario Wilderness* (Toronto: University of Toronto Press 1989).

13 See, for example, the various editions of *Summer Tours by the Canadian Pacific Railway; Fishing Resorts along the Canadian Pacific Railway, Eastern Division* (Montreal 1887).

14 W.F. Whitcher, *Nepigon Trout: An Ottawa Canoeist's Experience of the Northern Shore of Lake Superior* (Montreal 1887), 4.

15 Hudson's Bay Company Archives, Provincial Archives of Manitoba, B.134/c/173/433, quoted in Hamilton and Ritchie, *Rediscovering Red Rock House*.

16 PAM, HBC B. 134/c127, fo. 98dd-99: R. Crawford and J. Bissett, Red Rock, 20 July 1874. I owe this reference to David Arthurs, who kindly made available his file, 'References to Tourism North of Lake Superior.'

17 'The Nepigon,' *Rod and Gun* (June 1902), 23. Also see W.H.H. Murray, *Daylight Land* (Boston 1888), 53–67; D.C. Scott, 'Lake Nepigon,' *Rod and Gun* (January 1900), 152–3.

18 PAM, HBC, B.134/c/159 fo.176, N. Flannigan and S.K. Parson, Red Rock, 15 August 1888.

19 Whitcher, *Nepigon Trout*, 4; 'The Giant Trout of Nipigon,' *Rod and Gun* (April 1913), 1139–40.

20 'Nepigon,' 21.

21 'Giant Trout,' 1140.

22 'Ten Days on the Nipigon,' *Globe* (19 July 1884).

23 'Giant Trout,' 1140.

24 Whitcher, *Nepigon Trout*, 36.

25 'Giant Trout,' 1140.

26 'Ten Days on the Nipigon,' *Globe* (19 July 1884, 1 August 1884).

27 Sladen, *On the Cars*, 205.

28 Interview with an Ojibway elder at Couchiching Reserve, December 1992. Interview conducted, translated, and transcribed by Julie Byzewski.

29 'Summer Playgrounds of Canada' (July 1911), 142. On the development of the tourist industry in Temagami, see Hodgins and Benidickson, *Temagami Experience*. Also see Frank Yeigh, 'Touring in Temagami Land,' *Rod and*

Gun (October 1906), 324–7; *Guide to the Fishing and Hunting Resorts in the Vicinity of the Grand Trunk Railway of Canada: Season 1890; Fishing Resorts along the Canadian Pacific Railway Eastern Division* (Montreal 1887).

30 Quoted by Hodgins and Benidickson, *Temagami Experience*, 114.

31 'Temagami, Mississagua, French River and That Sort of Thing,' *Rod and Gun* (April 1906), 586; Donald B. Smith, *From the Land of the Shadows: The Making of Grey Owl* (Saskatoon: Western Producer Prairie Books 1990), 42.

32 E. and S.W., 'John Green, Guide,' *Rod and Gun* (June 1908), 9.

33 Charles G. Campbell, 'A North Country Trouting Trip,' *Rod and Gun* (August 1904), 108–9.

34 On the Ojibway of Bear Island, see Smith, *From the Land of the Shadows*, and Hodgins and Benidickson, *Temagami Experience*.

35 'Timagami, French River, and That Sort of Thing,' *Rod and Gun* (April 1905), 592. On Tom Polson, see H. Barnard, 'Northern Ontario,' *Rod and Gun* (March 1903), 350.

36 Hodgins and Benidickson, *Temagami Experience*, 122, 218.

37 Frank Yeigh, 'Touring in Temagami Land,' *Rod and Gun* (October 1906), 305.

38 Frank Carrell, 'Our Fishing and Hunting Trip in Northern Ontario,' *Rod and Gun* (April 1907), 936.

39 Ibid., 939.

40 Hodgins and Benidickson, *Temagami Experience*, 57, 81.

41 Yeigh, 'Touring in Temagami Land,' 302.

42 St Croix, 'Second Sight and the Indian,' *Rod and Gun* (August 1902), 103–4; C.C. Farr, 'Indians and the Weather,' *Rod and Gun* (January 1904), 429–30.

43 Farr, 'In the Woods with Indian Guides,' *Rod and Gun* (October 1906), 328.

44 St Croix, 'Second Sight,' 103.

45 Barnard, 'Northern Ontario,' *Rod and Gun* (April 1903), 387.

46 George G. Cotton, 'Mississauga,' *Rod and Gun* (February 1904), 449, 456.

47 C.C. Farr, 'A Trip to Matachuan,' *Rod and Gun* (December 1901), 3.

48 C.C. Farr, 'Ducks and Duck Shooting on Lake Temiscamingue,' *Rod and Gun* (March 1901), 475.

49 G.M. Richards, 'In the Indian Country,' *Rod and Gun* (January 1903), 413.

50 'Timigami, Mississauga, French River, and That Sort of Thing,' 592.

51 Farr, 'Trip to Matachuan,' 1.

52 Barnard, 'Northern Ontario,' 388.

53 C.C. Farr, 'Indian's Spring,' *Rod and Gun* (June 1902), 28.

54 Whitcher, *Nepigon Trout*, 26–9.

55 'Giant Trout,' 1142.

56 C.C. Farr, 'The Old and the New,' *Rod and Gun* (April 1904), 540.

57 Ibid.
58 Farr, 'Trip to Matachuan,' 5

Conclusion

1 Varley, 'Tourist Attractions,' 24–30.
2 For example, see Paul Fussell, *The Great War and Modern Memory* (London: Oxford University Press 1977).

Index

Picture Credits

Archives of Ontario: W.T. Craig's *Falls of Niagara on the River St Lawrence*, S1679; The entrance to Horseshoe Falls cavern, S1681; English writer Anna Jameson, Acc 2305 S4299; Tourists posed in front of Horseshoe Falls, ambrotype, Acc 6760 S4279; The Duke and Duchess of York shooting the rapids, photograph by Underwood and Underwood, Acc 2373 ST101; Family members in front of their home on the Garden River Reserve, Acc 10748 S16361; A Garden River Reserve family dressed for the Hiawatha pageant, Acc 10748 S16354; The steamer *Frances Smith*, Acc 16657-154; A poster advertising an excursion through Parry Sound, 2411; Boating on the Muskoka River, Acc 11747 ST1203; A party of men and women camp out on 'Yoho-cucoba,' stereograph by Jas. Esson, Preston, Acc 12025 S1209; Excursionists returning from a picnic, Acc 6616 S4781; A cottage living room on Chief's Island, Acc 14054-32; *S.S. Luella* discharges passengers, Acc 12026-232; Forster's Hunt Club, S1049; Fisherman and guides at Nipigon, albumen print, J.R. Miller Collection, Acc 13098-14; A guide and his family at Temagami, Acc 9348 S14654; An Ojibway guide and his family at Fort Matachuwan, from *Temagami: A Peerless Region for the Sportsman, Canoeist, Camper* (1906), Acc 4793 S6611; Temagami guide Bill Friday and companions, Acc 9348 S14651

National Library of Canada: Guidebook view of the ruins of Fort Erie, from John W. Orr, *Pictorial Guide to the Falls of Niagara* (Buffalo 1842), 17452

Toronto Metropolitan Reference Library: Tourist attractions along the Niagara frontier, map from *Travels through Part of the United States and Canada in 1818 and 1819* (Glasgow 1823); W.H. Bartlett's *General Brock's Monument*, *Scene among the Thousand Isles*, *St Regis Indian Village*, and *A Forest Scene*, from

N.P. Willis and W.H. Bartlett, *Canadian Scenery Illustrated*, vol. 1 (London 1842), 17450; Bartlett's *Timber Slide*, from ibid., vol. 2; Shopping for souvenirs, from *A Pleasure Trip, Toronto to Duluth, July 1880* (Toronto 1880); A rest cure in a canoe, from *Rod and Gun in Canada* (July 1910); The Muskoka Club, albumen print, 1866, T15202; Hanlan's Hotel, T10178; 'Bella Villa' cottage, T1130

Canadian Institute for Historical Reproductions: A romantic portrait of an Indian pilot, from *Hunter's Panoramic Guide from Niagara to Quebec* (Cleveland 1857), 35724; The Grand Trunk Railway and its connections, from *Handbook of Canadian Excursion Tours via Grand Trunk Railway and Canadian Navigation Company* (1878), 40999; A poster advertising an excursion through the Thousand Islands, 59969; The routes north from Toronto, A healthy, happy family, and The Beaumaris Hotel touts its advantages, from Muskoka and Nipissing Navigation Co., *Guide to Muskoka Lakes* (Toronto 1888), 07149

Chancellor Paterson Library, Lakehead University: The excitement of running the rapids and *Duck Shooting at Lake Rosseau*, from W.H. Withrow, *Our Own Country Canada* (Toronto 1889); F.B. Schell's *Lake of the Isles* and View of the Thousand Islands, and Schell and Hogan's *Muskoka Scenery*, from G.M. Grant, ed., *Picturesque Canada*, vol. 2 (Toronto 1882); L.R. O'Brien's picture of a steamer passing round Thunder Cape, *The Sleeping Giant*, *Kakabeka Falls*, Schell and Hogan's *Toronto from the Island*, and The Hudson's Bay post at Red Rock, from ibid., vol. 1; The Grand Trunk Railway advertising deer hunting, from *Canadian Magazine* (November 1899); The lure of Muskoka and 'A vacation *without* a Kodak,' from *Canadian Magazine* (July 1909); The Grand Trunk Railway advertises the wild and magnificent Temagami region, from *Canadian Magazine* (October 1909); A CPR sleeping-car by day, from *On the Cars and Off* (London 1895)